D1355780

Saint Foucault

▲ ▲ ▲ ▲ ▲ ▲ ▲ ▲ ▲

Saint Foucault

Towards a Gay

Hagiography

▼ ▼ ▼ ▼ ▼ ▼ ▼ ▼ ▼

DAVID M. HALPERIN

New York   Oxford
OXFORD UNIVERSITY PRESS
1995

Oxford University Press

Oxford   New York
Athens   Auckland   Bangkok   Bombay
Calcutta   Capetown   Dar es Salaam   Delhi
Florence   Hong Kong   Istanbul   Karachi
Kuala Lumpur   Madras   Madrid   Melbourne
Mexico City   Nairobi   Paris   Singapore
Taipei   Tokyo   Toronto

and associated companies in
Berlin   Ibadan

Copyright © 1995 by David M. Halperin

Published by Oxford University Press, Inc.,
198 Madison Avenue, New York, New York 10016

Oxford is a registered trademark of Oxford University Press

Library of Congress Cataloging-in-Publication Data
Halperin, David M., 1952–
    Saint Foucault : towards a gay hagiography / David M. Halperin.
       p.   cm.   Includes index.
    ISBN 0-19-509371-2
    1. Homosexuality—Political aspects.   2. Homosexuality—Philosophy.
  3. Foucault, Michael.   I. Title.
  HQ76.5.H35   1995
  306.76'6—dc20   94-41136

9 8 7 6 5 4 3 2 1

Printed in the United States of America
on acid-free paper

▲ ▲ ▲ ▲ ▲ ▲ ▲ ▲

▲ ▲ ▲ ▲ ▲ ▲ ▲ ▲

Acknowledgments

The idea for this little book came to me originally from Paul Foss; to him, first of all, go my thanks and acknowledgments. My work was generously supported by fellowships from the Humanities Research Centre at The Australian National University in Canberra and from the Society for the Humanities at Cornell University in Ithaca, New York. I am more grateful to these institutions than I can say for what they provided: splendid working conditions, warm hospitality, an immensely stimulating intellectual atmosphere, and superb collegiality; I wish to extend my appreciation particularly to G. W. Clarke, John Ballard, Jill Julius Matthews, Dominick LaCapra, and Jonathan Culler for making these visits possible and for looking after me so handsomely during the course of them.

The impetus to compose the first of these two essays came from a lecture program at Vassar College called "The Philosopher's Holiday." The seriousness, interest, and support demonstrated by the students and faculty during my visit to Vassar in the spring of 1992 provided strong encouragement for me to persevere with this project. The impetus for the second essay came from Jim Miller, whose friendship and generosity have withstood—quite remarkably—the strain of my severe criticisms of his work.

My thinking about Foucault was aided by early discussions with Arnold Davidson, David N. Dobrin, Mark Maslan, Jim Miller, Paul Morrison, and Emery J. Snyder. I also wish to thank Douglas Crimp, Gary Dowsett, Lee Edelman, Didier Eribon, Ann Ferguson, Gary Gutting, Barry Hindess, Morris Kaplan, David Kent, Michael Lucey, Biddy Martin, Ellen Meese, D. A. Miller,

Ruth Perry, Joe Powers, Patrick Roff, David Román, Gayle Rubin, Jana Sawicki, Eve Kosofsky Sedgwick, and Alain Vizier—all of whom have contributed to my thinking in various ways. For opportunities to present my work on Foucault, I am grateful to Robert Aldrich, Lourdes Arguelles, John Ballard, Michael Bartos, Nicholas Baume, Sandy Bem, Ruth Blair, Mary Lynn Broe, Ann Ferguson, Simon Goldhill, Kevin Hart, Terence Irwin, Carlos Jerez-Farrán, Peter Larmour, Suzanne MacAlister, Jim Miller, Peter Nardi, Martha Nussbaum, Clare O'Farrell, Paul Patton, Roger Pitcher, Art Pomeroy, Laurie Shrage, Edward Stein, Chris Straayer, Harold Tarrant, David Thorburn, and Marcus Wilson. Additional specific debts are acknowledged in the headnote to each essay.

I wish to thank Jody Greene for invaluable assistance, support, and encouragement. I'm almost inexpressibly grateful to Liz Maguire, my editor at Oxford University Press, for her belief in me and in this book, without which I cannot quite imagine ever having been able to finish it.

Finally, I want to express my gratitude to Paul Morrison for his companionship and support, his criticisms and provocations, and most of all for his unswerving loyalty and friendship during the composition of this book—a period in my life during which such items were otherwise in short supply.

Ithaca, N.Y.   D.M.H.
May 1994

▲ ▲ ▲ ▲ ▲ ▲ ▲ ▲

Contents

Saint Foucault

Ross Moore, *Of the Visible and Hidden*
(1992–93). Triptych center panel. Reprinted
by permission of the artist.

▲ ▲ ▲ ▲ ▲ ▲ ▲ ▲

Saint Foucault

IN A RECENT book devoted to the commendable task of promoting and defending what, in its title, are called *Gay Ideas*, the philosopher Richard Mohr singles out for extended criticism one idea in particular that, despite its sometime popularity among lesbian and gay historians and cultural theorists, evidently does not qualify, in his eyes, as properly "gay": namely, the idea that sexuality is socially constructed. Mohr blames the queer vogue for this un-gay idea on the baneful influence of the late French philosopher and historian Michel Foucault—a gay man whose life and work have come to represent, especially since his death from AIDS in 1984, important sources of intellectual and political inspiration to many lesbians and gay men, as well as to numbers of variously identified cultural radicals.

"Within the emerging academic discipline of lesbian and gay studies," Mohr contends,

> there is nearly universal agreement among scholars that social factors are in some sense determinant in homosexuality, that homosexuality is culturally constituted or produced. Indeed, especially as espoused by Michel Foucault, this variant of cultural determinism—the social construction of homosexuality—has achieved hagiographical status within lesbian and gay studies, where it is almost always an object for witness rather than of analysis.[1]

Before proceeding to give the idea that sexuality is socially constructed the lengthy drubbing he believes it deserves, Mohr refers his readers to my 1990 book *One Hundred Years of Homosexuality*, which, I confess, used a social-constructionist model to analyze the erotics of male culture in ancient Greece,

3

even as it appealed to the recorded facts of sexual life in ancient Greece in order to support a social-constructionist model for analyzing the constitution of sexual identity. Mohr adduces my book as a prime example of what he terms—in a formula that has stayed with me ever since I first encountered it—"generic worship of Saint Foucault."[2]

It is hard not to feel defensive in the face of such criticism, and my first impulse on reading that passage in manuscript three years ago—when Mohr himself sent me advance drafts of several chapters in his book—was to protest against its multiple injustices. Mohr was wrong, it seemed to me, on several counts.[3] First of all, Foucault, so far as I know, never took a position on such empirical questions as what causes homosexuality or whether it is constituted socially or biologically; he contented himself with studying the history of the conditions that made possible the institutional and discursive formation of homosexuality (as well as other "kinds" of "sexuality"). Although he did heap scorn on the assumption that homosexuality has always existed,[4] and although his decision to write the history of sexuality "from the viewpoint of a history of discourses"[5] rather than from the viewpoint of the history of science admittedly had the effect of privileging historical and cultural modes of explanation over scientific ones, he never explicitly "espoused," as Mohr claims he did, the notion that homosexuality is socially constructed.[6] In fact, when on one occasion he was asked about "the distinction between innate predisposition to homosexual behavior and social conditioning," and whether he had "any conviction one way or the other on this issue," Foucault emphatically replied, "On this question I have absolutely nothing to say. 'No comment.' "[7]

Second, although I may have been the only professional classicist in North America to give the second volume of Foucault's *History of Sexuality* (which dealt with classical Greece) a favorable review, it simply is not true that I was uncritical of

Foucault at the time I wrote *One Hundred Years of Homosexuality*. Here, for example, is something I said in my review and repeated in my book, and it expresses an attitude rather far removed from worship:

> Volume One [of Foucault's *History of Sexuality*], for all its admittedly bright ideas, is dogmatic, tediously repetitious, full of hollow assertions, disdainful of historical documentation, and careless in its generalizations: it distributes over a period spanning from the seventeenth to the twentieth centuries a gradual process of change well known to Foucault only in its later, mid-nineteenth-century manifestations.[8]

I would not write such a sentence today.

Finally, by accusing me of worshiping Saint Foucault, Mohr in effect differentiates my engagement with Foucault from his own enthusiasms for the various thinkers and artists whom *he* admires. He implies that his own evaluative judgments are sober, reasonable and considered, exactly proportional to the merits of their objects, honest and honorable tributes to the actual accomplishments of talented people (e.g., "the pinnacle of Western civilization [was] reached in the secular cantatas of Anton Webern": p. 135), whereas *my* admiration for Foucault has something irrational and excessive about it—something illiberal, idolatrous, fanatical, indiscriminate, hyperbolic, obscurantist, dogmatic, weak-minded, and superstitious.

▼ ▼ ▼ ▼ ▼ ▼ ▼ ▼

WHAT MOHR'S caricature of me makes clear is that Michel Foucault has become the sort of intellectual figure with whom it is no longer possible to have a rational or nonpathological relationship. One of the most brilliant and original thinkers of our era, Foucault now appears to represent such a powerful, volatile, and sinister influence that his ideas—if they are not to contaminate and disqualify whoever ventures to make use of them—must first be sanitized by being passed through an acid bath of derogation and disavowal. As I have watched the cautionary spectacle of Foucault's demonization unfold, and noted the specific terms in which it has been carried out, my own attitude to Foucault has gradually changed, correspondingly, from one of distant admiration to one of passionate personal and political identification. For I see in the posthumous reversal of Foucault's critical fortunes the fate of every oppositional thinker who is also gay and who undertakes explicitly to combine scholarship and politics in his own practice. Far from being intimidated into towing a more normative line by the prospect or threat of getting herded together with Foucault into the stigmatized company of "militant," "radical," or "extreme" gay male intellectuals and activists, I have been driven by an instinct of survival to want to expose the political operations that have brought about such a phobic construction of Foucault in the first place. And in the course of pursuing that project, my admiration for Foucault and my identification with his discursive and political positioning have increased exponentially.

So let me make it official. I may not have worshiped Foucault at the time I wrote *One Hundred Years of Homosexuality*, but I do worship him now. As far as I'm concerned, the guy was a fucking saint.

Not that I imagine Foucault to have led either a sexually or a morally perfect life. In fact, I know almost nothing about his life beyond what I've read in three recent biographies, whose will-to-truth about Foucault constitutes the subject of the second of the two long essays published here. I never met Foucault myself. I never even laid eyes on him. My relation to him is indirect and secondary: like my relation to virtually every other great writer, ancient or modern, that I have ever studied, it is entirely mediated, imaginary, and—why bother to deny it?—hagiographical. But if Foucault did not have to lead a perfect life in order to qualify as an object of my worship, I certainly do consider him to have led an intellectually and politically exemplary life. I believe he grasped his total political situation as a gay intellectual and scholar better than anyone else has ever done. Moreover, Foucault's acute and constantly revised understanding of his own social location enabled him to devise some unsystematic but effective modes of resistance to the shifting discursive and institutional conditions which circumscribed his own practice. As I shall argue, it was that ability to reflect critically on and to respond politically to the circumstances that both enabled and constrained his own activity that accounts for why Foucault's life—as much as or perhaps even more than his work—continues to serve as a compelling model for an entire generation of scholars, critics, and activists.

As if that weren't enough, I have some additional reasons of both a personal and a political nature to identify with Foucault (I'll specify them in a moment). A series of recent attacks on Foucault has therefore had a galvanizing effect on me. I have come to realize that whenever I come across people saying stupid, uninformed, uncomprehending, or derogatory things about any of the *other* French theorists who seem to have become fashionable of late, though for different reasons, among both academic cultural critics and anti-intellectual cultural reactionaries—even when, as happens more and more often, I hear people saying ignorant and poisonous things about my closest and most esteemed collaborators in the field of lesbian/gay studies—I may be disgusted or outraged, but I don't take it personally, I don't get angry or resentful, and I don't stew over it for days. But that *is* how I feel when Foucault is attacked—and not only because the attacks are often homophobic or because so many of them have (flatteringly) used me as his whipping boy, appropriating my work on ancient Greece as the vehicle and pretext for attempts to discredit his scholarship, his theoretical hypotheses, or his politics.[9] Rather, what strikes me most forcefully about such attacks is the brutal, cheap, and effortless way they mobilize the attackers' social credit and cultural authority, pressing them into service against the views of someone whose stigmatized personal identity invites precisely such an onslaught even as it disarms his ability to withstand it. For that reason Foucault and his posthumous vicissitudes have gradually come to embody for me the political truth of my own personal, professional, and scholarly vulnerability. In short, *Michel Foucault, c'est moi.*

Before that last remark starts to make me sound delusional, let me explain what I mean by it. I do not intend to compare myself to Foucault in any substantive sense. My identification with him is purely positional. If I share nothing else with Foucault, what I do share with him is the problem of how, as a gay man, an academic, and a public intellectual, I can acquire and maintain the authority to speak, to be heard, and to be taken seriously *without* denying or bracketing my gayness. It's not just a matter of being publicly or visibly out; it's a matter of being able to devise and to preserve a positive, undemonized connection between my gayness and my scholarly or critical authority. That problem of authorization, to be sure, presents itself in its most acute form only to otherwise socially accredited gay men of the professional classes, but it dramatizes the more general social and discursive predicament of lesbians and gay men in a world where a claimed homosexual identity operates as an instant disqualification, exposes you to accusations of pathology and partisanship (even by other gay men, as we have seen), and grants everyone else an absolute epistemological privilege over you.[10] What Foucault and I have in common, in short, is our vexed and inescapable relation to the sexual politics of truth.

▼   ▼   ▼   ▼   ▼   ▼   ▼   ▼

JUST HOW VEXED that relation is can be illustrated by means of two stories from my recent life, stories which I consider revealing in their exemplarity. I'll begin with what, in a sense, is closest to my own experience, to my everyday practice as a writer and a critic: namely, the story of how I came to write the second of the two essays in this volume. I had been invited, along with a number of philosophers and historians, to contribute a paper on James Miller's book *The Passion of Michel Foucault* to a roundtable discussion that was to be published in *Salmagundi*, a quarterly journal of criticism and comment with a liberal-centrist readership. I was acquainted with Jim Miller, had read a draft of the first chapter of his book, and had discussed the project with him as it neared completion. At first I was excited by Miller's proposal to interpret Foucault's life and work as a single, daring, exemplary personal/philosophical experiment; in fact, as a result of Miller's influence, I have come to interpret it that way myself. However, when I received the unrevised typescript of Miller's book, I was appalled. I won't go into my reasons here (I expound them at considerable length in the essay itself) except to say that Miller's biography, perhaps more than anything else I had ever read, seemed to me to demonstrate—not by argument but by its own negative example—the value and urgency of Foucault's critique of the discursive politics of truth. Having gotten clear about that, I sat down to write the essay. But nothing happened. I sat at my desk, working continuously for about six weeks and by the end of that period I had succeeded only in becoming totally obsessed with my topic; I had written nothing worth preserving.

In retrospect, I can see that what had paralyzed me was a sense of the futility of the task before me. While I was grateful to Miller for treating Foucault's sexual life as a matter of serious philosophical interest, I also wanted to protest strongly and effectively, if I could, against Miller's lurid portrayal of it; even more, I wanted to protest against Miller's tendency to vaporize the political meaning of Foucault's sexual practices by presenting them not as techniques of resistance but as symptoms of personal pathology, thereby reducing the significance of Foucault's struggle from an exemplary to a highly idiosyncratic one. The problem for me was this: Could I specify what I found politically odious about Miller's personalizing strategy without at the same time convicting myself of narrow-minded partisanship in the eyes of *Salmagundi*'s readership? Would not the overall effect of my political defense of Foucault and my political critique of Miller be to discredit myself through a kind of guilty association with the former and an insufficient generosity toward the latter? Would I not simply fail to convince my readers and instead come off as a rabid gay polemicist determined to defend Foucault at all costs from the sensational and newly revealed "truth" about his stigmatized sexual practices, a "truth" that to those readers could only look like bad news for Foucault's intellectual standing and reputation? In short, I felt that, under the circumstances, I couldn't *not* defend Foucault, yet I couldn't defend him either.

It's always interesting to find oneself in a situation that one can't write one's way out of. The impasse may be a clue to something real, an indication that one has stumbled upon something of potentially wider significance than one's own limitations, onto some major organizing structure of social meaning or some irreducible law of cultural discourse.[11] In this case, what I had stumbled upon turned out to be at least one basis for my identification with Foucault: namely, the permanent crisis of authority faced by any intellectual in our society who is also gay. I could not figure out a way of writing about the politics of writing about a gay life without enmeshing myself in that politics to my own disadvantage, thereby suffering in my own person precisely the political disqualifications that Miller's biography seemed calculated to inflict on Foucault.

My second story is less edifying but perhaps more illuminating. On April 7, 1992, Cynthia Griffin Wolff, then the most senior faculty member (in rank and salary) in my academic department at the Massachusetts Institute of Technology, filed a lawsuit against MIT charging it with "wrongful acquiescence in and perpetuation of a persistent and continuing pattern of professional, political and sexual harassment towards Professor Wolff in the workplace." That harassment turned out, on closer inspection, to consist of a series of political disagreements between Wolff and her colleagues, myself among them; her lawyers portrayed us in the lawsuit as a cabal of politically correct professors who had allegedly persecuted Wolff because she had exposed our abuses of power. The lawsuit claimed that I had "demanded" that MIT interview a job candidate because I said I was in love with this person; in another incident Wolff's lawyers represented her as having informed the provost of MIT that departmental decisions "were being dominated by political views and sexual preferences" and, in particular, that "Professor Halperin could readily be harassing undergraduates, *especially* as Professor Halperin had been charged and funded by the Administration to create an undergraduate program in Gay and Lesbian Studies."[12] (The last item is no less imaginary, alas, than the rest of Wolff's grievances: the MIT administration has no plan, so far as I know, to create such a program.)

The *Chronicle of Higher Education* received by fax a complete copy of the text of the lawsuit on the very day it was filed, and for several months the whole affair produced considerable, if short-lived, publicity. My friends speculated that Wolff's purpose in bringing the lawsuit was not so much to win in court as to embarrass the MIT administration into acceding to her personal demands. If so, the strategy seems to have worked. Wolff's lawsuit was a great success with the media. The headline in the *New York Times* read, SUIT DEPICTS FIGHT ON M.I.T. FACULTY: LITERATURE PROFESSOR ASSERTS PROMOTIONS WERE TIED TO SEXUAL PREFERENCES.[13] MIT settled the lawsuit out of court on undisclosed terms in November 1992. Meanwhile, I had become, for fifteen minutes at least, the Willie Horton of lesbian/gay studies.

That turned out not to be quite so much fun as it sounds, but I don't want to exaggerate my sufferings. No one I really cared about disowned me. I continued to get grants. My lecture invitations did not diminish; in fact, my lecture fee increased. My students defended me in person and in print. Even the right-wing campus newspaper—which made an obligatory and rather pathetic attempt to produce examples of what it tried to present as "appearance[s] of impropriety" on my part, such as holding occasional classes at my home (all of which was immediately reported in the right-wing campus press around the country and even got broadcast on Pat Robertson's cable TV show)—had to admit that "there had been no report of sexual harassment of Prof. Halperin against a student."[14] Martha Nussbaum gallantly came to my defense in the pages of *The New Republic*.[15] Wolff transferred out of my department and into another one. And MIT offered me two years of leave at a generous level of financial support, along with a research budget whose magnitude I shall probably not see the likes of again. For my part, unable to undo whatever damage the extensive publicity had already done to my professional reputation, I decided to take MIT's offer and accordingly dropped all plans to bring a formal complaint against Wolff at MIT. There, at least for the moment, the matter now rests.

The incident has come to represent for me an object lesson in the institutional crisis of gay authority. It indicates, first of all, the kind of moral panic that can be unleashed in the public mind by the presence of socially recognized authority figures who are openly, visibly gay and who work to promote lesbian/

gay political causes within their own institutions. Also, the incident indicates precisely what constitutes authoritative speech about a gay subject: who is authorized to speak, to whom, and with what truth-effects. It dramatizes the remarkable ease with which socially authorized individuals can communicate certain "truths" about a gay subject: if the message is already waiting at the receiver's end, it doesn't even need to be sent; it just needs to be activated. Ultimately, what the Wolff affair brought home to me is the very real vulnerability which until that moment, I hadn't realized I shared with all other lesbian and gay people in our society, a vulnerability I foolishly thought I had managed to escape *by coming out.* The point of coming out, I had thought, was precisely to deprive other people of their privileged knowingness about me and my sexuality; coming out had seemed to me to furnish a means of seizing the initiative from them, a means of claiming back from them a certain interpretative authority over the meaning of my words and actions. As I discovered to my cost, however, it turns out that if you are known to be lesbian or gay your very openness, far from preempting malicious gossip about your sexuality, simply exposes you to the possibility that, no matter what you actually do, people can say absolutely whatever they like about you in the well-grounded confidence that it will be credited. (And since there is very little you can do about it, you might as well not try to ingratiate yourself by means of "good behavior.")

▼   ▼   ▼   ▼   ▼   ▼   ▼   ▼

THOSE ISSUES of authority, vulnerability, and sexual politics are the very ones that I have seen being played out lately in the public critical discourse about Foucault. This book represents an attempt to intervene in that discourse. It is divided into two parts. The first essay tries to account for the fact that whereas Foucault has often been attacked because of his politics by non-gay-identified liberal critics, he has now become, in the eyes of many lesbian and gay cultural activists, something like an author-function attached to whatever we may deem to be our most effective and empowering techniques of social and political resistance. The second essay attempts to account for the fact that Foucault's life has provided a powerful model, and a vehicle of intense personal identification, for many lesbian and gay intellectuals who strive to combine critical analysis and political activism in their own practice. The second essay also offers a series of reflections on the politics of *writing* a gay life as well as the *effect* of writing *on* a gay life.

These two essays do not aim to expound or elucidate Foucault's thought either in part or as a whole. I am well aware that my treatment of his thought is often crude, reductive, overly general, abstracted from its contexts, and signally lacking in the subtlety which Foucault himself never ceased to display. I am also aware that by concentrating on Foucault's importance to lesbian/gay culture, I shall seem to be trivializing his work or, at the very least, to be privileging a single aspect of his intellectual contribution at the expense of what many may be pleased to consider its "general significance," "wider relevance," or "broader appeal."[16] But my intention is not to present Foucault's overall achievement or to account for his attractiveness to non-gay people. Rather, this book is a study of one of the ways that Foucault's thought has operated in the world since his death in 1984. It is an inquiry into what has been called "the Foucault effect"—an inquiry, more specifically, into how different people on various sides of the recent culture wars have responded to the challenge that Foucault has posed to our established ways of thinking, reading, writing, and doing politics.

▲　▲　▲　▲　▲　▲　▲　▲

The Queer Politics
of Michel Foucault

> The critical ontology of ourselves has to be
> considered not, certainly, as a theory, a doc-
> trine, nor even as a permanent body of knowl-
> edge that is accumulating; it has to be
> conceived as an attitude, an ethos, a philo-
> sophical life in which the critique of what we
> are is at one and the same time the historical
> analysis of the limits that are imposed on us
> and an experiment with the possibility of go-
> ing beyond them. . . . I continue to think that
> this task requires work on our limits, that is,
> a patient labor giving form to our impatience
> for liberty.
>
> —Michel Foucault, "What Is Enlightenment?"

FILL IN THE blank. *X* is to contemporary AIDS activists as
Norman O. Brown or Herbert Marcuse was to student radicals
of the New Left. Alternatively, if American labor organizers of
the 1930s might all be imagined to have carried about with them
in their back pockets a copy of *The Communist Manifesto,* and
if antiwar demonstrators and campus protesters of the late
1960s might all be imagined to have carried about with them in
their jeans a copy of *Life Against Death* or *Love's Body, Eros
and Civilization* or *One-Dimensional Man,* what book do we
imagine the more reflective members of ACT UP to carry about
with them in their leather jackets? What is the single most
important intellectual source of political inspiration for contemporary AIDS activists—at least for the more theoretically-

minded or better-outfitted among them? When I conducted an admittedly unsystematic survey in 1990 of various people I happened to know who had been active in ACT UP/New York during its explosive early phase in the late 1980s, and when I put those questions to them, I received, without the slightest hesitation or a single exception, the following answer: Michel Foucault, *The History of Sexuality, Volume I.*

Now that may come as something of a surprise, especially to those left-liberal critics of Foucault who had been scandalized specifically by what they took to be the *political* implications of Foucault's notion of power, as that notion was originally articulated in *Discipline and Punish*, in the interviews collected under the title *Power/Knowledge*, and most provocatively of all in a ten-page chapter smack in the middle of *The History of Sexuality, Volume I.* Few left-wing philosophers and literary critics would have suspected, even less than a decade ago, that Foucault was headed for political sainthood, let alone that he was about to be canonized as the founding spirit of a newly militant form of popular resistance. For it was the received opinion among many on the Left that Foucault's hypothesis, advanced in *The History of Sexuality, Volume I*, that "power is everywhere"[1] effectively robbed people of freedom and made successful political opposition impossible.

It's not very hard to figure out what it was about Foucault's notion of power that traditional liberals found so sinister, so dangerous, and even so reactionary. First of all, on Foucault's view, power is not a substance but a relation. Power is therefore not *possessed* but *exercised*. That means that power should not be conceptualized as the property of someone who can be identified and confronted, nor should it be thought of (at least in the first instance) as embedded in particular agents or institutions. Power is not a possession of the Monarch or the Father or the State, and people cannot be divided into those who "have" it and those who don't. Instead, power is what characterizes the complex relations among the parts of a particular society—and the interactions among individuals in that society—as relations of ongoing struggle. Power is thus a dynamic *situation,* whether personal, social, or institutional: it is not a quantum of force but a strategic, unstable relation. Because power, for Foucault, is intrinsically relational in character, specific political struggles are properly described not in terms of power *tout court* but in terms of "relations of power."[2]

Power, then, is not to be understood according to the model of a unidirectional vector from oppressor to oppressed. Rather, it's a fluid, all-encompassing medium, immanent in every sort of social relation—though unevenly concentrated or distributed, to be sure, and often stabilized in its dynamics by the functioning of social institutions. Foucault doesn't deny the reality of domination, in other words; what he denies is that domination is the whole story there is to tell when it comes to power. And Foucault even asserts—famously—that "power comes from below."[3]

Hence, power is not intrinsically, nor is it only, negative: it is not just the power to deny, to suppress, to constrain—the power to say no, you can't. Power is also positive and productive. It produces possibilities of action, of choice—and, ultimately, it produces the conditions for the exercise of freedom (just as freedom constitutes a condition for the exercise of power). Power is therefore not opposed to freedom. And freedom, correspondingly, is not freedom *from* power—it is not a privileged zone outside power, unconstrained by power—but a potentiality internal to power, even an effect of power.[4]

Power, then, is everywhere. Resistance to power takes place from within power; it is part of the total relations of power, "part of the strategic relationship of which power consists." What escapes from relations of power—and something always does escape, according to Foucault—does not escape from the reach of power to a place outside power, but represents the

limit of power, its reversal or rebound.[5] *The aim of an opposi-*
tional politics is therefore not liberation but resistance.[6]

▼   ▼   ▼   ▼   ▼   ▼   ▼   ▼

ALTHOUGH SOME of Foucault's critics on the Left may simply have misunderstood his claim, "power is everywhere," to
imply that contemporary forms of social domination are so total
in their operations and so overwhelming in their effects as to
leave no possibility for individual or collective resistance, what
most of them are likely to have reacted against in his political
theorizing is not a totalitarian concept of power that would deny
the possibility of resisting domination—a concept of power
that, in any case, is quite alien to Foucault's thinking—but
something resembling its opposite: namely, Foucault's *reversal*
of the standard liberal critique of totalitarianism. When he says
that "power is everywhere," Foucault is not talking about power
in the sense of coercive and irresistible force (which in his lex-
icon goes by the name not of "power" but of "determination");
rather, he is referring to what might be called *liberal power*—
that is, to the kind of power typically at work in the modern
liberal state, which takes as its objects "free subjects" and defines itself wholly in relation to them and to their freedom.[7]
Modern forms of governmentality actually *require* citizens to be
free, so that citizens can assume from the state the burden of
some of its former regulatory functions and impose on themselves—of their own accord—rules of conduct and mechanisms of control. The kind of power Foucault is interested in,
then, far from enslaving its objects, constructs them as subjective agents and preserves them in their autonomy, so as to invest
them all the more completely. Liberal power does not simply
prohibit; it does not directly terrorize. It normalizes, "respon-
sibilizes," and disciplines. The state no longer needs to frighten
or coerce its subjects into proper behavior: it can safely leave

them to make their own choices in the allegedly sacrosanct private sphere of personal freedom which they now inhabit, because within that sphere they *freely and spontaneously* police both their own conduct and the conduct of others—and so "earn," by demonstrating a capacity to exercise them, the various rights assigned by the state's civil institutions exclusively to law-abiding citizens possessed of sound minds and bodies.

What shocked traditional liberals about Foucault's dictum that power is everywhere, then, is the dark vision of modernity, of the liberal state, and of progressive, Enlightenment-era values (such as freedom, truth, and rationality) that it expresses. For according to Foucault's analysis, civil society, scientific research, intellectual activity, and personal life are not in fact free zones from which power has progressively retreated since the Enlightenment but colonized spaces into which it has steadily expanded, proliferated, and diffused itself. In one book after another, but most of all in *The History of Sexuality, Volume I*, Foucault attempts to show that the separation of public and private, of power and knowledge, which is characteristic of modern liberal societies, has not limited (as it is often supposed to have done) the operative field of power but instead has functioned strategically to extend the reach of power and to multiply techniques of social control. Modern liberalism has eliminated certain modes of domination only to produce many others (which do not present themselves as modes of domination and are all the more difficult to challenge or oppose); it has championed an ethic and an ideal of personal freedom while making the exercise of that freedom conditional upon personal submission to new and insidious forms of authority, to ever more deeply internalized mechanisms of constraint.

Foucault's political vision becomes darkest and most radically anti-emancipatory when it focuses on sex. "It is the original thesis of [*The History of Sexuality, Volume I*]," as Leo Bersani succinctly summarizes it, "that power in our societies functions primarily not by repressing spontaneous sexual drives but by producing multiple sexualities, and that through the classification, distribution, and moral rating of those sexualities the individuals practicing them can be approved, treated, marginalized, sequestered, disciplined, or normalized."[8] On Foucault's view, the modern political movements for sexual liberation have been complicitous with—indeed, they have been a part of—the modern regime of sexuality; the sexual revolution has merely strengthened the political powers that it has purported to overthrow. For the effect of sexual liberation has been not, or not only, to *free* us to express our sexuality but to *require* us to express—freely, of course—our sexuality. Although we can now choose more easily *how* to be sexually free, we can no longer choose so easily *whether* to be sexually free, *what* to count as sexual freedom, *where* to draw the distinction between sexual and nonsexual expression—or how to interrelate our sexual behaviors, our personal identities, our public lives, and our political struggles.[9] Sexual liberation may have liberated our sexuality but it has not liberated us *from* our sexuality; if anything, it has enslaved us more profoundly to it. In that sense, the kind of freedom that sexual liberation has produced imposes on us an even more insidious unfreedom. Or, at the risk of sounding Orwellian, it enslaves us to a specific mode of freedom and thereby makes the exercise of other freedoms almost unthinkable. To paraphrase the Sex Pistols, the modern regime of sexuality takes away our freedom in the name of liberty—or, to be more precise, it takes away our freedom by imposing on us its own brand of liberty, by requiring us to be "free" according to its own definitions of freedom, and by constructing freedom as a "privilege" that we must, on pain of forfeiting it, use responsibly and never abuse. In our present context, then, liberation movements bind us more closely to the very thing from which we may need most urgently to emancipate ourselves. What we ultimately have to liberate ourselves from may be nothing less than "freedom" itself—that is, from the liberal concept of freedom as a regulative or normative ideal of responsible and self-respecting human conduct.

▼   ▼   ▼   ▼   ▼   ▼   ▼   ▼

Such NOTIONS, not surprisingly, proved to be scandalous in 1978 when *The History of Sexuality, Volume I*, was translated into English—scandalous especially, it would seem, to non-gay-identified academic left-wing men. Typical of that reaction is an exasperated protest by Edward Said, a sometime admirer of Foucault's, in *The World, the Text, and the Critic* (1983). "The problem," Said writes,

> is that Foucault's use of the term *pouvoir* moves around too much, swallowing up every obstacle in its path . . . obliterating change and mystifying its microphysical sovereignty. . . . In fact, Foucault's theory of power is a Spinozist conception, which has captivated not only Foucault himself but many of his readers who wish to go beyond Left optimism and Right pessimism so as to justify political quietism with sophisticated intellectualism, at the same time wishing to appear realistic, in touch with the world of power and reality, as well as historical and antiformalistic in their bias. The trouble is that Foucault's theory has drawn a circle around itself, constituting a unique territory in which Foucault has imprisoned himself and others with him. . . . Resistance cannot equally be an adversarial alternative to power and a dependent function of it, except in some metaphysical, ultimately trivial sense. . . . The disturbing circularity of Foucault's theory of power is a form of theoretical overtotalization. . . . [10]

In a more moderate vein, Peter Dews complains that power, for Foucault, "having nothing determinate to which it could be opposed, loses all explanatory content and becomes a ubiquitous, metaphysical principle"; Foucault's work therefore reveals "the inability of Nietzschean naturalism, of a pure theory of forces, to provide a substitute for the normative foundations of political critique."[11] A similar complaint appears in a well-meaning and perceptive but resolutely disengaged essay by the philosopher Charles Taylor entitled "Foucault on Freedom and Truth." Taylor argues that "power, in [Foucault's] sense, *does not make sense* without at least the idea of liberation.... Foucault's Nietzschean theory can only be the basis of utterly monolithic analyses...."[12] The Marxist critic Frank Lentricchia, in the course of a brilliant, detailed, nuanced, and otherwise sympathetic reading of *Discipline and Punish*, singles out Foucault's conception of power as the most objectionable feature of the book's argument. Contending correctly that "Foucault's theory of power, because it gives power to anyone, everywhere, at all times, provides a means of resistance, but no real goal for resistance," Lentricchia concludes, "Because he leaves no shaded zone, no free space for real alternatives to take form, Foucault's vision of power, despite its provisions for reversals of direction, courts a monolithic determinism . . . and determinism courts despair."[13] Jürgen Habermas simply categorized Foucault, along with other supposed "antimodernists" such as Jacques Derrida, as a "Young Conservative."[14] Similar objections to the political implications of Foucault's thought—or to Foucault's failure to produce a substantively critical political theory or to articulate a positive program of political action—were raised by many others; they have been scrupulously examined and persuasively refuted by Keith Gandal, Mark Maslan, Ed Cohen, Judith Butler, and Joseph Rouse.[15]

In any case, if "political quietism" actually was the covert message of Foucault's inquiries into the nature of power, as Said implies, that message was certainly lost on the AIDS Coalition to Unleash Power, or ACT UP. ACT UP has been accused of many things, but not even Larry Kramer at his most exasperated has exactly accused ACT UP of quietism (so far as I know).

After all, ACT UP is the organization that blocked traffic on San Francisco's Golden Gate Bridge, halted trading on the New York Stock Exchange, and disrupted the broadcast of the *CBS Evening News*, among many other spectacular actions.[16] The quietist reading of Foucault is also at stark odds with Foucault's own well-documented practice of political engagement. At the very time that he was crafting his heretical formulations about power, in fact, the fifty-year-old philosopher was regularly engaging in street battles with the police, fighting at sufficiently close quarters to sustain a variety of serious physical injuries—including, on at least one occasion, a broken rib. "It is the cop's job to use physical force," Foucault explained in the pages of *Libération* on September 24, 1975, in reference to another episode; "anyone who opposes cops must not, therefore, let them maintain the hypocrisy of disguising this force behind orders that have to be immediately obeyed."[17] What Foucault referred to at the end of his life as his "hyperactivism" amounted to a great deal more than a few high-profile, celebrity political endeavors—such as founding *Libération*, or holding an audacious press conference in Franco's Madrid to denounce the fascist government's planned execution of ten young Basque militants. (Foucault and his fellow VIPs were quickly arrested and deported, five of the militants later put to death.) From the late 1960s on, Foucault tirelessly took part in the real dirty work of political organizing—going to meetings, writing manifestos, handing out leaflets, and even driving three thousand kilometers from Paris to Warsaw in the fall of 1982, less than two years before his death, leading a convoy of medical supplies and smuggled printing materials that he had helped to collect for the beleaguered members of Solidarnosc.[18]

All that highly visible political activity, however, far from reassuring Foucault's liberal critics, seems actually to have contributed to their mistrust of him. Richard Rorty, for example, judged Foucault's "anarchist politics" to amount to little more than "self-indulgent radical chic."[19] The term of criticism that stands out most strikingly in that formulation is, of course, "self-indulgent." By so labeling the queer brand of street politics that Foucault engaged in, Rorty manages to imply that getting beaten up by the police presents to academic philosophers the sort of seductive appeal that only an austere and strong-minded person, capable of holding out against the temptation to indulge his taste for fashionable causes, can withstand—as if keeping one's distance from violent street demonstrations did not in fact represent to intellectuals the path of least resistance to their own innate tendencies but required of them instead a rare and laudable fortitude. (Foucault's biographer David Macey mildly observes that Rorty's judgment on Foucault reflects "little concrete knowledge and a lot of credit in hearsay.")[20] Liberal critiques of Foucault's politics, suffice it to say, merit detailed political interrogation in their own right.

▼   ▼   ▼   ▼   ▼   ▼   ▼   ▼

DESPITE THE rigorously anti-empancipatory thrust of his work, and despite the mistrust of his critics, Foucault insisted that he fully intended his intellectual activities to have a political impact. Even his most arcane scholarly investigations were undertaken with the aim of intervening in contemporary social struggles. He was surprised, but ultimately very pleased, by the political use to which the British antipsychiatry movement put his first major book, *Madness and Civilization*. He expected— quite realistically, as it turned out—that the publication of *Discipline and Punish* would create turmoil in the administration of the French prison system. *The History of Sexuality, Volume I*, also aimed to intervene in contemporary sexual politics. Reflecting on the political reception of his work in an (awkwardly translated) 1978 interview, Foucault described the relationship between his historical inquiries and contemporary political movements as follows:

> [My] investigation makes use of "true" documents, but in such a way as to furnish not just the evidence of truth but also an experience that might permit an alteration, a transformation, of the relationship we have with ourselves and our cultural universe: in a word, with our knowledge.
>
> Thus this game of truth and fiction—or if you prefer, of evidence and fabrication—will permit us to see clearly what links us to our modernity and at the same time will make it appear modified to us. This experience that permits us to single out certain mechanisms (for example, imprisonment, penalization, etc.) and at the same time to separate ourselves from them by perceiving them in a totally different form, must be one and the same experience.
>
> This procedure is central to all my work. And what are its consequences? . . . [That], starting from experience, it is necessary to clear the way for a transformation, a metamorphosis which isn't simply individual but which has a character accessible to others: that is, this experience must be linkable, to a certain extent, to a collective practice and to a way of thinking. That is how it happened, for example, for such movements as anti-psychiatry, or the prisoners' movement in France.[21]

One test of a book's success for Foucault was whether or not it got linked up with, and helped to mobilize or at least contributed to, a larger process of social transformation.

Still, it would probably be a mistake to give Foucault too much credit for the emergence of contemporary styles of direct-action politics or to infer from Foucault's perennial vogue among cultural radicals that his notions about power played a decisive or formative role in the development of the new social movements. For all its subsequent influence on those movements, Foucault's thought may actually owe more to them than they owe to him. At least some of Foucault's most important theoretical reflections on power were directly inspired by political struggles that he saw already going on around him—political struggles waged (to cite some of the examples Foucault himself mentions) by the student movements, the children's rights movement, the prisoners' rights movement, the antipsychiatry movement, the women's movement, and the lesbian and gay movement.[22] And in any case it is improbable that the prestige accorded to Foucault even by such intellectually sophisticated groups as ACT UP/New York reflects the direct influence of *The History of Sexuality, Volume I.* Foucault's influence is more likely to be an effect of the ways in which his work has been mediated by other texts of greater contemporary relevance—by recent texts, say, in art history and criticism, lesbian and gay studies, or political theory—as well as by such larger social developments as the emergence of theoretically informed practices of subcultural resistance or the academic vogue for "poststructuralist" critical theory.[23] But whatever relation of cause and effect may obtain between Foucault's thought and the new social movements, it is noteworthy that his speculations about power seem to have found their most receptive audience among cultural activists, members of political direct-action groups, participants in various social resistance movements with some connection to universities, and—most of all, perhaps—lesbian and gay militants.

It is curious, then, that the text of Foucault's that has positioned him, if only in retrospect, as the intellectual architect of what is arguably the most significant recent development in progressive politics in the United States (and perhaps elsewhere)— the text that, everyone now says, *you can't even begin to practice queer politics without reading*—it is curious that *this* text of Foucault's should turn out to be the very text that, at the time of its publication, aroused such vehement criticism from leftists on political grounds and earned its author so much vilification from self-styled exponents of progressive politics on both sides of the Atlantic. What did gay activists see in Foucault, and specifically in *The History of Sexuality, Volume I*, that his straight-liberal critics missed, and why?[24] That is the question that will occupy me, in one form or another, for the remainder of this essay.

▼   ▼   ▼   ▼   ▼   ▼   ▼   ▼

A NUMBER OF plausible answers suggest themselves, and I'll run through a few of them briefly before lingering over the one I wish to emphasize. The most obvious impetus for gay activists to find political inspiration in *The History of Sexuality, Volume I*, has come, of course, from AIDS. In fact, it would be difficult to imagine a more powerful or urgent demonstration than the AIDS crisis of the need to conceptualize sexuality, after the manner of Foucault, as "an especially concentrated point of traversal [*point de passage*] for relations of power."[25] (Feminists, to be sure, had been making similar arguments for many years about gender, and about sexual relations between women and men in the context of gender inequality; perhaps it has taken AIDS to drive home a similar message to gay men. But perhaps Foucault's focus on sexuality, and his refusal to subordinate the analysis of its instrumentality to the politics of gender, race, or class, made his work particularly useful for addressing the irreducibly *sexual* politics of the AIDS crisis.)[26] It would also be difficult to imagine a better illustration than the public response to AIDS of the mutual imbrication of power and knowledge, which manifests itself in endless relays between expert discourse and institutional authority, between medical truth and social regulation, as well as between popular knowledge practices (for example, the dissemination of safer-sex information in gay male enclaves) and local struggles for survival and resistance. Or, as Foucault put it in *The History of Sexuality, Volume I*, "Between techniques of knowledge and strategies of power, there is no exteriority, even if they have specific roles and are linked together on the basis of their difference."[27] Finally, AIDS has focused attention on the modalities of what Foucault calls, in *The History of Sexuality, Volume I,* "bio-power"—specifically on the state's administration of the technology for producing and regulating life.

AIDS activism has taken its distinctive (and indicatively modern) shape from the social and institutional embodiments of the power/knowledge nexus with which it has had to struggle. In order to be effective, AIDS activism has had to challenge traditional modes of empowering knowledge as well as traditional modes of authorizing and legitimating power. It has had to find ways of breaking down monopolies of professional expertise, ways of democratizing knowledge, and ways of credentializing the disempowered so that they can intervene in the medical and governmental administration of the epidemic. AIDS activism has thereby accelerated a multiplication of the sites of political contestation beyond such traditional arenas as the electoral process, the power structure, and the industrial economy, to immigration policy, public health policy (including such matters as anonymous HIV-antibody testing and needle exchange), the practice of epidemiology and clinical medicine (right down to the determination of optimum dosage levels for new drugs), the conduct of scientific research (the elimination of placebo trials in experiments on human subjects), the operation of the insurance and pharmaceutical industries, the role of the media in representing the epidemic, the decisions of rent-control boards, the legal definition of "family," and ultimately the public and the private administration of the body and its pleasures. Foucault's *History of Sexuality, Volume I,* had already treated the body as a site of political struggle. ACT UP—which has led a kind of uprising of the sick against their doctors, insurers, health care providers, blood banks, public welfare administrators, prison wardens, medical researchers, drug vendors, and media experts, not to mention their employers and landlords—would seem to furnish a perfect example of a strategic power reversal, a form of resistance made possible by the very apparatus of power/knowledge it was invented to resist.[28]

Next, the notion that freedom is internal to power finds an echo in the experiences of many gay men. W. H. Auden's question of 1942—"When shall we learn, what should be clear as day, We cannot choose what we are free to love?"—is perfectly Foucauldian in spirit.[29] Perhaps a similar understanding of the relation between power and freedom is encoded in the distinctively gay male practice known as *camp*. Camp, after all, is a form of cultural resistance that is entirely predicated on a shared consciousness of being inescapably situated within a powerful system of social and sexual meanings. Camp resists the power of that system from within by means of parody, exaggeration, amplification, theatricalization, and literalization of normally tacit codes of conduct—codes whose very authority derives from their privilege of never having to be explicitly articulated, and thus from their customary immunity to critique. (I'm thinking of codes of masculinity, for example.)[30]

Finally, nothing communicates the sense that power is everywhere more eloquently than the experience of the closet.[31] The closet is nothing, first of all, if not the product of complex relations of power. The only reason to be *in* the closet is to protect oneself from the many and virulent sorts of social disqualification that one would suffer were the discreditable fact of one's sexual orientation more widely known. To "closet" one's homosexuality is also to submit oneself to the social imperative imposed on gay people by non-gay-identified people, the imperative to shield the latter not from the knowledge of one's homosexuality so much as from the necessity of acknowledging the knowledge of one's homosexuality.[32] The experience of the closet, then, is hardly an experience of freedom (although the closet certainly does afford its occupants an otherwise unattainable latitude and admits them to some of the privileges reserved for those who are heterosexually identified). By contrast, if there is something self-affirming and indeed *liberating* about coming *out* of the closet, that is not because coming out enables one to emerge from a state of servitude into a state of untrammeled liberty. On the contrary: to come out is precisely to expose oneself to a different set of dangers and constraints, to make oneself into a convenient screen onto which straight people can project all the fantasies they routinely entertain about gay people, and to suffer one's every gesture, statement, expression, and opinion to be totally and irrevocably marked by the overwhelming social significance of one's openly acknowledged homosexual identity.[33] If to come out is to release oneself from a state of unfreedom, that is not because coming out constitutes an escape from the reach of power to a place outside of power: rather, coming out puts into play a different set of power relations and alters the dynamics of personal and political struggle. *Coming out is an act of freedom, then, not in the sense of liberation but in the sense of resistance.*

There are doubtless many other factors that may explain the overdetermined appeal for gay activists of Foucault in general and *The History of Sexuality, Volume I,* in particular. For the purpose of this essay, however, I want to concentrate on only one motive for the gay-militant appropriation of Foucault. I believe that Foucault's political approach to discourse, specifically his inquiry into what might be called the political economy of sexual discourse,[34] enables us to devise some effective strategies for confronting and resisting the discursive operations of contemporary homophobia. For one thing, Foucault's example teaches us to analyze discourse strategically, not in terms of what it *says* but in terms of what it *does* and how it *works*. That does not mean that we learn from Foucault to treat the *content* of particular discourses as uninteresting or irrelevant (after all, one has to understand what discourses say in order to be able to analyze what they do and how they work); it does mean that we learn from him not to allow the truth or falsity of particular propositions to distract us from the power-effects they produce or the manner in which they are deployed within particular systems of discursive and institutional practice.[35] The effect of Foucault's political approach to discourse is not to collapse truth into power but to *shift the focus* of our attention from matters of truth to matters of power.[36] That shift has proven extremely profitable for the analysis of homophobic discourse;[37] it has also proven crucial for the larger projects of delegitimating heterosexist authority and empowering gay practices of knowledge and community. I shall take up each of these three points in turn.

▼ ▼ ▼ ▼ ▼ ▼ ▼ ▼

FOUCAULT DID NOT always occupy such an honorific position in the pantheon of gay political theory, and when such a position was offered him he repudiated it, evading occasional efforts by left-wing gay intellectuals to credit his writings with contributing to the gay liberation movement: "My work has had nothing to do with gay liberation," he reportedly told one admirer in 1975.[38] And, indeed, it was precisely the anti-emancipatory rhetoric of *The History of Sexuality, Volume I*, that led so many of Foucault's liberal critics to denounce it.

But that was a long time ago, and times have changed. Gay liberation seems a strangely antiquated formula. Nowadays, when gay men in the United States talk about politics, chances are the talk is not so much about change or reform or liberation as it is about *survival* and *resistance*. That shift does not merely reflect a fundamental despair, and consequently diminished expectations, brought on by AIDS, by the intensified and newly fashionable homophobia evoked by it, and by the recent wave of antigay pogroms in U.S. cities (there was a 172 percent increase in antigay violence between 1988 and 1992),[39] which the Catholic church and the Republican party, among other institutions, have incited or applauded. Nor does the disenchantment with liberation proceed merely from a growing awareness that gay life has generated its own disciplinary regimes, its own techniques of normalization, in the form of obligatory haircuts, T-shirts, dietary practices, body piercing, leather accoutrements, and physical exercise (would you say, for example, that your daily workout at the gym feels more like liberation or forced labor?). Ultimately, I think, what the shift away from a liberation model of gay politics reflects is a deepened understanding of the discursive structures and representational systems that determine the production of sexual meanings, and that micromanage individual perceptions, in such a way as to maintain and reproduce the underpinnings of heterosexist privilege.[40]

To put the point more plainly, it has become increasingly clear to gay men in the United States that what we are up against in our struggles to survive this genocidal era is not only—and perhaps not ultimately—specific agents of oppression, such as gay-bashers or the police, nor formal, explicit interdictions, such as sodomy laws, nor even particular, hostile institutions, such as the Supreme Court, but rather pervasive and multiform strategies of homophobia that shape public and private discourses, saturate the entire field of cultural representation, and, like power in Foucault's formulation, are everywhere. The discourses of homophobia, moreover, cannot be refuted by means of rational argument (although many of the individual propositions that constitute them are easily falsifiable); they can only be resisted. That is because homophobic discourses are not reducible to a set of statements with a specifiable truth-content that can be rationally tested. Rather, homophobic discourses function as part of more general and systematic strategies of delegitimation. If they are to be resisted, then, they will have to be resisted strategically—that is, by fighting strategy with strategy.

▼   ▼   ▼   ▼   ▼   ▼   ▼   ▼

Homophobic discourses contain no fixed propositional content. They are composed of a potentially infinite number of different but functionally interchangeable assertions, such that whenever any one assertion is falsified or disqualified another one—even one with a content exactly contrary to the original one—can be neatly and effectively substituted for it. A good example of the opportunistic and propositionally indeterminate nature of homophobic discourses is provided by the history of legal disputes over whether homosexuality constitutes an "immutable characteristic." The story begins in the nineteenth century, when German gay-rights advocates who were attempting to decriminalize sodomy decided it would be to their advantage to represent homosexuality to their contemporaries as a natural condition into which a minority of individuals are born rather than as a sin or moral failing or acquired perversity for which homosexuals themselves should be held criminally liable; these militants succeeded so well in convincing the early sexologists of their view that a number of influential, mid- and late-nineteenth-century accounts of "sexual inversion" relied for their data on the self-representations of gay polemicists. That victory did not bring about the reform of the Prussian penal code—despite some initial, and quite promising, results. It did diminish the practice of sending homosexuals to jail for fixed terms; from now on, instead, they would be incarcerated for life in insane asylums—and ultimately exterminated in concentration camps by the Nazis—as members of a degenerate *species*. Judicial history has recently been repeating itself in the United States. American courts have ruled repeatedly that homosexuals possess no rights, as a minority group, to equal protection under the law, in part because homosexuality—unlike race or gender, supposedly—is not an "immutable characteristic." At the same time, the courts have held that homosexuals as a group do share at least one immutable characteristic: by definition we all commit sodomy, apparently, which is a felony in half of the United States. As of April 15, 1991 (when my information runs out), four separate judicial decisions had, on the basis of such reasoning, legally defined homosexuals to be criminals *as a class*.[41] In short, if homosexuality *is* an immutable characteristic, we lose our civil rights, and if homosexuality is *not* an immutable characteristic, we lose our civil rights. Anyone for rational argument on these terms?

Homophobic discourses are incoherent, then, but their incoherence, far from incapacitating them, turns out to empower them. In fact, homophobic discourses operate strategically *by means of* logical contradictions. The logical contradictions internal to homophobic discourses give rise to a series of double binds which function—incoherently, to be sure, but nonetheless effectively and systematically—to impair the lives of lesbians and gay men.

The best illustration of this phenomenon is provided by what Eve Kosofsky Sedgwick has memorably called the "epistemology of the closet."[42] Sedgwick has shown that the closet is an impossibly contradictory place: you can't be in it, and you can't be out of it. You can't be in it because—so long as you *are* in the closet—you can never be certain of the extent to which you have actually succeeded in keeping your homosexuality secret; after all, one effect of being in the closet is that you are precluded from knowing whether people are treating you as straight because you have managed to fool them and they do not suspect you of being gay, or whether they are treating you as straight because they are playing along with you and enjoying the epistemological privilege that your ignorance of their knowledge affords them. But if you can never be in the closet, you can't ever be out of it either, because those who have once enjoyed the epistemological privilege constituted by their knowledge of your ignorance of their knowledge typically refuse to give up that privilege, and insist on constructing your sexuality as a secret to which they have special access, a secret which always gives itself away to their superior and knowing gaze.[43] By that means they contrive to consolidate their claim to a superior knowingness about sexual matters, a knowingness that is not only distinct from knowledge but is actually opposed to it, is actually a form of ignorance, insofar as it conceals from the knowing the political nature of their own considerable stakes in preserving the epistemology of the closet as well as in maintaining the corresponding and exactly opposite epistemological construction of heterosexuality as *both* an obvious fact that can be universally known without "flaunting itself" *and* a form of personal life that can remain protectively private without constituting a secret truth.

The closet is an impossibly contradictory place, moreover, because when you *do* come out, it's both too soon and too late. You can tell that it's too soon by the frequency with which the affirmation of your homosexuality is greeted with impatient dismissal, which may take either an abusive form—of the "Why do you have to shove it in our faces?" variety—or, in better circles, the supremely urbane form of feigned boredom and indifference: "Why did you imagine that we would be interested in knowing such an inconsequential and trivial fact about you?"[44] (Of course, you told them *not* because you thought they would be interested—although in fact they obviously *are* interested, intensely interested—but because you didn't want them to presume that you were straight.) Nonetheless, whenever you do come out of the closet, it's also already too late, because if you had been honest you would have come out earlier.

That double bind operates not only informally, in personal relations, but institutionally—for instance, in the courts. I quote

Eve Kosofsky Sedgwick's powerful account of one particularly telling example.

In Montgomery County, Maryland, in 1973, an eighth-grade earth science teacher named Acanfora was transferred to a nonteaching position by the Board of Education when they learned he was gay. When Acanfora spoke to the news media, such as "60 Minutes" and the Public Broadcasting System, about his situation, he was refused a new contract entirely. Acanfora sued. The federal district court that first heard his case supported the action and rationale of the Board of Education, holding that Acanfora's recourse to the media had brought undue attention to himself and his sexuality, to a degree that would be deleterious to the educational process. The Fourth Circuit Court of Appeals disagreed. They considered Acanfora's public disclosures to be protected speech under the First Amendment. Although they overruled the lower court's rationale, however, the appellate court affirmed its decision not to allow Acanfora to return to teaching. Indeed, they denied his standing to bring the suit in the first place, on the grounds that he had failed to note on his original employment application that he had been, in college, an officer of a student homophile organization—a notation that would, as school officials admitted in court, have prevented his ever being hired. The rationale for keeping Acanfora out of his classroom was thus no longer that he had disclosed too much about his homosexuality, but quite the opposite, that he had not disclosed enough. The Supreme Court declined to entertain an appeal.

It is striking that each of the two rulings in *Acanfora* emphasized that the teacher's homosexuality "itself" would not have provided an acceptable ground for denying him employment. Each of the courts relied in its decision on an implicit distinction between the supposedly protected and bracketable fact of Acanfora's homosexuality proper, on the one hand, and on the other hand his highly vulnerable management of information about it. So very vulnerable does this latter exercise prove to be, however, and vulnerable to such a contradictory array of interdictions, that the space for simply existing as a gay person who is a teacher is in fact bayonetted through and through, from both sides, by the vectors of a disclosure at once compulsory and forbidden.[45]

Sedgwick's whole account of the epistemology of the closet owes a great deal, as she acknowledges, to Foucault. It is inspired, specifically, by a passage in *The History of Sexuality, Volume I*, which Sedgwick quotes at the outset of her study:

> Silence itself . . . is less the absolute limit of discourse . . . than an element that functions alongside the things said. . . . There is no binary division to be made between what one says and what one does not say; we must try to determine the different ways of not saying such things, how those who can and those who cannot speak of them are distributed, which type of discourse is authorized, or what form of discretion is required in either case.

But Sedgwick's entire project can perhaps be summed up more precisely by transposing Foucault's terms and suggesting instead that Sedgwick does for "knowledge" and "ignorance" what Foucault himself did for "speech" and "silence." One has only to substitute "ignorance" for "silence" and "epistemology" for "discourse" in the concluding sentence of the passage Sedgwick quotes in order to grasp this point: "There is not one but many silences," Foucault writes, "and they are an integral part of the strategies that underlie and permeate discourses."[46]

The great virtue of Sedgwick's analysis is that it delivers lesbians and gay men from the temptation to play what is ultimately a mug's game of refuting the routine slanders and fantasies produced by the discourses of homophobia. The reason it is pointless to refute the lies of homophobia is not that they are difficult or impossible to refute—on the contrary, taken one at a time they are easily falsifiable, as I've already suggested—but that refuting them does nothing to impair the stra-

tegic functioning of discourses that operate precisely by
deploying a series of mutually contradictory premises in such a
way that any one of them can be substituted for any other, as
different circumstances may require, without changing the final
outcome of the argument. Sedgwick's account recalls us, specifically, from our natural impulse to try and win, move by move,
the game of homophobic truth being played against us and to
respond to each fresh defeat in this losing game by determining
to play it harder, better, more intelligently, more truthfully.
Sedgwick encourages us, instead, to stop playing long enough
to stand back from the game, to look at all its rules in their
totality, and to examine our entire strategic situation: how the
game has been set up, on what terms most favorable to whom,
with what consequences for which of its players. In this she
exemplifies the basic method of Foucauldian discourse analysis, which is to refuse to engage with the content of particular
authoritative discourses—in this case, with the content of homophobic discourses—and to analyze discourses in terms of
their overall strategies.

▼　　▼　　▼　　▼　　▼　　▼　　▼　　▼

FOUCAULT'S tendency to analyze discourses not substantively but strategically dates back to his early work on "madness
and unreason." In the original preface to *Madness and Civilization*, for example, Foucault describes his project, famously,
as follows:

> In the serene world of mental illness, modern man no
> longer communicates with the madman. . . . As for a com-
> mon language, there is no such thing; or rather, there is no
> such thing any longer; the constitution of madness as a
> mental illness, at the end of the eighteenth century, affords
> the evidence of a broken dialogue, posits the separation
> as already effected, and thrusts into oblivion all those

stammered, imperfect words without fixed syntax in which the exchange between madness and reason was made. The language of psychiatry, which is a monologue of reason *about* madness, has been established only on the basis of such a silence.

I have not tried to write the history of that language, but rather the archaeology of that silence.[47]

Rather than examine and critique the representations or concepts of madness produced by psychiatric scientists, in other words, Foucault inquires into the process whereby madness came to occupy its present discursive position vis-à-vis reason and rationality—how it came to be deauthorized, silenced, relegated to the status of a voiceless object of scientific discourse, and positioned both institutionally and discursively in relation to evolving practices of reason. Madness, on Foucault's view, is not a thing but a relation. As Foucault explained in an interview in *Le Monde* on July 22, 1961, "Madness cannot be found in a wild state. Madness exists only within a society, it does not exist outside the forms of sensibility which isolate it and the forms of repulsion which exclude it or capture it."[48] Madness, in effect, is a by-product of the processes that constructed the modern form of reason itself: madness is constituted in such a way as to answer to the functional requirements of reason (which comes to define itself as the knowledge of the difference between reason and madness) and thereby furnishes an element indispensable to the discursive and institutional operation of reason.[49] Or, as Roland Barthes, reviewing Foucault's book, put it, "[M]adness is not an object of understanding, whose history must be rediscovered; it is nothing more, if you like, than this understanding itself. . . ."[50] And Michel Serres, in his own review, went further: "[T]he object of archaic psychiatric knowledge is not so much the madman . . . as a projection of the classical cultural universe on to the space of confinement."[51] Substitute "homosexuality" for "madness" and "heterosexuality" for "reason" in these formulations and you have (despite the obvious disanalogies between the two sets of terms) many of the grounding axioms of contemporary queer theory.

In *The History of Sexuality, Volume I*, Foucault took the same approach to "sexuality" as he had to "madness": he treats sexuality not as a thing, a natural reality, but as the necessary instrument and determinate effect of an entire series of discursive and political strategies. "Sexuality," he writes, "must not be thought of as a kind of natural given which power tries to hold in check, or as an obscure domain which knowledge tries gradually to uncover."[52] Sexuality, in the first instance at least, is nothing more than "the correlative of that slowly developed discursive practice which constitutes the *scientia sexualis*"; its essential features correspond "to the functional requirements of a discourse that must produce its truth."[53] If sexuality is located by that discourse in nature, in bodies—in what, in other words, are the most literal and objective of realities[54] that positivism can conceive—that is because sexuality is defined by its function, which is to ground the discourse of which it is the object. Without a stable object to study, there can be no positive science of sexuality. It is part of the function of sexuality, in its role as "a specific domain of truth,"[55] to provide an epistemological anchor for that science, a secure ground of knowledge on which the new science of sexuality can be built.

Foucault's shift of perspective, his insistence on writing the history of sexuality "from the viewpoint of a history of discourses"[56] rather than from the viewpoint of the history of science,[57] enables him both to denaturalize and to politicize sexuality. Conceived according to Foucault in discursive terms, sexuality can now be analyzed according to the strategies immanent in its discursive operation. When sexuality is viewed from that angle, it appears not as a natural drive but instead (as we have seen) as "an especially concentrated point of traversal for relations of power." Sexuality is in fact part of an "apparatus" or "device" (*dispositif*)[58] that serves to connect new forms of power and knowledge with new objects and new domains. It can therefore be described as "a great surface network in which the stimulation of bodies, the intensification of pleasures, the incitement to discourse, the formation of special knowledges, the strengthening of controls and resistances, are linked to one another, in accordance with a few major strategies of knowledge and power."[59] The political importance of sex consists in the way it supports the modern regime of "bio-power," which Foucault defines, contrasting it with the old regime of "power over life and death," as an "entire political technology of life." "Bio-power" refers to the modern political procedure of regulating human life by means of expert techniques (statistics, demographics, eugenics, sterilization, etc.)—techniques that make possible a strategic alliance between specialized knowledge and institutionalized power in the state's management of life. Sex contributes to this technology, specifically, by connecting the body and the nation, linking "the procedures of power that characterized the disciplines" of sexuality (the "anatomo-politics of the human body") with "an entire series of . . . regulatory controls: a bio-politics of the population."[60]

Foucault's conceptual reorientation of sexuality, his transformation of it from an object of knowledge into a cumulative effect of power—"the sum of effects produced in bodies, behaviors, and social relations by a certain apparatus that emerges from a complex political technology"[61]—enables him effectively to displace conventional ontologies of the sexual and thereby to resist the preemptive claims of various modern expert knowledges, of positivist epistemologies that constitute sexuality as a (or as the) real thing, an objective natural phenomenon to be known by the mind. Foucault's own discursive counterpractice seeks to remove sexuality from among the objects of knowledge and thereby to deauthorize those branches of expertise grounded in a scientific or quasi-scientific understanding of it; it also seeks to delegitimate those regulatory disciplines whose power acquires the guise of legitimate authority by basing itself on a privileged access to the "truth" of sexuality. By analyzing modern knowledge practices in terms of the strategies of power immanent in them, and by treating "sexuality" accordingly not as a determinate thing in itself but as a *positivity* produced by those knowledge practices and situated by their epistemic operations in the place of the real, Foucault politicizes both truth and the body: he reconstitutes knowledge and sexuality as sites of contestation, thereby opening up new opportunities for both scholarly and political intervention.

▼   ▼   ▼   ▼   ▼   ▼   ▼   ▼

THE POLITICAL implications of Foucault's discursive approach to sexuality have not been lost on lesbians and gay men,[62] who for too long have been the objects rather than the subjects of expert discourses of sexuality—who have been the objects, in particular, of murderously pathologizing, criminalizing, and moralizing discourses, one of whose comparatively minor effects has been to deauthorize our subjective experiences and to delegitimate our claims to be able to speak knowledgeably about our own lives. (To be sure, we no longer live in an era when reputable books can be published with such titles as *The Homosexuals: As Seen by Themselves and Thirty Authorities*,[63] but a glance at the recent scientific literature reveals a plethora of equally idiotic and authoritative publications: "Physical and Biochemical Characteristics of Homosexual Men," for example, demonstrates that "homosexuals" have "less subcutaneous fat and smaller muscle/bone development," narrower shoulders in relation to pelvic width, and lesser muscular strength, among many other things, than heterosexuals; "Female Homosexuality and Body Build" establishes that "homosexual women have narrower hips, increased arm and leg girths, less subcutaneous fat, and more muscle than heterosexual women.")[64] It is not surprising, therefore, that a number of lesbian and gay critical and cultural theorists have tended to follow Foucault's example and to resist being drawn in by what he called the *bavardage*, or "chatter,"[65] of psychiatry, sexology, criminology, and social science. Like Sedgwick, they have concerned themselves less with refuting homophobic discourses than with describing how those discourses have been constituted, how they function, how they have constructed their subjects and objects, how they participate in the legitimation of oppressive social practices, and how they manage to make their own operations invisible.[66] In a sense, all gay-positive analysis of the discursive, epistemological, and institutional operations of homophobia begins where Foucault left off: its inaugural gesture, as I already suggested, is to do for the relation between "heterosexuality" and "homosexuality" what Foucault did for the relation between "reason" and "madness."

▼   ▼   ▼   ▼   ▼   ▼   ▼   ▼

How CAN SUCH a discursive or strategic analysis help to explain the puzzling features of homophobic discourse already noted—namely, its paradoxical combination of incoherence, propositional indeterminacy, and social efficacy? Lesbian and gay theorists, influenced by Foucault, have advanced two related explanations, the first in a deconstructive and the second in a psychoanalytic mode. The modes are distinguishable, but they are in fact often and easily combined.[67] According to the first, "the homosexual" is not a stable or autonomous term but a supplement to the definition of "the heterosexual"—a means of stabilizing heterosexual identity.[68] According to the second, "the homosexual" is an imaginary "Other," whose flamboyant "difference" deflects attention from the contradictions inherent in the construction of heterosexuality; heterosexuality thrives precisely by preserving and consolidating its internal contradictions at the same time as it preserves and consolidates its own ignorance of them, and it does that by constructing and deploying the figure of "the homosexual."[69] I'll expand on each of these two points in turn.

The heterosexual/homosexual binarism is itself a homophobic production, just as the man/woman binarism is a sexist production. Each consists of two terms, the first of which is unmarked and unproblematized—it designates "the category to which everyone is assumed to belong" (unless someone is specifically marked as different)—whereas the second term is marked and problematized: it designates a category of persons whom *something differentiates* from normal, unmarked people.[70] The marked (or queer) term ultimately functions not as a means of denominating a real or determinate class of persons but as a means of delimiting and defining—by negation and opposition—the unmarked term. If the term "homosexuality" turns out, as we have seen, not to describe a single, stable *thing* but to operate as a placeholder for a set of mutually incompatible, logically contradictory predicates, whose impossible conjunction does not refer to some paradoxical phenomenon in the world so much as it marks out the limits of the opposed term, "heterosexuality," that is because homosexuality and heterosexuality do not represent a true pair, two mutually referential contraries, but a hierarchical opposition in which heterosexuality defines itself implicitly by constituting itself as the negation of homosexuality.[71] Heterosexuality defines itself without problematizing itself, it elevates itself as a privileged and unmarked term, by abjecting and problematizing homosexuality. Heterosexuality, then, *depends* on homosexuality to lend it substance—and to enable it to acquire *by* default its status *as* a default, as a *lack of difference* or an *absence of abnormality*.[72] ("A source of heterosexual comfort," Paul Morrison suggests: " 'Whatever else you might say about [heterosexuality], at least it's not that.'" But also "a source of heterosexual anxiety: 'There is nothing else to say about it but that.'")[73] Although the unmarked term *claims* a kind of precedence or priority over the marked term, the very logic of supplementarity entails the unmarked term's dependence on the marked term: the unmarked term needs the marked term in order to generate itself as unmarked. In that sense the marked term turns out to be structurally and logically prior to the unmarked one. (In the case of heterosexuality and homosexuality, the marked term's priority to the unmarked term is not only structural or logical but historical as well: the invention of the term and the concept of homosexuality preceded by some years the invention of the term and concept of heterosexuality—which was originally the name of a perversion [what we now call bisexuality] and only gradually came to occupy its familiar place as the polar opposite of homosexuality.)[74] "Homosexual," like "woman,"[75] is not a name that refers to a "natural kind" of thing; it's a discursive, and homophobic, construction that has come to be misrecognized as an object under the epistemological regime known as *realism*. Which is not, of course, to say that homosexuality is unreal. On the contrary, constructions are very real.[76] People live by them, after all—and nowadays, increasingly, they die from them. You can't get more real than that. But if homosexuality is a reality, it is a constructed reality, a social and not a natural reality. The social world contains many realities that do not exist by nature.

"The homosexual," then, is not the name of a natural kind but a projection, a conceptual and semiotic dumping ground for all sorts of mutually incompatible, logically contradictory notions. These contradictory notions not only serve to define the binary opposite of homosexuality by (and as a) default; they also put into play a series of double binds that are uniquely oppressive to those who fall under the description of "homosexual," double binds whose operation is underwritten and sustained by socially entrenched discursive and institutional practices. As constructed by homophobic discourse, "the homosexual" is indeed an impossibly—and, it now appears, fatally—contradictory creature. For "the homosexual" is simultaneously (1) a social misfit, (2) an unnatural monster or freak, (3) a moral failure, and (4) a sexual pervert. Now it is of course impossible, under a post-Kantian system of ethics at least, for anyone to be all of those things at the same time—to be, for example, both *sick* and *blameworthy* in respect of the same defect—but no matter: such attributes may be mutually incompatible in logical terms, but they turn out to be perfectly compatible in practical, that is to say political, terms. Not only do they not cancel out one another in practice, they actually reinforce one another and work together systematically to produce, over and over again, the same effect: namely, the abjection of "the homosexual."

But if the logical contradictions internal to "the homosexual," as the term and concept are deployed in the political economy of sexual discourse, are crippling to those unfortunates who fall under that designation, they also enable—correspondingly—a crucially *empowering* incoherence to attach to the unmarked term and concept of "the heterosexual." They serve to define heterosexuality, implicitly and therefore all the more efficaciously, as simultaneously (1) a social norm, (2) a perfectly natural condition into which everyone is born and into which everyone grows up if no catastrophic accident interferes with normal, healthy development, (3) a highly laudable accomplishment that one is entitled to take pride in and for which one deserves no small amount of personal and social credit, and (4) a frighteningly unstable and precarious state that can easily be overthrown—by such contingent events as coming into contact with a gay or lesbian role model, being seduced by a member of the same sex during adolescence, hearing homosexuality spoken of too often, or having a gay man as a primary school teacher (as if there is anyone who has ever had a *nongay* man as a primary school teacher)—and that therefore needs to be militantly protected, defended, and safeguarded by a constant mobilization of social forces.

What allows those mutually incompatible and internally contradictory notions about heterosexuality not only to coexist but to thrive, to reinforce one another, and to be politically efficacious is their privileged invisibility and the ignorance that surrounds them. The crucial, empowering incoherence at the core of heterosexuality and its definition never becomes visible because heterosexuality itself is never an *object* of knowledge, a target of scrutiny in its own right, so much as it is a *condition* for the supposedly objective, disinterested knowledge of *other* objects, especially homosexuality, which it constantly produces as a manipulably and spectacularly contradictory figure of transgression so as to deflect attention—by means of accusation—from its own incoherence.[77] (If there are no academic Departments of Heterosexual Studies, even in our more liberal universities, that is not only because all branches of the human sciences are already, to a greater or lesser degree, departments of heterosexual studies but also because heterosexuality has thus far largely escaped becoming a *problem* that needs to be studied and understood.)[78] By constituting homosexuality as an object of knowledge, heterosexuality also constitutes itself as a privileged stance of subjectivity—as the very condition of knowing—and thereby avoids becoming an object of knowledge itself, the target of a possible critique.[79] In this, it is of course unlike homosexuality, which is a perennial object of inquiry but never a viable subjective stance, never a disinterested, nonpartisan, legitimate position from which to speak, and is therefore never authorized except as the occasional voice of an already discounted and devalued subcultural minority. Thus, heterosexuality can be a repository for all sorts of contradictory notions without forfeiting its privileges. For the notions that go into heterosexuality, however contradictory they may be, turn out not to be collectively disabling because they operate not as a set of double binds but as a set of mutually authorizing credentials which, despite their patchwork quality, become all the more unimpeachable for *never having to be presented.* Indeed, if heterosexual credentials ever *do* have to be presented, they not only fail to work but tend to invalidate themselves in the process: as all the world knows, there's no quicker or surer way to compromise your own heterosexuality than by proclaiming it. After all, if you really were straight, why would you have to say so? (Heterosexuality, not homosexuality, then, is truly "the love that dare not speak its name.")[80]

▼　　▼　　▼　　▼　　▼　　▼　　▼　　▼

NOW, **IF POWER** is everywhere, according to Foucault, and if freedom—along with the possibilities for resisting power—is contained within power itself, then where shall we locate the pressure points, the fault lines, the most advantageous sites within the political economy of heterosexist/homophobic discourse for disrupting and resisting it? What opportunities does the discursive formation of sexuality create for discursive counterpractices? What sort of antihomophobic strategies does the apparatus of homophobia make possible? Several of them come immediately to mind.

Creative appropriation and resignification. I remember being told that shortly after the newspapers reported the results of Simon LeVay's notorious study purporting to discover the anatomical and neurological cause of sexual orientation,[81] there appeared in San Francisco a new gay disco named Club Hypothalamus. The point was clearly to reclaim a word that had contributed to our scientific objectification, to the remedicalization of sexual orientation, and to transform it ludicrously into a badge of gay identity and a vehicle of queer pleasure.

FIGURE 1

Appropriation and theatricalization. An example of this procedure was furnished by the San Francisco *Bay Times* in its response to the infamous June 21, 1993, "lesbian issue" of *Newsweek* (see Figures 1 and 2). The *Newsweek* article had presented lesbianism to its presumptively straight readership as an interesting but deeply problematic phenomenon that might be socially tolerated but only within certain narrow limits (the

FIGURE 2

"limits of tolerance" formula has been a standard accompaniment to *Newsweek*'s reporting of homosexuality),[82] and it had provided a short glossary of technical terms, such as "butch" and "femme," in order to assist its readers in acquiring a worldly conversancy with the basic if admittedly arcane and exotic features of lesbianism. The *Bay Times* responded ten days later with its own parodic cover story. Picturing the front cover of a publication called *Dykeweek*, it imagined a mainstream weekly magazine addressed presumptively to a readership of lesbians who might on occasion be curious to learn more about the bizarre sexual rituals of heterosexuals. It provided a devastatingly precise and wonderfully alienated perspective on heterosexual roles through its own glossary, which contained such items as "Wife: Traditionally the 'feminine' partner [in a heterosexual relationship] responsible for domestic tasks and child care" and "Vanilla: He comes in five minutes. She just wants to be held."[83] In this way the *Bay Times* implied that heterosexuality, not lesbianism, is what demands to be problematized by sensational journalistic treatment; it also sought to foreground the role-playing, gender polarization, and power asymmetries that are both fundamental and essential to heterosexual relationships— and that heterosexuals take far more seriously than do even the most butch and femme lesbians (insofar as heterosexuals tend to see them not as role-playing, gender polarization, and power asymmetries but as the natural facts of life). Such a response to *Newsweek* is an attempt not to engage with the content of its assertions but to theatricalize its strategies.[84]

Exposure and demystification. If, as Foucault claims in *The History of Sexuality, Volume I*, power's "success is proportional to its ability to hide its own mechanisms,"[85] then the careful mapping and exposure of those mechanisms may do something to frustrate its operations. That, after all, was the task Foucault set himself in his scholarly career. His books on the history of the insane asylum, of the clinic, of the prison, of the human sciences, and of sexual discourse constitute *political histories of the production of "truth"*[86]—scholarly attempts to historicize and defamiliarize, so as the better to sabotage, the technologies of a socially empowered rationality that phobically constructs, then scrupulously isolates and silences, the mad, the sick, the delinquent, and the perverse. As Foucault put it in an interview in *Le Monde* on February 21, 1975,

All my books, whether [*Madness and Civilization*] or this one [*Discipline and Punish*], are little toolboxes, if you will. If people are willing to open them and make use of such and such a sentence or idea, of one analysis or another, as they would a screwdriver or a monkey wrench, in order to short circuit or disqualify systems of power, including even possibly the ones my books come out of, well, all the better.[87]

One way to fight homophobia, accordingly, might be to expose, as I have just tried to do, the operations of homophobic discourses, to reveal the strategies by which the discourses of medicine, law, science, and religion deauthorize lesbians and gay men, to subject those discourses to a political critique, and thereby to attempt to find ways of frustrating the political strategies immanent in their deployment, of delegitimating their claims to authority and dismantling their institutional base.

▼　▼　▼　▼　▼　▼　▼　▼

IN HIS POLITICAL work, by contrast, Foucault tried a different tactic. As one of his biographers sums it up, "The goal of Foucault's political activity was the empowering of others by giving, for instance, prisoners the voice they were denied. His own voice tended therefore to fade, or to be merged into a collective discourse." Rather than intervene immediately in a situation affecting others, and propose reforms in institutions, or improvements in material conditions, on their behalf, Foucault typically used his intellectual skills and his prestigious social location to create specific opportunities for the voices of the disempowered to be heard, recorded, published, and circulated. Except in the case of political struggles affecting the university system, in which he was both a knowledgeable and an interested participant,[88] Foucault tended to see his political role as a facilitator rather than a leader: he consistently refused to speak for others, working instead to create conditions in which others could speak for themselves, and his driving ethical ambition expressed itself in his resistance to any attempt to subordinate the political efforts of particular groups to universalizing or generalizable standards of ethical value. He was wary of formulating specific proposals or programs, because he believed such programs nearly always amount to a power grab; they lead to "abuse or political domination from a bloc" (he claimed instead that political experimentation "without a program can be very useful and very original and creative, if it does not mean without proper reflection about what is going on, or without very careful attention to what's possible").[89] Foucault strongly resisted any attempt to construct abstract ideals against which political change would have to be measured or to prescribe ethical criteria for governing the political actions of others. "[I]f I don't ever say what must be done, it isn't because I believe that there's nothing to be done," Foucault insisted; "on the contrary, it is because I think that there are a thousand things to do, to invent, to forge, on the part of those who, recognizing the relations of power in which they're implicated, have decided to resist or escape them."[90] Foucault saw political collaboration itself as a matter for evolving negotiation among the potential collaborators, whose collective identity and commonality of interests had to be constructed rather than presumed.[91]

Keith Gandal has attempted to explicate Foucault's political attitudes and practices, and his account is worth quoting at some length:

> Foucault developed a new political role for intellectual work and a new sort of political activism that was informed by historical analysis. What has often been thought of as his nihilism was, first of all, his sense that articulating

a set of values inhibits effective and ethical political action, and, secondly, his understanding that resistance cannot stand in pure opposition to the powers that be, but that, instead, struggle and change always take place through co-optation, that, in fact, change is made possible by co-optation because, in the process of co-optation, in assimilating the resistance, the terms of power change. . . . [H]e wanted to establish an activism that was predicated, not on the enumeration of values or the proposal of social policy, but on tactical considerations and ethical practice (including a practice of reform that would not depend upon the expert reformer). Foucault was concerned above all with the *effects* of his thinking and political activity. . . . He pursued struggles where the situation was "intolerable," but also where an alteration of power relations was possible. . . . Those who come to Foucault's work looking for political solutions will be perpetually disappointed. Foucault's project—in both his politics and his histories—was not to lay out solutions, but rather to identify and characterize problems. . . . For Foucault, Truth did not reside in a set of ideas about the way things should be, but in a practice that talked about problems in a manner that opened up new possibilities for action. Identifying and sizing up a problem was the most determinate act of thought. . . . Foucault challenged the intellectual activism whose claim to a progressive politics is a theoretical apparatus, or a correct set of values, or a program for a legitimate political system. He believed that a progressive politics needed, not a vision of what should be, but a sense of what was intolerable and an historical analysis that could help determine possible strategies in political struggles. . . . If Foucault remained fairly silent on the subjects of answers and principles, it was because he was acting ethically and strategically, it was because he believed that asserting principles would get in the way of an ethic of "popular" participation. He wanted to allow and even inspire a practice of criticism which proceeded, not with expert, theoretical or scientific knowledges, but with "low-ranking knowledges."[92]

For example, the aim of the Groupe d'Information sur les Prisons (GIP), which Foucault founded and led in the early 1970s, was not to formulate proposals for the reform of the French prison system but to gather and disseminate information about it and to put that information to the maximum possible disruptive effect. Foucault accordingly devised questionnaires which he distributed to the inmates of prisons, inviting them to record their experiences, identify problems, or specify abuses; he then collated and published the results. His purpose was to expand the available sources of information, and to authorize those who are normally the objects of expert discourses, who are spoken about while remaining silent themselves, to speak on their own behalf—not so that they might confess to the authorities the truth of their being, of course, but so that they could articulate their own needs, point out the conditions that were particularly odious to them, and advance their own political projects.

The first pamphlet issued by the GIP proclaimed the organization's objectives in the following terms:

> The GIP does not propose to speak in the name of the prisoners in various prisons: it proposes, on the contrary, to provide them with the possibility of speaking themselves and telling what goes on in prisons. The GIP does not have reformist goals; we do not dream of some ideal prison: we hope that prisoners may be able to say what it is that is intolerable for them in the system of penal repression. We have to disseminate as quickly and widely as possible the revelations that the prisoners themselves make—the sole means of unifying what is inside and outside the prison, the political battle and the legal battle, into one and the same struggle.[93]

The aim, then, was to democratize the distribution of information so as to facilitate the emergence of new circuits of knowledge and power, circuits that might generate different distributions of authority and thereby alter the overall strategic

situation in which the governors and the governed found themselves. The goal of the struggle was not revolutionary victory
so much as popular autonomy; its purpose was not to win access to state power so much as to further self-empowerment.
Foucault's aim, in short, was not *liberation* but *resistance*. As
the 1980 manifesto of the Association Défense Libre (a legal-
defense organization), which Foucault helped to draft, puts it,
"Let us avoid the hackneyed problem of reformism and anti-
reformism. It is not up to us to take responsibility for institutions which need to be reformed. It is up to us to defend
ourselves so well that the institutions will be forced to reform
themselves."[94] The immediate aim of many of Foucault's political undertakings, in fact, was to alter, insofar as possible, the
strategic positions of the various participants in the endless and
ongoing social struggle that, to his eyes at least, comprised the
whole of "politics" (which he consistently likened, inverting
Clausewitz's formula, to the pursuit of war by other means).[95]
In particular, his efforts were directed to resisting specific forms
of social domination effected and legitimated by specific apparatuses of power/knowledge, and his characteristic tactic was
to attempt to reverse the subject- and object-positions typically
assigned by those apparatuses to the empowered and the disempowered, respectively. Indeed, perhaps it is not too much to
say that such a differential assignment of subject- and object-
positions constitutes the basic mode by which systems of
power/knowledge produce effects of social domination in the
first place.

▼　▼　▼　▼　▼　▼　▼　▼

THE HISTORY of the ongoing struggles for homosexual
emancipation and gay liberation has consisted largely in the
story of how lesbians and gay men fought to wrest from non-
gay-identified people control over such matters as who gets to

speak for us, who gets to represent our experience, who is authorized to pronounce knowledgeably about our lives.[96] It has been the story of one long struggle to reverse the discursive positioning of homosexuality and heterosexuality: to shift heterosexuality from the position of a universal subject of discourse to an object of interrogation and critique, and to shift homosexuality from the position of an object of power/knowledge to a position of legitimate subjective agency—from the status of that which is spoken about while remaining silent to the status of that which speaks.[97] The possibility of producing such a shift in the status of homosexuality from object to subject illustrates what Foucault has called in *The History of Sexuality, Volume I*, "the tactical polyvalence of discourses": "We must not imagine," he insists, "a world of discourse divided between accepted discourse and excluded discourse, or between the dominant discourse and the dominated one.... Discourses are not once and for all subservient to power or raised up against it, any more than silences are. We must make allowance for the complex and unstable process whereby discourse can be both an instrument and an effect of power, but also a hindrance, a stumbling-block, a point of resistance and a starting point for an opposing strategy."[98]

It is precisely because the characteristic and defining political strategy of gay liberation is one of discursive reversal that Foucault situates his sole theoretical analysis of the gay liberation movement in the context of his discussion of "the tactical polyvalence of discourses" in *The History of Sexuality, Volume I*.

There is no question that the appearance in nineteenth-century psychiatry, jurisprudence, and literature of a whole series of discourses on the species and subspecies of homosexuality, inversion, pederasty, and "psychic hermaphrodism" made possible a strong advance of social controls into this area of "perversity"; but it also made possible the formation of a "reverse" discourse: homosexuality began to speak in its own behalf, to demand that its legitimacy or "naturality" be acknowledged, often in the same vocabulary, using the same categories by which it was medically disqualified.[99]

To the extent that the "reverse discourse" produced by the early homosexual emancipationists as well as by recent gay liberationists recapitulates (albeit in a positive mode) the sexual terms, categories, and concepts of the pathologizing medical and psychological discourses to which it opposes itself—and to the extent that it thereby extends, prolongs, and fortifies the regime of power/knowledge responsible for constructing the homosexual/heterosexual binarism in the first place—Foucault remains critical of sexual liberation discourse in particular, and of discursive reversal in general, as a political strategy. Nonetheless, Foucault made it very clear on a number of occasions that he considered the early homosexual emancipation movement's discursive reversal of medical discourse to have been, in its time, an absolutely necessary strategic move,[100] and therefore an important, politically progressive development. "I believe that the movements labeled 'sexual liberation' ought to be understood as movements of affirmation 'starting with' sexuality," Foucault explained to an interviewer in 1977.

> Which means two things: they are movements that start with sexuality, with the apparatus of sexuality inside of which we're caught, and that make it function right up to the limit; but, at the same time, they are in motion relative to it, disengaging themselves and surmounting it. Take the case of homosexuality. Psychiatrists began a medical analysis of it around the 1870s—a point of departure for a whole series of new interventions and controls. . . . But [we see homosexuals] taking such discourses literally, and thereby turning them about; we see responses arising in the form of defiance: "All right, we are what you say we are—by nature, disease, or perversion, as you like. Well, if that's what we are, let's be it, and if you want to know

what we are, we can tell you ourselves better than you can." . . . It is the strategic turnabout of one and the "same" will to truth.[101]

By putting "the 'same' " in quotation marks, Foucault scoffs at the hostile liberal reading of *The History of Sexuality, Volume I*, that understands it to be making the implausible and odious claim that there is no difference between repression and liberation, or that a "reverse discourse" is one and the same as the discourse it reverses. On the contrary: to recapitulate in an affirmative vein, as the nineteenth-century homosexual emancipationists did, the oppressive, medicalizing discourse to which they were subjected, while strategically reversing the object- and subject-positions assigned by it to themselves and to the medical authorities, respectively, is, in Foucault's eyes, to perform a significant act of political resistance.

If Foucault did indeed find fault with the modern project of liberating a supposedly repressed sexuality, then, the reason was not that "the repressive hypothesis" was *wrong* but that it was politically bankrupt: "[W]e had arrived at a situation in which notions of sexual repression found themselves overburdened, worn out, and it was a matter of asking oneself how to make those notions function at the interior of a struggle, a battle, a debate."[102] Foucault's explanation for his emphasis on resistance rather than liberation indicates that his critique of liberation in *The History of Sexuality, Volume I*, should not be read as a blanket condemnation or disqualification of it. Foucault's objection to liberation as the goal of sexual politics does not express his theoretical position on the issue—it is not an enunciation of some cardinal principle or abstract law—but reflects his understanding of a specific historical situation, of concrete political realities and techniques of power: "a complex strategic situation in a particular society."[103]

In any case, to conceive gay politics as a reverse discourse and a form of resistance is not to assign to it an entirely reactive, or negative, character—to deny it a claim to independence or creativity. After all, a reverse discourse, as Foucault describes it, does not simply produce a mirror reversal—a pure, one-to-one inversion of the existing terms of the discourse it reverses. Gay liberation is not the upside-down reflection of medical pathologization, nor is it the exact opposite of homophobic stigmatization and oppression. Gay liberation, rather, is a surprising, unexpected, dynamic, and open-ended movement whose ultimate effects extend beyond its immediate tactics. Gay politics is not a politics of pure reactivity, then, even though its conditions of possibility are admittedly rooted in an oppressive regime of power/knowledge. It is a reversal that takes us in a new direction. To quote a formulation with which Foucault registered strong agreement when it was put to him some years later, once again in reference to the lesbian and gay movement, "To resist is not simply a negation but a creative process."[104]

Similarly, the project of shifting the discursive position of homosexuality from that of object to subject does not constitute a mere attempt to *reform* sexual discourses. It is not an exercise in restraining the supposed "excesses" of homophobic bigotry, eliminating the supposed "distortions" produced by homophobic "prejudice," and reasserting a new and more rigorous standard of unbiased sexual knowing, available in principle to "everyone" (meaning nongay people). The aim is not to produce a supposedly kinder, gentler, more objective, less tendentious form of expertise about homosexuality, to be licensed presumably by non-gay-identified authorities—or by lesbians and gay men accredited by straight institutions; it is not to reconstitute homosexuality as a real object to be studied and understood, definitively if sympathetically, by those in a legitimate position to know.[105] The aim, rather, is to treat homosexuality as a position from which one *can* know, to treat it as a legitimate *condition* of knowledge. Homosexuality, according to this Foucauldian vision of *un gai savoir*, "a gay science," is not something to be got right but an eccentric positionality to be exploited and explored: a potentially privileged site for the criticism and analysis of cultural discourses.[106]

In order to reverse the discourses of contemporary homophobia, then, it is not enough to attempt simply to reclaim and transvalue homosexuality. The most radical reversal of homophobic discourses consists not in asserting, with the Gay Liberation Front of 1968, that "gay is good" (on the analogy with "black is beautiful")[107] but in assuming and empowering a marginal positionality—not in rehabilitating an already demarcated, if devalued, identity but in taking advantage of the purely oppositional location homosexuality has been made to occupy by the logic of the supplement and by the fantasmatic character of homophobic discourse. "The homosexual" constituted by that discourse is, as we have seen, an impossibly contradictory creature, not a natural reality but a fantasmatic projection, an incoherent construction that functions to stabilize and to consolidate the cultural meaning of heterosexuality by encapsulating everything that is "other" than or "different" from it. "The homosexual" is defined by negation and opposition as everything the heterosexual is not. In short, "the homosexual" is an identity without an essence.

To shift the position of "the homosexual" from that of object to subject is therefore to make available to lesbians and gay men a new kind of sexual identity, one characterized by its lack of a clear definitional content. The homosexual subject can now claim an identity without an essence. To do so is to reverse the logic of the supplement and to make use of the vacancy left by the evacuation of the contradictory and incoherent definitional content of "the homosexual" in order to take up instead a position that is (and always had been) defined wholly relationally, by its distance to and difference from the normative. (Homo)sexual identity can now be constituted not substantively but oppositionally, not by *what* it is but by *where* it is and *how* it operates. Those who knowingly occupy such a marginal location, who assume a de-essentialized identity that is purely positional in character, are properly speaking not gay but *queer*.

▼   ▼   ▼   ▼   ▼   ▼   ▼   ▼

UNLIKE GAY identity, which, though deliberately proclaimed in an act of affirmation, is nonetheless rooted in the positive fact of homosexual object-choice, queer identity need not be grounded in any positive truth or in any stable reality. As the very word implies, "queer" does not name some natural kind or refer to some determinate object; it acquires its meaning from its oppositional relation to the norm. Queer is by definition *whatever* is at odds with the normal, the legitimate, the dominant. *There is nothing in particular to which it necessarily refers.* It is an identity without an essence. "Queer," then, demarcates not a positivity but a positionality vis-à-vis the normative—a positionality that is not restricted to lesbians and gay men but is in fact available to anyone who is or who feels marginalized because of her or his sexual practices: it could include some married couples without children, for example, or even (who knows?) some married couples *with* children—with, perhaps, *very naughty* children. "Queer," in any case, does not designate a class of already objectified pathologies or perversions; rather, it describes a horizon of possibility whose precise extent and heterogeneous scope cannot in principle be delimited in advance. It is from the eccentric positionality occupied by the queer subject that it may become possible to envision a variety of possibilities for reordering the relations among sexual behaviors, erotic identities, constructions of gender, forms of knowledge, regimes of enunciation, logics of representation, modes of self-constitution, and practices of community—for restructuring, that is, the relations among power, truth, and desire.[108]

Perhaps I should say that I don't intend this argument to be understood as advocating the adoption of the term "queer" in preference to the term "gay" or as providing partisan support for the politics of Queer Nation. First of all, it is not for me to suggest what words the members of sexual constituencies should use to designate or identify themselves. Second, the only thing that need be said about Queer Nation in this context is that it is significantly less *queer*, in the sense in which I am using the term, than, say, ACT UP, whose style of direct-action politics and activist glamor Queer Nation has attempted to replicate for the purpose of creating a movement of young lesbian and gay radicals defined by no other issue than that of sexual orientation.[109] (ACT UP, by contrast, draws in members of all the constituencies affected by the AIDS catastrophe, creating a political movement that is genuinely *queer* insofar as it is broadly oppositional; AIDS activism links gay resistance and sexual politics with social mobilization around issues of race, gender, poverty, incarceration, intravenous drug use, prostitution, sex phobia, media representation, health care reform, immigration law, medical research, and the power and accountability of "experts": in fact, it was precisely ACT UP's contamination of sexual with nonsexual politics, and its supposedly myopic focus on AIDS, that generated the felt need for a movement like Queer Nation in the first place.) Finally, the endless and fruitless debates among lesbians and gay men over the respective merits of "gay" or "lesbian" versus "queer" have not only wasted a lot of energy and generated a lot of ill feeling but, more important, have inhibited careful evaluation of the *strategic* functioning of those terms, as if there could be any safety or security in adhering single-mindedly to "the right" one (whichever one that might be). It is crucial to keep in focus the specific *effects* our terminology of choice will produce when it is deployed—to understand what, concretely, it will make happen. The problem of choosing a particular term should not distract us from the analysis of its instrumentality, from the scrutiny of its strategic investment by various forces, from the critique of the modalities of its incorporation into various techniques of power.

Looked at from such a strategic perspective, the term "queer" in and of itself reveals a number of serious liabilities. Considered purely in terms of its political efficacy, in fact, the term may now be almost hopelessly compromised, and not only because it has become the vehicle of unproductive political conflict and generational division among lesbians and gay men. More critically, "queer" 's very lack of specificity, which I consider its chief advantage, has also become its most serious drawback, and for several reasons. First, as the term is used, it sometimes gives a false impression of inclusiveness, of embracing in equal measure all species of sexual outlaws. It thereby promotes the misleading notion that a queer solidarity has decisively triumphed over historical divisions between lesbians and gay men (or between lesbians and gay men, on the one hand, and [for example] sadomasochists, fetishists, pederasts, and transgender people, on the other) and that differences of race or gender no longer pose political problems for queer unity that require urgently to be addressed. As it happens, one chapter of Queer Nation after another has broken up over the failure to acknowledge and to remedy what in fact have remained painful imbalances of privilege among the members of various local constituencies—imbalances temporarily masked but not redressed by the dream of a single, albeit heterogeneous, queer identity.[110] Second, and perhaps even more important, the lack of specifically homosexual content built into the meaning of "queer" has made that term all too handy—not for generating a de-essentialized identity or defining a marginal positionality so much as for multiplying the opportunities for disidentification, denial, and disavowal. While some uses of "queer" treat it as a virtual synonym of "gay," repackaging an old-fashioned homosexual essentialism under a fashionable and suspiciously non–homosexually specific label,[111] other uses evoke the ancient and persistent specter of sexual despecification. What makes "queer" potentially so treacherous as a label is that its lack of definitional content renders it all too readily available for appropriation by those who do not experience the unique political disabilities and forms of social disqualification from which lesbians and gay men routinely suffer in virtue of our sexuality.[112] "Queer" therefore invites the kind of hostile political manipulation that already is all too familiar to lesbians and gay men from the deployment of the label "bisexual": it provides a means of de-gaying gayness.

Like "bisexual," though for different reasons, "queer" would seem to provide a ready-made instrument of homophobic disavowal: inasmuch as it reconstitutes sexual identity under the sign of the political, it has the capacity to despecify the realities of lesbian and gay oppression, obscuring what is irreducibly *sexual* about those practices and persons most exposed to the effects of sexual racism. "Queer" can even support the restigmatization of lesbians and gay men, who can now be regarded (once again) as sad, benighted folks, still locked—*unlike* postmodern, non–sexually labeled, self-theorized queers—into an old-fashioned, essentialized, rigidly defined, specifically sexual (namely, *lesbian* or *gay*) identity. Lesbians and gay men can now look forward to a new round of condescension and dismissal at the hands of the trendy and glamorously unspecified sexual outlaws who call themselves "queer" and who can claim the radical chic attached to a sexually transgressive identity without, of course, having to do anything icky with their bodies in order to earn it. There is nothing enviable about the lot of lesbians and gay men who wind up living in the sort of queer world where, as a friend of mine reports about a certain New England women's college, all the women who are sleeping with men identify themselves as lesbians and all the women who are sleeping with women identify themselves as bisexuals. Hence the stunning headline of a recent lesbian 'zine: LESBIANS WHO SLEEP WITH WOMEN![113]

Despite all its present political liabilities, however, "queer" can still stand for the possibility of a radical reversal in the logic of homophobic discourses such as I sketched out earlier, and my little manifesto in defense of it was framed with that possibility in mind. My purpose was not to advocate the use of the term, to divert attention from its various strategic liabilities, or to declare my support for the brand of identity politics currently advanced under the banner of "queer," so much as to highlight and to preserve a dimension of that category's meaning which seems to me uniquely useful and worth cherishing, whether or not it is realized as the term is deployed in current political practice. I want to keep open a possibility that may remain, for all I know, largely potential, that may indeed already be foreclosed, but that represents one of the important possibilities that some of its earlier advocates saw in the term "queer" and that may yet constitute one of its crucial uses: namely, the ability of "queer" to define (homo)sexual identity oppositionally and relationally but not necessarily substantively, not as a positivity but as a positionality, not as a thing but as a resistance to the norm.[114] Such resistance is not merely a radicalism for its own sake, a fashionable attachment to whatever may look new in the way of personal or political styles, or a simplistic and facile habit of denigrating whatever forms of lesbian and gay life may seem insufficiently up to date—all of which tendencies find expression, admittedly (though in a disarmingly antipuritanical form), in Queer Nation's call to liberation through commodification (as in the slogan "Don't militarize, accessorize!"). Resistance to normativity is not purely negative or reactive or destructive, in other words; it is also positive and dynamic and creative. It is by resisting the discursive and institutional practices which, in their scattered and diffuse functioning, contribute to the operation of heteronormativity that queer identities can open a social space for the construction of different identities, for the elaboration of various types of relationships, for the development of new cultural forms. As Lee Edelman cautiously suggests,

> Though "queer" as the endlessly mutating token of non-assimilation (and hence as the utopian badge of a would-be "authentic" position of resistance) may reflect a certain bourgeois aspiration to be always *au courant*, its vigorous and unmethodical dislocations of "identity" create, at the risk, to be sure, of producing a version of identity politics as postmodern commodity fetishism, a zone of possibilities in which the embodiment of the subject might be experienced otherwise.[115]

Edelman's "diagnosis concerning the nature of the present" state of queer politics proceeds along the lines suggested by Foucault—that is, "in accordance with [the] kinds of virtual fracture which open up the space of freedom understood as a space of concrete freedom, i.e. possible transformation."[116] And it is precisely such a queer understanding of homosexual identity that best agrees with Foucault's own vision of gay politics.

▼　▼　▼　▼　▼　▼　▼　▼

F OUCAULT himself would seem to have anticipated and embraced a queer conception of both homosexual identity and gay politics. In a 1981 interview, at least, he took something like the position I have been defending here: "Homosexuality is a historic opportunity to open up new relational and affective potentialities [*virtualités*], not in virtue of qualities intrinsic to the homosexual, but because *the position of the homosexual 'off-center,'* somehow, together with the diagonal lines which the homosexual can draw through the social fabric, makes it possible to bring to light these potentialities."[117] Foucault saw homosexuality not as a newly liberated species of sexual being but as a strategically situated marginal position from which it might be possible to glimpse and to devise new ways of relating to oneself and to others.[118] As the focus of his work shifted, in the last years of his life, from politics to ethics, from an analytics of power to an interest in the relation of the self to itself, he became attracted to the notion, which he encountered in ancient Greek and Roman writers, of *an aesthetics, or stylistics, of existence*, and he brought that notion to bear on his political thinking about the future of the lesbian and gay movements. Conversely, Foucault's growing exposure, in the same period of his life, to the burgeoning political, social, and sexual cultures of the new lesbian and gay communities in the United States significantly shaped the interpretative lenses he brought to bear on the ancient ethical texts and provided a framework for his deepening inquiries into ethical self-fashioning. "[I]f I was interested in Antiquity," Foucault remarked two months before his death, "it was because, for a whole series of reasons, the idea of a morality as obedience to a code of rules is now disappearing, has already disappeared. And to this absence of morality corresponds, must correspond, the search for an aesthetics of existence."[119] In order to make sense of Foucault's pronouncements about lesbian and gay politics, then, it will be necessary to situate his remarks in the context of his late work on ancient ethics and, in particular, to summarize his understanding of sexual morality in Greece and Rome.

Ancient ethics, Foucault maintained, concerned itself less with the forbidden than with the voluntary: it was a practice of self-regulation with regard to pleasure, and as such it constituted for some elite males an entire "art of life" or "art of existence" (*technē tou biou* in Greek). "What I mean by the phrase [the 'arts of existence']," Foucault explained in his introduction to the second volume of *The History of Sexuality*, in terms he also applied to homosexual "practices of the self" (*pratiques de soi,* "are those voluntary and deliberate practices according to which men not only set themselves rules of conduct but also seek to transform themselves, to change themselves in their singular being, and to make their life into a work of art [*une oeuvre*] that carries certain aesthetic values and meets certain stylistic criteria."[120] By practicing such transformative "arts of life," or "technologies of the self" (*techniques de soi*), certain self-selected members of the Greek upper classes were able to live a moral life grounded in what Foucault called "an aesthetics of existence." This he defined, in the first instance, as

> a manner of living whose moral value did not depend either on its conformity to a code of behavior or on an effort of purification but on certain forms, or rather certain general formal principles in the use of pleasures, in the way one distributed them, in the limits one observed, in the hierarchy one respected. Through the *logos*—through the rationality and the relation to truth—that governed it, such a life joined in the maintenance and reproduction of an ontological order; moreover, it took on the brilliance of a beauty that was revealed to those able to behold it or keep its memory present in mind.[121]

Principles of ethical conduct in such a system operated more like the rules of a bodybuilding regimen or a daily workout routine than like universal moral imperatives: they functioned not as standards by which to normalize populations but as elements in a procedure that a few people might adopt with the aim of living what they considered a beautiful and praiseworthy life. If such a life was necessarily, given the cultural ideals of classical antiquity, a sexually austere one, its austerity was nevertheless to be achieved not by multiplying and enforcing sexual interdictions but rather by *stylizing freedom.*[122] The ultimate goal of all this ethical work was mastery over self and others. What Foucault understood by an "art of existence," then, was an ethical practice that consisted in freely imposing on the form of one's life a distinctive shape and individual style, and thereby transforming oneself in accordance with one's own conception of beauty or value.

Foucault's most detailed picture of the ancient "arts of existence," and of the corresponding sorts of ethical stylistics to which they gave rise, can be found in his writings on what he called, in reference to the ancient Stoics and other late antique philosophers, *la culture de soi*: "the culture and cultivation of the self."[123] Foucault insisted that for the late antique moralists "taking care of one's self . . . [did] not mean simply being interested in oneself, nor [did] it mean having a certain tendency to self-attachment or self-fascination."[124] Ancient self-cultivation was not simply a habit of introspection but a specific "art of life" or "art of existence" dominated, in this case, by the principle of "caring for oneself."[125] Foucault emphasized, accordingly, that the "care of the self" (*epimeleia heautou* in Greek, *cura sui* in Latin), as the late antique philosophers came to understand this venerable notion, designated "not just a preoccupation but a whole set of occupations." It was not an attitude but a strenuous activity, a practical exercise, a constant, demanding, laborious exertion: "[T]aking care of oneself [was] not a rest cure." Furthermore, the care of the self was "a true social practice . . . an intensification of social relations." It led one to seek help and guidance from others, and it was undertaken together with others in philosophical communities, aristocratic households, and other institutional settings.[126] Far from being a mere vehicle of aesthetic recreation or personal self-absorption, the ancient cultivation of the self consisted in a set of elaborate and rigorous practices designed to produce a heightened scrutiny of oneself, a constant monitoring of one's behavior and dispositions, a holistic and therapeutic regimen of mind and body. The result of self-cultivation was not only self-mastery but self-sufficiency and happiness. For in the process of styling and perfecting oneself, the late antique philosophers taught, one came eventually to find a source of pleasure, a means of happiness, in oneself. As Foucault put it, summarizing the writings of certain late antique moralists, "[T]he relation to self is also defined as a concrete relationship enabling one to delight in oneself, as in a thing one both possesses and has before one's eyes. . . . The individual who has finally succeeded in gaining access to himself is, for himself, an object of pleasure."[127] Self-cultivation ultimately produced a self that could afford the same kinds of pleasures to its owner as a beautiful physique or a work of art.

Such an ambitious program of self-transformation imposed on its participants the need for strict self-regulation, and such self-regulation carried with it in turn increased demands for sexual austerity. Nonetheless, "this added emphasis on sexual austerity in [late antique] moral reflection [took] the form," Foucault argued, "not of a tightening of the code that defined prohibited acts, but of an intensification of the relation to oneself by which one constituted oneself as the subject of one's acts."[128] The more stringent standards of sexual austerity that distinguished the late antique "culture of the self" took the form of a new and more intense mode of ethical subjectivation—and of new and more elaborate technologies of self-transformation that nonetheless remained continuous with earlier classical Greek models, insofar as they were still designed to enable one to master oneself and to *style* one's entire existence in conformity with one's own vision of the most beautiful way to live.

Modern systems of morality, by contrast, have tended to allocate little or no role in ethical practice to comparable techniques of self-fashioning, placing most of their emphasis instead on personal obedience to the dictates of reason, virtue, conscience, or the law (whether natural, human, or divine). Hence the significance Foucault attributed to the renewed possibilities for ethical artistry, self-cultivation, and various stylistics of the self produced by the emergence of lesbian and gay communities—and by the emergence, along with them, of original and distinctive lesbian and gay styles of life. The construction and evolution of openly lesbian and gay social worlds presented, to Foucault's way of thinking, unique historic opportunities for an elaboration of personal and ethical creativity analogous to that practiced by certain moral athletes in classical antiquity, only now such creativity need not be restricted to a social elite, or to a single, privileged gender, but could become the common property of an entire subculture.

To be sure, Foucault's notion of a "style of life," shaped as it was by his reading of the ancient ethical texts at least as much as by his personal contacts with the rapidly developing lesbian and gay communities, signified something very different from what is normally meant by a "lifestyle." As Paul Veyne—a classicist who worked closely with Foucault during the composition of the second and third volumes of *The History of Sexuality*— properly emphasizes, when Foucault spoke during the last months of his life about the creation of a "style of life," he was talking not about a standard mode of consumption shared by great masses of people, nor about a kind of stylishness, an elegance of comportment through which an individual attempts to distinguish himself or herself from others, but about a mode of ethical elaboration whose goal is precisely to "open up [within the sphere of individual existence] the space of freedom understood as a space of concrete freedom, i.e. possible [personal and social] transformation." Veyne explicates Foucault's notion as follows:

> *Style* does not mean distinction here; the word is to be taken in the sense of the Greeks, for whom an artist was first of all an artisan and a work of art was first of all a work. Greek ethics is quite dead, and Foucault judged it as undesirable as it would be impossible to resuscitate this ethics; but he considered one of its elements, namely, the idea of a work of the self on the self, to be capable of

reacquiring a contemporary meaning. . . . We can guess at what might emerge from this diagnosis: the self, taking itself as a work to be accomplished, could sustain an ethics that is no longer supported by either tradition or reason; as an artist of itself, the self would enjoy that autonomy that modernity can no longer do without. . . . [I]t is no longer necessary to wait for the revolution to begin to realize ourselves: *the self is the new strategic possibility.*[129]

The contemporary meaning that Greek ethics could reacquire emerges clearly from Foucault's statements about the potential usefulness and value of ethical artistry for the development of lesbian and gay culture. "I think that what the gay movement needs now," Foucault remarked in 1982, "is much more the *art of life* than a science or scientific knowledge (or pseudo-scientific knowledge) of what sexuality is. . . . We have to understand that with our desires, through our desires, go new forms of relationships, new forms of love, new forms of creation. Sex is not a fatality: it's a possibility for creative life."[130]

▼   ▼   ▼   ▼   ▼   ▼   ▼   ▼

IT MAY BE tempting to see in Foucault's delineation of an aesthetic or stylistic mode of ethical practice in general, and in his valuation of lesbian and gay styles of life in particular, a mere recapitulation of the much-execrated fin-de-siècle aestheticism typically associated with Oscar Wilde—or a revival, more specifically, of the "dandyism" championed by Baudelaire, which Foucault nonetheless took seriously as a form of ethical self-fashioning, of self-transformation, and which he defined as "tak[ing] oneself as object of a complex and difficult elaboration."[131] But it would be a political mistake as well as an exegetical error to treat Foucault's ethical aestheticism reductively, or to underestimate the radical possibilities contained in all these varieties of ethical stylistics—in the Wildean and Baudelairean varieties no less than in the Foucauldian one. Foucault in effect seizes on that most abjected and devalued feature of gay male self-fashioning, namely, *style*—the very category that has been repeatedly and phobically invoked against him (most notably by Hayden White)[132]—and finds in it a rigorous, austere, and transformative technology of the self which produces concrete possibilities for the development of personal autonomy.[133] Ultimately, what sets Foucault's own stylistics of the self apart from a reductively construed notion of "decadent style," and what allows the self to become a genuinely new strategic possibility, not merely an outmoded Romantic one, is the thoroughly *impersonal* conception of "the self" on which Foucault's entire model of stylistics rests.

Foucault himself did not explicitly thematize the impersonal character of "the self" as he conceived it, but everything he said about "the care of the self" in his late writings strongly implied such an impersonal understanding of it. When on one occasion, for example, he was asked whether "the Greek concern with the self" wasn't "just an early version of our self-absorption," Foucault replied, "[N]ot only do I not identify this ancient culture of the self with what you might call the Californian cult of the self, I think they are diametrically opposed."[134] In the classical Greek world, after all, the purpose of self-fashioning was not to discover one's "true self" but to work on one's self so as to transform it into a vehicle of personal autonomy and social preeminence. Self-regulation was a specific strategy for gaining power both over oneself and over others; it was not an ancient forerunner of New Age mysticism.

The late antique "culture of the self" presents an even starker contrast with the modern, normalizing, pop-psychological ethic of "self-realization." For the late antique philosophers whom Foucault studied identified the self with the soul, and the soul, as those philosophers conceptualized it, is not a principle of personal individuation but an errant particle of the Divine. The "self," on this ancient philosophical view of it, then, is not the locus of a unique and private psychological depth (on the model of bourgeois humanism) but the site of a radical alterity: it is the space within each human being where she or he encounters the not-self, the beyond. Ancient self-cultivation aimed accordingly not at realizing a personal self but at actualizing or instantiating an impersonal essence—a generalized moral quality such as self-restraint (*sophrosynē*), for example, or an intellectual capacity such as "reason." In its late antique versions, self-fashioning typically sought to purify the individual soul of its accidental characteristics and to reunite it with universal Mind. The ancient practice of self-cultivation, highly individualistic as it was, did not constitute a technology for producing unique individuals; rather, it took the form of an ascetic art, a spiritual exercise designed to *empty* the self of precisely those passions and attachments that make the self, according to the modern view, something individual, personal, and unique.

Here one detects the pervasive influence on Foucault of the magisterial work on "spiritual exercises and ancient philosophy" by Pierre Hadot, a French scholar of the ancient philosophical tradition with whom Foucault worked constantly and closely during the composition of *The Care of the Self* and from whose work he seems to have taken the notion of philosophy as a transformative mode of existence, an art or style of life.[135] That for the ancients the soul is not a self in the modern sense but a fragment of divine reason, or an indwelling of some larger reality that transcends the self, is a theme of Hadot's work. Summarizing one of the common threads of the late antique philosophical tradition, for example, he emphasizes that "man appears, in that which is most his own, as something that is more than man, or, to speak more precisely, the true self of each individual transcends each individual."[136]

Similarly, according to Foucault's conception, "the self" which is to be cultivated by means of an "art of life" (whether in the ancient world or in the modern) is not a personal *identity* so much as it is a *relation of reflexivity*, a relation of the human subject to itself in its power and its freedom.[137] Foucault's "self" is not an Emersonian "self": it is not a personal substance or essence but, exactly as Veyne emphasizes, a strategic possibility. Hence, to cultivate oneself—and the "self" referred to here, both in the ancient texts and in Foucault's French text, is nothing but the bare reflexive pronoun—is not to explore or experience some given self, conceived as a determinate private realm, a space of personal interiority, but instead to use one's relation to oneself as a potential resource with which to construct new modalities of subjective agency and new styles of personal life that may enable one to resist or even to escape one's social and psychological determinations. To practice a stylistics of the self ultimately means to cultivate that part of oneself that leads beyond oneself, that transcends oneself: it is to elaborate the strategic possibilities of what is the most *impersonal* dimension of personal life—namely, the capacity to "realize oneself" by becoming other than what one is. That is what Foucault came to see himself as having done all his life through his writing ("one writes," he said, "in order to become other than what one is");[138] he also came to find the same possibility for self-transformation in gay sex.

▼   ▼   ▼   ▼   ▼   ▼   ▼   ▼

 F OUCAULT referred to the arduous activity of cultivating, fashioning, and styling the self—of working on the self in order to transform the self into a source of self-sufficiency and pleasure—as "ascesis" (*askēsis* in Greek), ascetics, or ethical work. "Ascesis," then, as Foucault conceived it, does not signify self-denial, austerity, or abnegation; rather, it means something like "training," almost in an athletic sense. Foucault defined "ascesis" as "an exercise of self upon self by which one tries to work out, to transform one's self and to attain a certain mode of being."[139] Foucault ultimately came to understand both philosophy and homosexuality as technologies of self-transformation, and therefore as modern versions of "ascesis." "For Foucault himself," Arnold Davidson writes, "philosophy was a spiritual exercise, an exercise of oneself in which one submitted oneself to modifications and tests, underwent changes, in order to learn to think differently."[140] In the preface to the second and third volumes of *The History of Sexuality*, published shortly before his death, Foucault articulated his conception as follows: "What is philosophy today," he asked famously, "if it does not consist *not* in legitimating what one already knows but in undertaking to know how and to what extent it might be possible to think differently?"[141] And Foucault went on to remark that the living substance of philosophy consists in a transformative experiment or test that one performs on oneself by playing games of truth: philosophy, in that sense, is still for Foucault "what it was in times past, namely, an 'ascesis,' an exercise of the self [*exercice de soi*] in the activity of thought."[142] The goal is *se déprendre de soi-même*,[143] to fall out of love with oneself, to get free of oneself, and to reconstitute oneself in a calculated encounter with otherness.

In his interviews with the gay press and other interested publications, Foucault spoke about homosexuality in strikingly similar terms:

> To be gay is to be in a state of becoming ... the point is not to be homosexual but to keep working persistently at being gay ... to place oneself in a dimension where the sexual choices one makes are present and have their effects on the ensemble of our life. ... [T]hese sexual choices ought to be at the same time creators of ways of life. To be gay signifies that these choices diffuse themselves across the entire life; it is also a certain

> manner of *refusing* the modes of life offered; it is to
> make a sexual choice into the impetus for a *change of
> existence*.[144]

Homosexuality for Foucault is a spiritual exercise insofar as it
consists in an art or style of life through which individuals transform their modes of existence and, ultimately, themselves. Homosexuality is not a psychological condition that we discover
but a way of being that we practice in order to redefine the
meaning of who we are and what we do, and in order to make
ourselves and our world more gay; as such, it constitutes a modern form of ascesis. Foucault proposes to us that instead of
treating homosexuality as an occasion to articulate the secret
truth of our own desires, we might ask ourselves "what sorts of
relations can be established, invented, multiplied, modulated
through [our] homosexuality. . . . The problem is not to discover
in oneself the truth of one's sex but rather to *use*, from now on,
one's sexuality to achieve a multiplicity of types of relations."[145]

As early as 1977 Foucault distinguished this ascetic, or creative, dimension of the current lesbian and gay political movement from the characteristic features of the older gay-liberation
struggle: "A movement is taking shape today which seems to
me to be reversing the trend of 'always more sex,' and 'always
more truth in sex,' which has enthralled us for centuries; it is a
matter—I don't say of 'rediscovering'—but rather of constructing other forms of pleasures, of relationships, coexistences, attachments, loves, intensities."[146] (Foucault's example of this
trend was Hervé Guibert's early fable *La Mort propagande*.)
Expanding on this theme four years later, Foucault expressed
himself as follows: "It's up to us to advance into *a homosexual
ascesis* that would make us work on ourselves and invent (I
don't say discover) a manner of being that is still improbable."[147]
By means of such a homosexual ascesis, a transformative queer
practice of the self, we may be able "to define and develop a
way of life" that in turn "can yield a culture and an ethics,"[148]

new forms of relationship, new modes of knowledge, new means of creativity, and new possibilities of love.

▼   ▼   ▼   ▼   ▼   ▼   ▼   ▼

F OUCAULT insisted that homosexuality did not name an already existing form of desire but was rather *"something to be desired."* Our task is therefore "to *become* homosexual, not to persist in acknowledging that we *are.*"[149] Or, to put it more precisely, what Foucault meant is that our task is to become queer. For his remarks make sense only if he understood his term "homosexual" according to my definition of "queer"—as an identity without an essence, not a given condition but a horizon of possibility, an opportunity for self-transformation, a queer potential. Because one can't *become* homosexual, strictly speaking: either one is or one isn't. But one can marginalize oneself; one can transform oneself; one can become queer. Indeed, "queer" marks the very site of gay becoming.

It was on the basis of such a queer ethic, of such a vision of gay becoming, that Foucault argued against concentrating too much political energy on the struggle to obtain specific juridical "rights" for lesbians and gay men.

> I think we should consider the battle for gay rights as an episode that cannot be the final stage. For two reasons: first because a right, in its real effects, is much more linked to attitudes and patterns of behavior than to legal formulations. There can be discrimination against homosexuals even if such discriminations are prohibited by law. It is therefore necessary to establish homosexual lifestyles, existential choices in which sexual relations with people of the same sex will be important. It's not enough as part of a more general way of life, or in addition to it, to be permitted to make love with someone of the same sex. The fact of making love with someone of the same sex can very naturally involve a whole series of choices, a whole series

of other values and choices for which there are not yet real possibilities. It's not only a matter of integrating this strange little practice of making love with someone of the same sex into pre-existing cultures; it's a matter of constructing cultural forms.[150]

And Foucault went on to add, "[I]f what we want to do is create a new way of life, then the question of individual rights is not pertinent."[151] The point is not to disparage the struggle for gay rights, which Foucault himself supported ("It is important . . . to have the possibility—and the right—to choose your own sexuality. Human rights regarding sexuality are important. . . . "),[152] but to look beyond that struggle to something else, to the possibility of inventing new rights and establishing new kinds of relationships that might entail their own privileges, duties, and rights.

That queerness constitutes not just a resistance to social norms or a negation of established values but a positive and creative construction of different ways of life seemed self-evident to Foucault. "As far back as I can remember," he told an interviewer for *Gai pied*,

> to desire boys meant to desire relationships with boys. That has always been, for me, something important. Not necessarily in the form of the couple, but as a question of existence: How is it possible for men to be together? to live together, to share their time, their meals, their room, their leisure, their sorrows, their knowledge, their confidences? What exactly is this thing—to be among men, "stripped down," outside institutionalized relationships, family, profession, obligatory forms of association?

The problem of inventing queer relationships can be further complicated by additional factors, such as differences between the partners in age or race or class or nationality: there exist no readily available social formulas for mediating and negoti-

ating those differences. "Two men of notably different ages—
what rule will they be able to use in order to communicate?"
Foucault asked; "they are face to face with one another, without
armor, without conventional phrases, without anything to stabilize the meaning of the movement which takes them one toward the other. They have to invent from A to Z a relationship
without form. . . . "[153] Self-invention is not a luxury or a pastime
for lesbians and gay men: it is a necessity. And it is therefore
part of the acquired practice of what Foucault called "becoming
homosexual."[154]

▼   ▼   ▼   ▼   ▼   ▼   ▼   ▼

WHAT, SPECIFICALLY, might constitute a queer way of
life? What might some of the new relationships of which Foucault spoke look like? Foucault gave a few hints about what he
had in mind in some of his interviews with the gay press. The
first challenge he saw was "to make ourselves infinitely more
susceptible to pleasures" and, accordingly, to devise relationships that might offer strategies for enhancing pleasure and
might enable us to escape the ready-made formulas already
available to us—formulas which offer no alternative to purely
sexual encounters, on the one hand, and the merging of identities in love, on the other.[155] Foucault protested against the
paucity of choices.

> We live in a relational world that institutions have consid-
> erably impoverished. Society and the institutions which
> frame it have limited the possibility of relationships be-
> cause a rich relational world would be very complex to
> manage. . . . In effect, we live in a legal, social, and insti-
> tutional world where the only relations possible are ex-
> tremely few, extremely simplified, and extremely poor.
> There is, of course, the fundamental relation of marriage,

and the relations of family, but how many other relations should exist . . . !

Hence Foucault's interest in classical antiquity and its social methods for institutionalizing friendships between men, methods which in their time gave rise to "a system of supple and relatively codified relations" with its own panoply of "obligations, tasks, reciprocal duties, [and] hierarchy."[156] Foucault made it clear that he did not recommend reviving that classical form of social relations; he invoked it merely to dramatize the possibility of multiplying the forms of association beyond the small number that presently exist.

One possibility that intrigued Foucault—one which he put forward as an example of how we might pluralize the currently available kinds of legally institutionalized personal relationships while nonetheless accommodating, to some degree, the established institutions of law and modern society—was the possibility of expanding the practice of legal adoption. "We should secure recognition for relations of provisional coexistence, adoption . . . of one adult by another," he urged. "Why shouldn't I adopt a friend who's ten years younger than I am? And even if he's ten years older? Rather than arguing that rights are fundamental and natural to the individual, we should try to imagine and create a new relational right which permits all possible types of relations to exist and not be prevented, blocked, or annulled by impoverished relational institutions."[157] Adoption might also provide a mechanism for formalizing differences of wealth or age or education between lovers, acknowledging informal inequality while providing a framework of mutual support in which such inequality, accompanied by clearly marked rights and duties, might not devolve into exploitation or domination.

Such a project may be profitably compared to the queer practices of self-fashioning pursued by the members of an Italian feminist collective, the Milan Women's Bookstore group, and documented in a 1987 volume which has recently been the subject of a fascinating and illuminating essay by Teresa de Lauretis. Like Foucault, the anonymous authors of this volume are very much concerned with the problem of collective ethical and political self-fashioning: self-invention is for them, just as it is for queer culture, a practical necessity, insofar as it means inventing a freedom and a form of unmediated relationship that women have never enjoyed. "This book is about the necessity to give meaning, exalt, and represent in words and images the relationship of one woman to another," the introduction states. "[W]e are dealing, in part, with things that had no name. . . . What we have seen taking shape [in our group over the course of decades] is a genealogy of women, that is, a coming into being of women legitimated by the reference to their female origin."[158] It is less a question of attempting to realize a preexisting female nature than of calling a new social and individual identity into being. Commenting on the book's title, *Non credere di avere dei diritti: La generazione della libertà femminile nell' idea e nelle vicende di un gruppo di donne* ("Don't Think You Have Any Rights: The Engendering of Female Freedom in the Thought and Vicissitudes of a Women's Group"), de Lauretis observes,

> The bold injunction of the title, "don't think you have any rights" (a phrase of Simone Weil's, cited in the epigraph), with its direct address to women and its unequivocal stance of negativity, sharply contrasts with the subtitle's affirmation of a freedom for women that is not made possible by adherence to the liberal concept of rights—civil, human, or individual rights—which women do not have *as women*, but is generated, and indeed engendered, by taking up a position in a symbolic community, a "genealogy of women," that is at once discovered, invented, and constructed through feminist practices of reference and address.[159]

Rather than put pressure on a homogeneous identity-concept, such as "woman," in the way that lesbians and gay men in the United States have tended to do, relying on the use of pseudo-ethnic identity categories to secure civil rights according to a politically regulative ideal of liberal pluralism, the Milan collective explored, as it evolved, various practical devices for coping with differences among its members, especially with disparities of power and wealth, so as to be able to continue to build relationships among women who were and who would no doubt remain to some extent differently positioned with respect to one another in terms of economic and social power. One device invented in order to meet the challenge posed to the group by the social disparities among its members was the practice of "entrustment" (*affidamento*), which de Lauretis explicates as follows:

> Briefly, the relationship of entrustment is one in which one woman gives her trust or entrusts herself symbolically to another woman, who thus becomes her guide, mentor, or point of reference—in short, the figure of symbolic mediation between her and the world. Both women engage in the relationship—and here is the novelty, and the most controversial aspect of this feminist theory of practice—not in spite, but rather because and in full recognition of the disparity that may exist between them in class or social position, age, level of education, professional status, income, etc. That is to say, the function of female symbolic mediation that one woman performs for the other is achieved, not in spite but rather because of the power differential between them, contrary to the egalitarian feminist belief that women's mutual trust is incompatible with unequal power.[160]

The theoretical basis for this practice apparently lies in the distinction drawn by the earlier Italian feminist Carla Lonzi (the author of *Sputiamo su Hegel*) between "equality" and "difference." According to Lonzi, who is quoted by the volume's collective authorship to this effect, "[E]quality is a juridical principle . . . what is offered as legal rights to colonized people. And what is imposed on them as culture. . . . Difference is an existential principle which concerns the modes of being human, the peculiarity of one's experiences, goals, possibilities, and one's sense of existence in a given situation and in the situations one may envision."[161] This definition of "difference," though in its original application it refers to sexual difference—that is, to the difference between men and women—would seem to apply equally well to the various social differences among women. And it helps to explain why the immediate goal of the Milan collective was not simply to eliminate difference or to impose equality but rather to invent ways of dealing with difference so as to guard against whatever effects it might produce that would pose obstacles to "the engendering of female freedom." Rather than insist on fabricating a purely formal or procedural equality that would leave intact existing social disparities among its members, the Milan collective experimented with ways of negotiating those existing differences not only to prevent them from producing damaging side effects but also to transform them into vehicles of mutual assistance and of communal as well as individual strength. In order to achieve that goal, however, the collective first needed to invent new styles of life, new arts of existence. The project seems recognizably Foucauldian. As Foucault put it, "I don't see where evil is in the practice of someone who, in a given game of truth, knowing more than another, tells him what he must do, teaches him, transmits knowledge to him, communicates skill to him. The problem is rather to know how you are to avoid in these practices . . . the effects of domination. . . . "[162]

▼   ▼   ▼   ▼   ▼   ▼   ▼   ▼

OF COURSE, the classic case of the strategic use of power differentials to produce effects of pleasure instead of effects of domination is sadomasochistic eroticism. And so it is not surprising, perhaps, that some of Foucault's clearest indications of what might count as *queer praxis* occur in the context of his discussions of S/M. It is also in those discussions that Foucault's belief in the transformative potential of queer sex emerges most eloquently, if still somewhat sketchily.

First of all, Foucault emphasizes that what goes by the name of "domination" in S/M is a strategy for creating pleasure, not a form of personal or political subjugation.

> What strikes me with regard to S/M is how it differs from social power. What characterizes power is the fact that it is a strategic relation that has been stabilized through institutions. So the mobility in power relations is limited, and there are strongholds that are very, very difficult to suppress because they have been institutionalized and are now very pervasive in courts, codes and so on. All that means that the strategic relations of people are made rigid.
>
> On this point, the S/M game is very interesting because it is a strategic relation, but it is always fluid. Of course, there are roles, but everyone knows very well that those roles can be reversed. . . . Or, even when the roles are stabilized, you know very well that it is always a game. Either the rules are transgressed, or there is an agreement, either explicit or tacit, that makes [the participants] aware of certain boundaries. This strategic game as a source of bodily pleasure is very interesting. But I wouldn't say that it is a reproduction, inside the erotic relationship, of the structure of power. It is an acting out of power structures by a strategic game that is able to give sexual pleasure or bodily pleasure.
>
> The practice of S/M is the creation of pleasure, and there is an identity with [i.e., a personal identity attached to] that creation. And that's why S/M is really a subculture. It's a process of invention. S/M is *the use* of a strategic relationship as a source of pleasure (physical pleasure). . . . What is interesting, is that in . . . heterosexual life those strategic relations [e.g., pursuit and flight] come before sex. It's a strategic relation in order to obtain sex. And in S/M those

strategic relations are inside sex, as a convention of pleasure within a particular situation.[163]

So S/M is a game in which power differentials are subordinated to the overall strategic purpose of producing human pleasure; it is not a form of domination in which human beings are subordinated to the functioning of rigidly structured power differentials.

Next, Foucault saw S/M, especially as it was cultivated and elaborated in gay male urban enclaves in the United States as part of a wider practice of subcultural community formation, not as the expression of a deep psychological impulse which a permissive society had finally enabled people to indulge but rather as something new that modern subjects could *do* with the sexuality to which their identities had become so closely attached. S/M represented to Foucault "a process of invention," insofar as it detaches sexual pleasure from sexuality (in an S/M scene, the precise gender and sexual orientation of one's sexual partner may lose some of their importance as prerequisites of sexual excitement) and insofar as it frees bodily pleasure from organ specificity, from exclusive localization in the genitals. S/M thereby makes possible a new relation between the body and pleasure, and one effect of continued S/M practice is to alter one's relation to one's own body.

> I don't think that this movement of sexual practices has anything to do with the disclosure or the uncovering of S/M tendencies deep within our unconscious, and so on. I think that S/M is much more than that; it's the real creation of new possibilities of pleasure, which people had no idea about previously. The idea that S/M is related to a deep violence, that S/M practice is a way of liberating this violence, this aggression, is stupid. We know very well what all those people are doing is not aggressive; they are inventing new possibilities of pleasure with strange parts of their body—through the eroticization of the body. I think it's a kind of creation, a creative enterprise, which has as

one of its main features what I call the desexualization [i.e., the "degenitalization"] of pleasure. The idea that bodily pleasure should always come from sexual pleasure, and the idea that sexual pleasure is the root of *all* our possible pleasure—I think *that's* something quite wrong. These practices are insisting that we can produce pleasure with very odd things, very strange parts of our bodies, in very unusual situations, and so on.[164]

The notion of "desexualization" is a key one for Foucault, and it has been much misunderstood. When he speaks of "desexualization," Foucault is drawing on the meaning of the French word *sexe* in the sense of sexual organ. What he means by S/M's "desexualization of pleasure" is not that S/M detaches pleasure from all acts of a conceivably sexual nature (even if it does destroy the absolute dependence of sexual pleasure on sexual intercourse narrowly defined) but that S/M detaches sexual pleasure from genital specificity, from localization in or dependence on the genitals. S/M, along with various related (though often quite distinct) practices of bondage, shaving, tit torture, cock and ball torture, piercing, humiliation, flagellation, and fist-fucking, produces intense pleasures while bypassing, to a greater or lesser extent, the genitals themselves; it involves the eroticization of nongenital regions of the body, such as the nipples, the anus, the skin, and the entire surface of the body. And it finds other erotic uses for the genitals than that of stimulation to the point of orgasm. S/M therefore represents a remapping of the body's erotic sites, a redistribution of its so-called erogenous zones, a breakup of the erotic monopoly traditionally held by the genitals, and even a re-eroticization of the male genitals as sites of vulnerability instead of as objects of veneration. In all of those respects, S/M represents an encounter between the modern subject of sexuality and the otherness of his or her body. Insofar as that encounter produces changes in the relations among subjectivity, sexuality, pleasure, and the body, S/M qualifies as a potentially self-transformative practice (which does not mean, of course, that S/M is the *only* sexual activity practiced by [some] lesbians and gay men that has the potential to be transformative).

By invoking his term "desexualization," Foucault seems to be referring back to a 1978 interview with Jean Le Bitoux which did not appear in French until ten years later (in what seems to have been an imperfect transcript), has never been reprinted, and has never been published in English.[165] A prominent theme in that interview is Foucault's insistence on a distinction between gay and straight machismo, between even the hypermasculine "clone" style of gay male comportment, as it was elaborated in New York and San Francisco in the late 1970s, and the larger "phallocratic culture" (Foucault's term) in which we live. Foucault welcomes the possibility of a strategic alliance between gay men and feminism, "which has enabled homosexuals to demonstrate that their taste for men is not another form of phallocracy." Clone culture is not an expression of male supremicism or separatism, according to Foucault: "[O]ne has to look closer in order to grasp that this entire theatrical display of masculinity does not at all coincide with a revalorization of the male *as* male."

> On the contrary: in daily life, the relations between these men are filled with tenderness, with communitarian practices of life and of sexuality. Beneath the sign and under the shelter of these masculine theatrical displays, the sexual relations that take place reveal themselves to be, rather, valorizations of a masochist sort. Physical practices of the fist-fucking sort are practices that one can call devirilized, that is desexed [i.e., degenitalized]. They are in effect extraordinary counterfeit pleasures which one achieves by means of various devices, signs, symbols, or drugs such as poppers or MDA.
>
> What these signs and symbols of masculinity are for is not to go back to something that would be on the order of

phallocratism, of machismo, but rather to invent oneself, to make one's body into the site of production of extraordinarily polymorphous pleasures, pleasures that at the same time are detached from the valorization of the genitals and especially of the male genitals. After all, the point is to detach oneself from this virile form of obligatory pleasure—namely orgasm, orgasm in the ejaculatory sense, in the masculine sense of the term.[166]

The hypermasculine look of gay clones is deceiving. What the new styles of gay virility represent, paradoxically, is a strategy for valorizing various practices of devirilization under the sign of masculinity, thereby forging a new association between masculinity and sexual receptivity or penetrability, while detaching male homosexuality from its phobic association with "femininity" (conceived in phallocratic terms as "passivity" or as an absence of phallic aggressivity). By desexing (that is, degenitalizing) bodily pleasure, gay male S/M practices make possible the creation of a masculine sexual identity that need no longer be centered in the penis (or that finds new uses for the penis which mortify rather than celebrate it). Masculinity can now be reconstituted in a devirilized form: that is, it can be constituted not phallocentrically but symbolically, or *performatively*. (If there is an argument to be made about the possible political congeniality of gay male hypermasculinity and feminism, it will have to be made on the basis of some such analysis of gender performativity, not—as Richard Mohr makes it—on the basis of a sentimental valorization of gay male active/passive role-switching, to which are imputed the standard liberal values of equality, fraternity, reciprocity, and democratic egalitarianism.)[167] Foucault similarly interprets lesbian S/M as the expression of a parallel struggle on the part of women to escape from constraining stereotypes of femininity.[168]

The creative and transformative potential of queer sex is especially clear in the case of fist-fucking,[169] the practice that Foucault singles out for mention and that he seems to have in mind when he speaks of "produc[ing] pleasure with very odd things, very strange parts of our bodies." Fist-fucking, after all, is a sexual practice that nonetheless differs in several important respects from "sexual intercourse" as the latter is conventionally defined. It is less an end-driven, teleological action aimed at achieving release of sexual tension through orgasm (as in the Freudian model of "full heterosexual genitality")[170] than a gradual, lengthy process—"an art," as Gayle Rubin describes it, "that involves seducing one of the jumpiest and tightest muscles in the body."[171] Intensity and duration of feeling, not climax, are the key values: the process can sometimes go on for hours, and it is possible that neither partner may come—or (in the case of men) even maintain an erection for long. It is also possible for the receptive male partner to come without being in a state of erection at the time. Hence, fist-fucking has been spoken of by its practitioners not as sex but as a kind of "anal yoga." As such, it would seem to represent a practical refutation of what Foucault considered, as we have seen, the mistaken "idea that bodily pleasure should always come from sexual pleasure, and the idea that sexual pleasure is the root of *all* our possible pleasure." The emergence of fist-fucking as both a sexual and a subcultural phenomenon therefore has the potential to contribute to redefining both the meaning and the practice of sex along the lines sketched out by Foucault in 1977 when, in an interview entitled "Down with the Dictatorship of Sex!" he announced, "I am for the decentralization, the regionalization of all pleasures."[172]

▼   ▼   ▼   ▼   ▼   ▼   ▼   ▼

FOUCAULT'S is not the last word on the subject of S/M, of course. His pronouncements represent only one man's reflections, and those reflections are not necessarily the most accurate, the most honest, or the most illuminating.[173] But on at least one point Foucault was demonstrably right: his claim that what gay men of his era were up to was "the real creation of new possibilities of pleasure, which people had no idea about previously," is amply borne out by the example of fist-fucking. For whatever else one might say about fist-fucking, there is no doubt about the fact that it *is*, historically speaking, a new pleasure. According to one expert writing in 1983, for example, fist-fucking "may be the only sexual practice invented in the twentieth century" (or, to be more precise, it *was* the only such practice invented in the twentieth century until the fin-de-siècle discoveries of phone sex and fax sex).[174] Perhaps Foucault himself was the source of that verdict, if his biographer David Macey is correct in identifying him as the nameless "French *savant*" whom Edmund White credits in his 1980 book *States of Desire* with the remark that "fist-fucking is our century's only brand-new contribution to the sexual armamentarium."[175] How "brand new" it was has been ascertained only recently: Rubin dates the emergence of fist-fucking as an elaborated collective practice and community formation to the late 1960s; by the 1970s it had furnished the basis for an entire subculture complete with its own clubs and organizations, its own urban spaces, its own artwork and insignia, and even its own public, communal events.[176]

To have invented a genuinely new form of pleasure represented, in Foucault's eyes, a major accomplishment—and no wonder: after all, as Foucault liked to complain to his friends, the nineteenth century had invented myriad species of perverse sexual *desire*, but virtually nothing new in the way of sexual *pleasure* had been created for millennia.[177] "The possibility of using our bodies as a possible source of very numerous pleasures is something that is very important," Foucault declared in 1982. "For instance, if you look at the traditional construction of pleasure, you see that bodily pleasure, or pleasures of the flesh, are always drinking, eating and fucking. And that seems to be the limit of the understanding of our body, our pleasures."[178] The production of a new pleasure is therefore a significant achievement in its own right, and it testifies powerfully and thrillingly to the creative potential of a gay praxis.

The distinction between desire and pleasure implicit in Foucault's comments on S/M was one he returned to and made explicit in several key passages, both in his books and in his interviews. The distinction may help to explain the specifically political significance Foucault attached to the invention of the new pleasures produced by fist-fucking or recreational drugs as well as to the invention of new sexual environments, such as saunas, bathhouses, and sex clubs, in which novel varieties of sexual pleasure could be experienced. "It is very interesting to note," he observed, "that for centuries people generally, as well as doctors, psychiatrists and even liberation movements, have always spoken about desire, and never about pleasure. 'We have to liberate our desire,' they say. No! We have to create new pleasure. And then maybe desire will follow."[179] As David Macey points out, Foucault's emphasis on pleasures rather than desire was deliberate: he "was distancing himself from the so-called philosophy of desire associated with Deleuze and Lyotard."[180] Foucault explained his emphasis in his interview with Jean Le Bitoux:

> I am advancing this term [pleasure], because it seems to me that it escapes the medical and naturalistic connotations inherent in the notion of desire. That notion has been used as a tool, as a grid of intelligibility, a calibration in terms of normality: "Tell me what your desire is and I will tell you who you are, whether you are normal or not, and then I can validate or invalidate your desire." One keeps running into this tactic which goes from the notion of Christian concupiscence all the way through the Freudian notion of desire, passing through the notion of the sexual instinct in the 1840s. Desire is not an event but a perma-

nent feature of the subject: it provides a basis onto which all that psychologico-medical armature can attach itself.

The term "pleasure" on the other hand is virgin territory, unused, almost devoid of meaning. There is no "pathology" of pleasure, no "abnormal" pleasure. It is an event "outside the subject," or at the limit of the subject, taking place in that something which is neither of the body nor of the soul, which is neither inside nor outside—in short, a notion neither assigned nor assignable.[181]

It was in order to intensify experiences of pleasure "at the limit of the subject" that Foucault advocated the use of what he called "*good* drugs."[182] He found similar possibilities in bathhouse sex:

I think it is politically important that sexuality be able to function the way it functions in the saunas, where, without [having to submit to] the condition of being imprisoned in one's own identity, in one's own past, in one's own face, one can meet people who are to you what one is to them: nothing else but bodies with which combinations, fabrications of pleasure will be possible. These places afford an exceptional possibility of desubjectivization, of desubjection, perhaps not the most radical but in any case sufficiently intense to be worth taking note of. [Anonymity is important] because of the intensity of the pleasure that follows from it. It's not the affirmation of identity that's important, it's the affirmation of non-identity. . . . It's an important experience in which one invents, for as long as one wants, pleasures which one fabricates together [with others].[183]

For Foucault, as for Plato (though for almost exactly opposite reasons), sex would seem to qualify as a low-level form of philosophical activity.[184] At least, intense sexual pleasure performs the function of decentering the subject and fragmenting personal identity; it thereby goes a certain way toward providing Foucault with what he had previously sought in the writings of Nietzsche and Bataille: namely, answers to such questions as

"Can't there be experiences in which the subject, in its consti-
tutive relations, in its self-identity, isn't given any more? And
thus wouldn't experiences be given in which the subject could
dissociate itself, break its relationship with itself, lose its identity?"[185] It is not desire but pleasure that, for Foucault, holds
out the promise of such a disaggregating experience. Unlike
desire, which expresses the subject's individuality, history, and
identity as a subject, pleasure is desubjectivating, impersonal:
it shatters identity, subjectivity, and dissolves the subject, however fleetingly, into the sensorial continuum of the body, into
the unconscious dreaming of the mind. As Foucault observed
in 1979 in the course of an address to Arcadie, the old French
homophile organization, on the subject of Herculine Barbin and
the nineteenth-century insistence on determining the "true sex"
of hermaphrodites, "Pleasure is something which passes from
one individual to another; it is not secreted by identity. Pleasure
has no passport, no identification papers."[186]

If we are to prevent personal identity from becoming "the
law, the principle, the rule" of individual existence,[187] then it is
ultimately sexuality itself that will have to be resisted, for it is
sexuality that amalgamates desire and identity into a unitary
and stable feature of the individual person and thereby imparts
to the subject a "true self"—a "self" that constitutes the "truth"
of the person and functions as an object both of social regulation and of personal administration. Modern techniques of
power make use of sexuality in order to attach to us a personal
identity, defined in part by our sexual identity; by attaching that
identity to us, they attach us to themselves. "Just because this
notion of sexuality has enabled us to fight [on behalf of our own
homosexuality] doesn't mean that it doesn't carry with it a certain number of dangers," Foucault remarked to Jean Le Bitoux.
"There is an entire biologism of sexuality and therefore an entire hold over it by doctors and psychologists—in short, by the
agencies of normalization. We have over us doctors, peda-

gogues, law-makers, adults, parents who talk of sexuality! . . . It is not enough to liberate sexuality; we also have to liberate ourselves . . . from the very notion of sexuality."[188] And in an interview given a few years earlier, Foucault made a number of positive recommendations. "We have to invent with our bodies—with their elements, their surfaces, their masses, their volumes—a non-disciplinary eroticism: an eroticism of the body in its volatile and diffuse potentialities, its chance encounters and uncalculated pleasures. . . . "[189] Foucault's famous and rather cryptic remarks, at the end of *The History of Sexuality, Volume I*, about the political importance of attacking sexuality itself and promoting pleasures at the expense of sex make a great deal more sense when they are set in the context of his insistent distinction between pleasure and desire, and his tendency to champion bodies and pleasures, on the one hand, at the expense of desire, identity, and sexuality, on the other. "We must not believe that by saying yes to sex, one says no to power," Foucault wrote;

> on the contrary, one thereby follows in the track of the entire apparatus of sexuality. It is from the agency of sex that one has to free oneself if one wishes, through a tactical reversal of the various mechanisms of sexuality, to assert, against the hold of power, the claims of bodies, pleasures, and knowledges in their multiplicity and their possibility of resistance. The rallying point for the counterattack against the apparatus of sexuality ought not to be sex-desire, but bodies and pleasures.[190]

The transformative power of the queer sexual practices that gay men have invented reveals in this context something of its political efficacy: through the invention of novel, intense, and scattered bodily pleasures, queer culture brings about a tactical reversal of the mechanisms of sexuality, making strategic use of power differentials, physical sensations, and sexual identity-categories in order to create a queer praxis that ultimately dispenses with "sexuality" and destabilizes the very constitution of identity itself. As Leo Bersani summarizes Foucault's position, "The most effective resistance to this disciplinary productivity [of power in the guise of sexuality] should, Foucault suggests, take the form not of a struggle against prohibition, but rather of a kind of counter-productivity. It is not a question of lifting the barriers to seething repressed drives, but of consciously, deliberately playing on the surfaces of our bodies with forms or intensities of pleasure not covered, so to speak, by the disciplinary classifications that have until now taught us what sex is."[191] Fist-fucking and sadomasochism appear in this light as utopian political practices, insofar as they disrupt normative sexual identities and thereby generate—of their own accord, and despite being indulged in *not* for the sake of politics but purely for the sake of pleasure—a means of resistance to the discipline of sexuality, a form of counterdiscipline—in short, a technique of ascesis. The shattering force of intense bodily pleasure, detached from its exclusive localization in the genitals and regionalized throughout various zones of the body, decenters the subject and disarticulates the psychic and bodily integrity of the self to which a sexual identity has become attached. By shattering the subject of sexuality, queer sex opens up the possibility for the cultivation of a more impersonal self, a self that can function as the substance of ongoing ethical elaboration—and thus as the site of future transformation.

▼   ▼   ▼   ▼   ▼   ▼   ▼   ▼

At the same time as he proposed practicing what Bersani calls "*jouissance* as a mode of ascesis,"[192] Foucault also argued implicitly against the tendency to associate resistance only with radically non-normative social and sexual practices. Despite his interest in the transformative potential of S/M, Foucault was far from insisting that gay life or gay sex had to be thoroughly transgressive, experimental, or avant-gardist in order to qualify as a form of political resistance. Given the way that society is currently organized, after all, even the most innocuous-seeming expressions of gay sexuality threaten the coherence of the social order. To reduce the inventiveness and creativity of gay life to sexual promiscuity, for example, is in Foucault's view to erase "everything that can possibly be upsetting about affection, tenderness, friendship, faithfulness, comradeship, companionship, for which a fairly controlled society cannot make room without fearing that alliances might be formed, that unexpected lines of force might appear."[193] And he added,

> Imagining a sexual act that does not conform to the law or to nature, that's not what upsets people. But that individuals might begin to love each other, that's the problem. That goes against the grain of social institutions: they are already crisscrossed by emotional intensities which both hold them in place and fill them with turmoil—look at the army, where love between men is endlessly solicited and stigmatized. The institutional regulations cannot approve such [emotional] relations [between men], with their multiple intensities, variable colorations, imperceptible movements, and changing forms—relations that produce a short circuit and introduce love where there ought to be law, regularity, and custom.[194]

Hence it is "the homosexual way of life" that, according to Foucault, is much more threatening "than the sexual act itself."[195] (Which may be why it is easier to legalize gay sex than gay marriage.) And he added that what straight society finds intolerable about gay people is not our specific pleasures or sexual practices but their outcome, their effect on the quality of our lives: straight people can forgive us our physical thrills, but what they ultimately cannot forgive us is our happiness.[196]

Similarly, the most interesting things about S/M and fist-fucking, in Foucault's eyes, may not have been their allegedly disaggregating impact on the individual subject of desire but their incongruous integration into "homosexual ways of life." As Rubin has recently documented, the 1970s were a time of vigorous and expansive community formation for gay leathermen in San Francisco and elsewhere in the United States.[197] What that meant is that fist-fucking and S/M did not remain merely occasional or isolated practices but became linked to other expressions of subcultural development, including dress, patterns of life and work, the transformation of neighborhoods, the growth of community organizations, the provision of public services, the staging of athletic events, and ultimately the emergence of locally based and funded social and political groups. These developments represented signal instances of the new sorts of things that gay men could *do* with their sexuality, and in fact what may have intrigued Foucault most about fist-fucking was the way a specific non-normative sexual practice could come to provide the origin and basis for such seemingly remote and unrelated events as bake sales, community fundraisers, and block parties. Those "communitarian practices of life and sexuality" which Foucault saw knitting together the social relationships of gay leathermen demonstrated dramatically how one could "use . . . one's sexuality to achieve a multiplicity of types of relations," "to define and develop a way of life," to "construct cultural forms."

▼   ▼   ▼   ▼   ▼   ▼   ▼   ▼

ULTIMATELY, in Foucault's opinion,

> [T]he gay movement has a future which goes beyond gays themselves. . . . [It may include the possibility of a] culture in the large sense, a culture which invents ways of relating, types of existence, types of values, types of exchanges between individuals that are really new and are neither the same as, nor superimposed on, existing cultural forms. If

that's possible, then gay culture will be not only a choice of homosexuals for homosexuals. It would create relations that are, at certain points, transferable to heterosexuals.

(Elsewhere Foucault cited gay bathhouses as an institution that heterosexuals might benefit from;[198] the codification of "relations of provisional coexistence" might enable other "types of exchanges" equally beneficial to heterosexuals).

> We have to reverse things a bit. Rather than saying what we said at one time: "Let's try to re-introduce homosexuality into the general norm of social relations," let's say the reverse: "No! Let's escape as much as possible from the type of relations which society proposes for us and try to create in the empty space where we are new relational possibilities." By proposing a new relational *right*, we will see that non-homosexual people can enrich their lives by changing their own schema of relations.[199]

The future Foucault envisages for us is not exclusively or categorically gay. But it is definitely queer.

All this may seem highly prescriptive, especially coming from someone who deplored the political effect of preformulated theories or programs on the wayward course of political struggle. Foucault, however, strenuously denied that he was prescribing anything to anyone.[200] In the context of discussions with other gay men and interviews with the gay press, Foucault felt able to advance proposals because he could do so not on the strength of some antecedently established authority but on the basis of personal experience, communal participation, and a situated knowledge which he shared with his interlocutors. Far from *pre*scribing courses of action to others in his interviews, Foucault was *de*scribing and reflecting on developments in gay culture that he saw already taking place all around him. Ed Cohen makes the point very well:

> Perhaps the most distinctive factor in Foucault's discussions of homosexuality, in part owing to the fact that they

took place primarily in the (non-academic) gay press, was the intimacy he adopted in relation to his topic. Unlike his interviews in other contexts—in which he consistently refused to use his role as a famous intellectual discussing the implications of his academic endeavours to propound . . . "political positions"—Foucault's forthright attitude in gay publications clearly exemplifies his willingness to use his intellectual activity strategically in the struggles of which he was a part. Since his inclusive relation to his audience established by a gay (con)text provided Foucault with a different relation of "authority" to his subject, it enabled him to make more explicit connections between his individual historical researches and the historical conditions from which they arose. . . . To take just one example, Foucault's lectures at The Barracks (a now defunct gay bathhouse in San Francisco) during the late 1970s must be seen as one concrete attempt to (re)situate his work on sexuality within the sexual field itself. Speaking as one member of the gay community who was also an intellectual, Foucault offered his opinions on the historical and tactical situation of the gay movement in order to deploy the knowledge which he elsewhere frames academically in those concrete fields of power that define everyday life for gay men and women.[201]

The story of Foucault's lectures at The Barracks "during the late 1970s" is almost certainly apocryphal (The Barracks had closed by 1976), and Cohen's careful attention to the distinction between "member of the community" and "intellectual" does not capture the unself-consciously enthusiastic and unpretentious tone that I find characteristic of Foucault's interviews with the gay press, but Cohen does convey the experimental quality of Foucault's practice of thinking out loud in groups of gay men.

▼   ▼   ▼   ▼   ▼   ▼   ▼   ▼

QUEER POLITICS itself, finally, is a kind of spiritual exercise, a modern practice of the self. "As strange as it may sound at first," Arnold Davidson concludes,

> Foucault pointed to homosexuality as one resource for an-
> swering the question of how to practice spiritual exercises
> in the twentieth century. Ultimately, for Foucault, one link
> between the ancient practices of self-mastery and contem-
> porary homosexuality is that both require an ethics or as-
> cetics of the self tied to a particular, and particularly
> threatening, way of life. I know it would have given Fou-
> cault genuine pleasure to think that the threat to everyday
> life posed by ancient philosophy had a contemporary an-
> alogue in the fears and disturbances that derive from [i.e.,
> that are evoked in straight society by] the self-formation
> and style of life of being gay.[202]

The forms of ascesis, the spiritual exercises of ethical self-
fashioning, by which modern subjects can achieve transcendence nowadays are obviously not identical to the ancient forms.
First of all, however suspiciously Catholic Foucault's notion of
ascesis may sound, the modern analogues Foucault describes are
entirely secularized. Second, modern modes of ascesis, for all
that they may have to do with effort and imagination and collective struggle, have little to do with austerity: what can impart to
human lives in the modern world something of the intensity of existence which philosophers in the ancient world sought out
through their strategic practices of austerity is not the elimination but the cultivation of pleasure. Foucault's "homosexual ascesis" calls not for less pleasure but for vastly more pleasure—
including the intense pleasures procured by means of drugs, sadomasochistic eroticism, and anonymous sex. "By taking the
pleasure of sexual relations away from the area of sexual norms
and its categories and in so doing making the pleasure the crys-
tallizing point of a new culture," gay people have taken what Foucault regards as "an important, interesting step."[203] In the ancient
world, the point of sexual austerity was, according to Foucault,
to enable "very cultivated people . . . to give to their life much

more intensity"; so "in a way it's the same in the twentieth century when people, in order to get a more beautiful life, tried to get rid of all the sexual repression of their society, of their childhood." Foucault goes on to hypothesize that "Gide in Greece would have been an austere philosopher";[204] by the same token, one might speculate that Seneca in San Francisco would have been a gay leatherman—and a butch bottom, at that.

The modern practice of pleasure as ascesis can be clearly and concretely illustrated by consulting Gayle Rubin's account of the Catacombs, a fist-fucking and S/M club in San Francisco in the late 1970s and early 1980s. Rubin's affectionate and nostalgic evocation of the Catacombs contains a number of elements that recall Foucault's conception of queer sex as a spiritual exercise and echo his interpretation of S/M as a creative and self-transformative practice. For example, Rubin is at pains to emphasize how much planning, deliberation, imagination, foresight, preliminary group formation, and shared sense of common purpose are necessary for the successful staging of parties where people who may not have previously met one another can achieve together intense sexual experiences; she also points out the transformative effects that can result from such experiences as well as the opportunities for making friends, exploring the body, and inventing pleasure that sexual experimentation affords. Like Foucault, then, Rubin underscores the importance of formulating in advance a personal or ethical goal, the necessity of expending laborious effort, the possibility of forming new social bonds, and the opportunities for self-transformation that accompany the uninhibited pursuit of sexual pleasure. "Good fisting and S/M require a great deal of attention, intimacy, and trust," she writes.

> Because of this, even casual encounters could lead to deep affection and enduring friendships. Moreover, in many cultures the application of carefully chosen physical stress is a method for inducing transcendental mental and emo-

tional states. People came to the Catacombs to do prodigious things to their bodies and minds, and some habitués reported having the kinds of transformational experiences more often associated with spiritual disciplines.

Rubin hastens to add, however, that although "Catacombs sex was often intense and serious . . . it also had a playful, kids-in-the-sandbox quality. . . . The Catacombs environment enabled adults to have an almost childlike wonder at the body. It facilitated explorations of the body's sensate capabilities that are rarely available in modern, western societies."[205]

▼   ▼   ▼   ▼   ▼   ▼   ▼   ▼

MODERN VERSIONS of ascesis may be thematically or materially opposed to the ancient ones, then, but the two versions can nonetheless be thought of as structurally isomorphic. What ultimately links the modern with the ancient forms of ascesis is the technique of cultivating a self that transcends the self—a radically impersonal self that can serve as a vehicle for self-transformation because, being nothing in itself, it occupies the place of a new self which has yet to come into being. The dimension of the self that makes it a site of irreducible alterity nowadays is no longer the divine spark that dwells within it, of course; instead, it is the subject's determination by history. It is no longer divinity but history (in which category I also include language and the Symbolic) that guarantees us an experience of the Other at the core of our own subjectivity and brings it about that any direct encounter with the self must also be a confrontation with the not-self.[206]

When I speak of the self's determination by *history*, I mean both past and future history. Foucault's philosophical work had occupied itself with history in the past tense, and had aimed to describe as rigorously and as systematically as possible the many alterities of the past. He had charted the various changes in European discursive and institutional practices that had rendered European culture different from itself and from the forms it had assumed in the present day. He had also described the species of deviance that European societies constructed, captured, excluded, and preserved in the process of defining their own identities. By doing so he had made those European societies themselves appear deviant: he had made their reason appear to be madness, their medicine sickness, their punishments forms of criminality, their sexual liberation a form of subjugation. Such is the effect of writing the history of Western rationality against the background of the figures whom it has so violently demonized and cast out.[207] Moreover, Foucault conceived of historical inquiry itself as a kind of spiritual exercise: "I aim at having an experience myself—by passing through a determinate historical content—an experience of what we are today, of what is not only our past but also our present. And I invite others to share the experience. That is, an experience of our modernity that might permit us to emerge from it transformed."[208] The study of history becomes a spiritual exercise when, through it, the self discovers its past as that which dwells within its present and thereby comes to recognize in itself its own alterity to itself. History is a scholarly thought-experiment that we perform on ourselves in order to decenter ourselves by revealing, through a genealogical analysis of our being in the present, our own otherness to ourselves. In the light of history we appear different from ourselves, or from what we thought we were, and so we recover a sense of ourselves as sites of difference—hence, sites of possible transformation.

Genealogical inquiry therefore has a proleptic, or ascetic, dimension. It is a "test of the limits that we may go beyond, and thus [a] work carried out by ourselves upon ourselves as free beings.... [I]t will not deduce from the form of what we are what it is impossible for us to do and to know; but it will separate out, from the contingency that has made us what we are, the possibility of no longer being, doing, or thinking what we are, do, or think. . . . [It thereby seeks] to give new impetus . . . to the undefined work of freedom."[209] Foucault's political efforts, including his contributions to the lesbian and gay movement, corresponded to that genealogical project. Foucault labored to discover and to exploit those potential spaces of concrete freedom, of radical possibility, that existed *virtually* in the present. "For me, what must be produced is not man identical to himself, exactly as nature would have designed him or according to his essence," Foucault emphasized (his remarks were made in the course of a rather recondite discussion of his relation to the Frankfurt School, but he might as well have been describing the difficulty, the excitement, and the risks of queer politics); "on the contrary, we must produce something that doesn't yet exist and about which we cannot know how and what it will be."[210] Political activism, insofar as it takes the form of concrete utopian vision, is an experiment we perform on ourselves so as to discover our otherness to ourselves in the experience of our own futurity. Politics is therefore a spiritual exercise by which we practice a kind of negative capability in relation to our own becoming. The self is a new strategic possibility, finally, not because it is the seat of our personality but because it is *the point of entry of the personal into history*, because it is the place where the personal encounters its own history—both past and future. What it means to practice a homosexual ascesis is precisely to cultivate in ourselves the ability to surpass ourselves, to enter into our own futurity. That sometimes dizzyingly scary, and obviously risky, but also exhilarating personal experiment, performed on ourselves by ourselves, is what ultimately defined for Foucault—as it still defines for many lesbian and gay people today—the transformative practice of queer politics.

▼　▼　▼　▼　▼　▼　▼　▼

A NUMBER OF objections to this conception of homosexuality as a spiritual exercise are obvious. First, it may be objected that Foucault's notion of homosexuality as ascesis provides just another ideological alibi for sex, another justification for sex functionally equivalent to the traditional ones of love, procreation, payment of the conjugal debt, psychic or somatic hygiene, and so on. One might well ask whether it shouldn't be the role of queer culture not to come up with new alibis, new rationales for sex but finally to dispense with such rationales altogether. Shouldn't our banner read, in the words of Boy With Arms Akimbo (the queer activist graphics collective from San Francisco), "Sex Is . . . Just Sex"?[211] For Foucault, however, the point of applying to queer sex and politics a concept of "spiritual exercise" derived from ancient asceticism (whatever redemptive value that concept may have acquired as I have deployed it in this essay) is not to dignify or to license sexual expression but to acknowledge—just as Gayle Rubin does—both that the imaginative and intelligent pursuit of pleasure *requires* a certain amount of work (in the sense of exertion) and that it *does* a certain amount of work (in the sense of transformation). Gay culture didn't just happen, after all: it is the outcome of considerable thought, strenuous effort, desperate longing, delirious excitement, and heart-stopping risks. Foucault's vision is rather darker than Rubin's, however: if he does seem to suggest that getting fisted is, in some sense, good for you, he does so only because he believes that getting fisted is, in another sense, extremely bad for you. Only something so very bad for the integrated person that the normalized modern individual has become can perform the crucial work of rupture, of social and psychological disintegration, that may be necessary in order to permit new forms of life to come into being. But there is no guarantee that they *will* come into being. Foucault, once again, is not formulating a blueprint for resistance so much as he is reflecting on the energy, dynamism, and collective bravery of a subculture that, without having a safe foundation to fall back on, has been pioneering new forms of life for many years now. The concept of "spiritual exercise," which I am emphasizing here as much for its impertinence as for its aptness, serves to indicate something of the effort required to produce the social and psychic ruptures that lesbians and gay men must engineer daily in order to detach ourselves from heteronormative society, so as to be able to lead our queer lives without apology or compromise, and to continue to forge new and better ways of being queer.

Here is a second objection to Foucault's notion of homosexuality as ascesis: just as gay liberation might be thought to aim at the elimination of alibis for sex, so might it be thought to aim at the dissociation of sex from work. What else does it mean, one might ask, to impose an ascetics on oneself but to submit to a new kind of discipline? Isn't the most insidious feature of the traditional disciplines the ease with which they manage to acquire a grip on the individual by enabling that individual to be more effective, to achieve more, to work better, and to work best of all when those disciplinary mechanisms are most thoroughly internalized and when submitting to them feels like the enjoyment of liberty?[212] The most concise response to this objection is to distinguish discipline from work. It is pointless to attempt to extract from Foucault a repudiation of work per se. On the contrary, what Foucault recommends to us, as we've seen, is to *keep working* at being gay. And he accepted as an approximation to his outlook the Nietzschean dictum that one should create one's life by giving style to it through long practice and daily work (*The Gay Science*, no. 290).[213] Not to work, in a context shaped by the multiple apparatuses of heteronormativity, is not to resist: it is to surrender any hope of autonomy. But if Foucault summons us to more work, the work to which he summons us is not the kind that is necessarily opposed to play—or that makes Jack a dull boy.

The possibility of differentiating ethical work from discipline in the modern sense—the possibility, that is, of defining a notion of ascesis distinct from modern technologies for extracting docility from the body and for normalizing human subjects—was partly what attracted Foucault to the study of ancient ethical thought in the first place. The ancient prescriptive texts fascinated Foucault because they presented him with concrete examples of a discourse that could construct norms *without* producing effects of normalization. For not only was submission to the norms of ancient morality a deliberate strategy, an entirely elective, voluntary matter, a method of self-stylization intentionally adopted by a few members of a male elite in order to enhance the beauty of their existences and to increase their mastery over both themselves and others (and, thus, to consolidate their own social authority within their local communities); rigorous and austere adherence to the norms of ancient morality was also an exceptional practice that, far from achieving for its practitioners a greater degree of normality, surrounded them with a brilliant and extraordinary distinction. The purpose, the function, and the effect of ancient moral self-fashioning, in other words, was not to enable those who conformed to ethical norms to become more normal, more average, more capable of losing themselves in the crowd, but, on the contrary, to enable a few moral athletes to stand out, appear special, and become conspicuous—either in an admirable way, as in the case of certain Greek civic leaders distinguished by their personal virtue and austerity, or in a ludicrous way, as in the case of Socratic philosophers and their even weirder Hellenistic progeny (such as Diogenes the Cynic, perhaps Foucault's favorite, who masturbated and defecated in public).[214]

The importance Foucault ascribes to the possibility of constructing norms without producing effects of normalization is what explains his insistence that ethical self-fashioning in antiquity was, for the tiny minority who elected to practice it, a matter not of conforming to established codes of conduct but of exercising freedom, of freely stylizing one's existence. Sexual austerity constituted for the elite male "the elaboration and stylization of an activity in the exercise of its power and the practice of its liberty."[215] Foucault has been very badly misunderstood on this point, and never more so than by professional classicists.[216] Foucault's emphasis on the significance of moral freedom in antiquity, far from expressing a sentimental and unrealistic idealization of classical civilization, a refusal to acknowledge the powerfully constraining force of ancient social conventions, or an uncritical surrender to the cultural glamor and prestige of the Greeks and Romans, reflects instead his unyielding determination to draw a clear and systematic distinction between self-fashioning or ascesis, on the one hand, and mass obedience or conformity to laws of conduct, on the other. Such a distinction, of course, is crucial to Foucault's ability to make his main conceptual point about the fundamental difference between ancient and modern sexual ethics:

> The moral reflection of the Greeks on sexual behavior did not seek to justify interdictions, but to stylize a freedom—that freedom which the "free" man exercised in his activity.... [The Greeks did not for the most part] seek to organize [sexual] behavior as a domain in which normal behavior might be distinguished from abnormal or pathological practices.... [T]he requirement of austerity that was implied by the constitution of this subject who was master of himself was not presented in the form of a universal law, which each and every individual would have to obey, but rather as a principle of stylization of conduct for those who wished to give their existence the most graceful and accomplished form possible.... For [the Greeks], reflection on sexual behavior as a moral domain was not a means of internalizing, justifying, or formalizing general

interdictions imposed on everyone; rather, it was a means of elaborating—for the smallest minority of the population, made up of free, adult males—an aesthetics of existence, the purposeful art of a freedom perceived as a power game. Their sexual ethics . . . rested on a very harsh system of inequalities and constraints (particularly in connection with women and slaves); but it was problematized in thought as the relationship, for a free man, between the exercise of his freedom, the forms of his power, and his access to truth.[217]

The study of Greek sexual morality discloses, in short, the possibility of an ascetic discipline whose effect—*unlike* that of the modern disciplines—is not to normalize but, if anything, to marginalize: that is, *to queer*. One of the motives behind Foucault's protracted engagement with ancient prescriptive and ethical texts, a motive rarely grasped by the critics of the later volumes of *The History of Sexuality*, was to recover a sense of the possibility of just such a queer mode of discipline. "Asceticism, in the sense of the renunciation of pleasure, has got itself a bad name these days," Foucault said in an interview with *Gai pied*; Foucault himself had given "discipline" a bad name in *Discipline and Punish*. But queer culture manages to detach certain forms of discipline—those conjoined with bondage, for example—from the normalizing functions it performs in modern liberal societies. As we have seen, sadomasochistic eroticism uses "discipline" strategically not only in order to produce effects of intense pleasure but also in order to disarticulate personal identity and to disrupt the order of the self on which the normalization of modern subjects depends. Like ancient Greek morality, then, S/M can also be understood as "the purposeful art of a freedom perceived as a power game." For a modern philosophical analogue to such a queer practice of the self, Foucault looked to the dandyism of Baudelaire or the "limit-experience" of Bataille, but ultimately he had to leave the modern world behind, entirely in order to document the existence of a mode of ascesis that functions differently from the way it does in modern disciplinary society—that functions, in other words, not as a technology of subjugation but as a strategy of freedom.

▼   ▼   ▼   ▼   ▼   ▼   ▼   ▼

WHAT ABOUT the objection that queer culture as it actually exists, far from producing practices of freedom, has simply promoted new forms of discipline and constructed even more insidious procedures of normalization? After all, it has become de rigueur among lesbians and gay men to confront straight society by deploying *just so much* queerness, just the right, premeasured dose of deviance and nonconformity: there is now a right way to be queer, to be radical, to be "in your face," to invert the norms of straight society, and well-socialized lesbians and gay men spend a lot of time—and, more tellingly, money—acquiring the requisite T-shirts, muscles, haircuts, tattoos, dietary habits, body piercings, and so forth. Isn't the marketing of queer identity a form of normalization-by-commodification? How can queer modes of consumption count as resistant cultural practices, as self-transformative ethical work, without trivializing the very notion of political resistance and compromising its oppositional function? Doesn't queer commodification reduce politics to a consumerist lifestyle? Foucault's response to that possibility was to refuse to identify any actually existing social group as a political vanguard and, instead, to search constantly for new practices, techniques, and modes of analysis that might, in the current historical situation, enlarge the possibilities for ongoing personal and political transformation. Queer politics may, by now, have outlived its political usefulness, but if its efficacy and its productive political life can indeed still be renewed and extended, the first step in this procedure will be to try and preserve the function of queer identity as an empty placeholder for an identity that is still in progress and has as yet to be fully realized, to conceptualize queer identity as an identity in a state of becoming rather than as the referent for an actually existing form of life. Queer politics, if it is to remain queer, needs to be able to perform the function of emptying queerness of its referentiality or positivity, guarding against its tendency to concrete embodiment, and thereby preserving queerness as a resistant relation rather than as an oppositional substance.[218]

Otherwise, queer culture is likely to suffer, on a larger political scale, the normalizing vicissitudes already undergone by so-called queer theory. Coined in 1990 by Teresa de Lauretis expressly in order to disturb the complacency embodied in the routine conjunction "gay and lesbian" (that "by now established and often convenient formula," as de Lauretis calls it), to introduce into a monolithic, homogenizing discourse of (homo)sexual difference a problematic of multiple differences, and to highlight everything that is perverse about the project of *theorizing* sexual pleasure and desire,[219] "queer theory" has since been transformed into an unproblematic, substantive designation for a determinate subfield of academic practice, respectable enough to appear in advertisements for academic jobs and in labels on the shelves of bookstores. Signifying little more than what used to be signified by "lesbian and gay studies," "queer theory" seems to have forfeited, in this process, much of its political utility. In any case, the more it verges on becoming a normative academic discipline, the less queer "queer theory" can plausibly claim to be.

It was for precisely such reasons that Foucault refused to codify practices of resistance, much less to assist in their institutionalization. At the same time, however, he also challenged the kind of logic that would interpret all existing techniques of resistance as recycled modes of domination and that would therefore see in gay subcultural practices nothing but the repetition and reproduction of oppressive social formations: "Yes,

[I know] , to live with a boy would be bourgeois, to make love furtively in a tearoom, that would be to accept the ghetto, to make love in a bathhouse would be consumerism. That's a discourse that pretends to be political, but is just naive."[220] But even without Foucault's reply to this particular objection, his political writings afford plenty of indication as to how he would have met it. For the objection is grounded, perhaps tacitly, in an ideological tendency that Foucault strenuously rejected, a tendency to invent and apply theoretical criteria in order to determine what is "truly" radical or resistant and what merely "seems" to be so but is really co-opted, is really reinscribed within the oppositions it was seeking to evade. "To be sure, some political groups have long felt this fear of being co-opted," Foucault once remarked, reflecting on his own political activity.

> Won't everything that is said be inscribed in the very mechanisms we are trying to denounce? Well, I think it is absolutely necessary that it should happen this way: if the discourse can be co-opted, that is not because it is vitiated by nature, but because it is inscribed in a process of struggle. Indeed, the adversary pushing, so to speak, on the hold you have over him in order to turn it around, this constitutes the best valorization of the stakes and typifies the whole strategy of struggles. As in judo, the best answer to the opponent's maneuver never is to step back, but to re-use it to your own advantage as a base for the next phase. . . . Now it is our turn to reply.[221]

As Foucault insisted over and over again, and as the example of the strategic advantages and perils of the term "queer" dramatizes, the point to emphasize "is not that everything is bad, but that everything is dangerous, which is not exactly the same thing as bad. If everything is dangerous, then we always have something to do. So my position leads not to apathy but to a hyper- and pessimistic activism. I think that the ethico-political choice we have to make every day is to determine which is the main danger."[222] And, in another interview, speaking of the problem of gay self-nomination, Foucault added, "One can never settle into a position. One has to determine the use one makes of each moment as it comes along."[223] There is no safety in the term "queer"; there is no safety in the self-transformative exercise of homosexual ascesis. Even before the advent of AIDS, the stakes in lesbian and gay self-fashioning were already very high. The point is not to retreat from the challenge but to think as carefully, creatively, intelligently, and imaginatively as possible about how to meet it, with a full awareness that whatever we decide will have far-reaching and immensely consequential effects that many of us may have to live with.

The last thing we should want to do, then, is to devise and distribute a kind of cultural resistance meter, a test to determine how radically transformative, or *truly queer*, one practice or another *really* is, so that there can finally be an authoritative knowledge about it and a magisterial discipline of it. Without advancing a notion of political ascesis so minimal and empty that it might include shopping for the right outfit, in other words, what we really need to do is to avoid formulating a set of criteria for resistance so rigorous and systematic that they would absolutely exclude the possibility that resistance could *ever* take the form of shopping for the right outfit. Obviously, not all gay technologies of the self are necessarily revolutionary, transformative, or self-transcending. But it is also important not to undervalue the transformative potential of popular subcultural practices.

Take the subcultural practice which has haunted much of my previous discussion of ascesis, namely, gay male bodybuilding. It is all too easy to think of reasons why working out ought not to qualify as a utopian political practice or as a proper vehicle of homosexual ascesis in Foucault's sense: it's too popular, too "narcissistic," too consumerist, too conformist, too unoriginal. Far from providing a means of translating into actuality an individual's freely chosen set of values or idiosyncratic vision of life, working out might seem rather to express a caving in to peer pressure, a form of submission to the normalizing disciplines produced by and within gay subcultures—the very disciplines that cultural radicals of all sorts ought to be resisting. And yet, I think gay people have equally good reasons against joining in the chorus of straight disapproval of gay male "body fascism," reasons above and beyond the constant suspicion that straight indignation at "fascism" becomes uncharacteristically righteous when gay men are its focus, a focus which seldom widens to include the vicious and, indeed, fascistic kind of antigay stereotyping exemplified by the accusation of gay male body fascism itself and according to which gay men are either too effeminate or too masculine, too sexual or too political, too self-hating or too narcissistic, too scrawny or too muscular. The more pertinent reason for rejecting a reductive, totalizing, and demeaning interpretation of gay male gym culture is that such an interpretation fails to take account of the many different meanings working out may have within the various life projects pursued by gay men who frequent gyms.

In particular, what the facile derogation of gay male gym culture misses is that many gay men (and others) work out in order to stimulate their immune systems, to live longer lives. It also misses the crucial fact that for serious gym-goers working out is more than just a cosmetic recreation: it is a strenuous, demanding, and transformative daily ritual which often alters the entire shape of one's life—including one's diet, routine, patterns of work and sleep, friendships, social habits, sense of community, and sense of personal possibilities. In all of those respects, working out is truly an "art of existence." Finally, and most important, queer muscles are not the same as straight muscles. Gay male body styles nowadays differ distinctly from heteronormative ones. The typical result of contemporary gay male body culture is to produce a physique that deviates noticeably from conventional, straight-male norms of masculinity. As D. A. Miller writes:

> Only those who can't tell elbow from ass will confuse the different priorities of the macho straight male body and the so-called gym-body of gay male culture. The first deploys its heft as a *tool* (for work, for its potential and actual intimidation of other, weaker men or of women)—as both an armored body and a body wholly given over to utility . . . whereas the second displays its muscle primarily as an *image* openly appealing to, and deliberately courting the possibility of being shivered by, someone else's desire.[224]

What distinguishes the gay male gym body, then, in addition to its spectacular beauty, is the way it advertises itself as an object of desire. Gay muscles do not signify power. They do not resemble the kind of muscles that are produced by hard physical labor. On the contrary, the exaggerated, arcane, highly defined, elaborately sculpted muscles of the gay male gym body derive from no useful pursuit and serve no practical function: they are the sort of muscles that could only have been developed in a gym. They are explicitly designed to be an erotic turn-on, and in their very solicitation of desire they deliberately flaunt the visual norms of straight masculinity, which impose discretion on masculine self-display and require that straight male beauty exhibit itself only casually or inadvertently, that it refuse to acknowledge its own strategies. If, as Foucault hypothesized in *Discipline and Punish*, those whom modern disciplinary society would destroy it first makes visible, then gay male bodybuilders, in visibly inscribing their erotic desires on the surfaces of their bodies, have not only exposed themselves to considerable social risks in the course of pursuing their ethical projects but have also performed a valuable political service on behalf of everyone, insofar as they have issued a challenge of defiance to the very mechanisms of modern discipline.[225] After all, many gay men work out not in order to conform to an average or received standard of male beauty but in order to develop a specific part of their body or a particular muscle group that holds a special significance for them or for their sexual partners: the goal of such a physical ascesis is not to look normal but to look weird, hypertrophic, even grotesque—that is, queer—and yet, for all that, intensely desirable.

If the example of gay male gym culture might seem to come dangerously close to trivializing or debasing Foucault's notion of ascesis, perhaps that's because working out isn't a sufficiently elitist practice, and even cultural radicals easily become suspicious of any technology of the self that is widely dispersed in a culture, and is genuinely popular. It may be worth emphasizing, in this context, that the examples of homosexual ascesis, such as fist-fucking, that Foucault himself singled out for discussion indicate how very far *his* notion of asceticism was from being avant-gardist. He did not study the ancient moralists in order to propound a private ethic for a few modern philosophers of the bedroom. Rather than prescribe modes of radical self-transformation for others, Foucault tried to articulate the radical possibilities he saw in those forms of homosexual ascesis that lesbians and gay men were already pioneering everywhere around him. To free Foucault's conception of gay asceticism from the elitism and austerity of his ancient sources may be, as Foucault would say, dangerous, but it is not necessarily or inevitably to trivialize that conception.

No doubt very few of the gay leathermen whom Foucault encountered in New York and San Francisco in the late 1970s and early 1980s modeled themselves on the figure of the Stoic sage or thought of themselves as philosophers. But many of them surely did believe, just as many of us who take part in various forms of lesbian and gay cultural politics still do, that they had embarked on an extraordinary life-experiment, an astonishing, unforeseen trajectory that had taken them from isolated, conventional lives, regulated by the routines of heterosexual society and dominated by the tyranny of homophobic attitudes, and had catapulted them into a new, exciting, unpredictable, and dangerous mode of existence, one which had to be made up as they went along and which turned out to be self-transforming beyond anything they could possibly have anticipated or imagined.

▼ ▼ ▼ ▼ ▼ ▼ ▼ ▼

"WHEREAS OTHER politics recognize only ideal necessities . . . or the free play of individual initiatives," Foucault observed, "a progressive politics is one which recognizes the historic conditions and the specified rules of a practice [and thus] defines in a practice the possibilities of transformation. . . ."[226] Both history *and* politics, then, are necessary for transformation. Both, moreover, are fictions, according to Foucault: history is like a historical romance; politics is like science fiction.[227] "I am well aware," he acknowledged,

> that I have never written anything but fictions. I do not mean to say, however, that truth is therefore absent. It seems to me that the possibility exists for fiction to function in truth, for a fictional discourse to induce effects of truth, and for bringing it about that a true discourse engenders or "manufactures" something that does not as yet exist, that is "fictions" it. One "fictions" history on the basis of a political reality that makes it true, one "fictions" a politics not yet in existence on the basis of a historical truth.[228]

And, in a passage I have quoted twice before, he added that

> the function of any diagnosis concerning the nature of the present . . . does not consist in a simple characterization of what we are but, instead—by following lines of fragility in the present—in managing to grasp why and how that-

which-is might no longer be that-which-is. In this sense, any description must always be made in accordance with these kinds of virtual fracture which open up the space of freedom understood as a space of concrete freedom, i.e. possible transformation.[229]

It is at this point of convergence between spiritual exercises and practices of resistance that a queer ethics of self-transformation appears as a defining and overarching feature of Foucault's philosophy and politics.

▼　▼　▼　▼　▼　▼　▼　▼

AND SO IF Michel Foucault had never existed, queer politics would have had to invent him—and perhaps it has indeed invented him, or at least partly reinvented him.[230] More powerfully than any other thinker I know, Foucault *politicizes* both truth and the body, an accomplishment of crucial importance for gay and lesbian political resistance in the age of AIDS. In particular, Foucault's political critique of sexual discourse gives queers of all sorts a powerful weapon with which to challenge and to resist the discursive operations of contemporary homophobia, if not always to prevail against the institutions in which its criminalizing, pathologizing, and moralizing discourses are entrenched. Beyond that, and even more important, Foucault gives us, in place of a theory of sexuality that would tell us the truth about sex, a critique of theoretical discourses about sexuality that effectively sidesteps the usual questions about its "fundamental nature": what sexuality really is, how we can discover our true sexuality, how we ought to express it, whether our specific expressions of it are healthy or diseased, and so forth. The value of Foucault's non-theory, of his critical intervention in the realm of theory, lies precisely in its brilliant strategic evasion of all those questions about *what sexuality is* and in its diversion of our attention, instead, to questions about *how sexuality functions* in both knowledge and society: what role sexuality has played, as a concept and an experience, in the history of European discursive and institutional practices. The effect of Foucault's inquiries into that latter set of questions about sex is to reconceptualize sexuality as a strategic device, as the linchpin of a complex socio-politico-scientific apparatus. Foucault thereby converts sex into the basis for a radical critique of, and political struggle against, innumerable aspects of modern disciplinary culture.

Even and exactly as Foucault politicizes sex, he also *depsychologizes* it. By conceptualizing sexuality as a device whose operation can be analyzed rather than as a thing whose nature can be known, by treating sexuality as the instrument and effect of a series of discursive and political strategies, Foucault translates sex from the realm of individual fantasy to the domain of social power and knowledge. That strategic repositioning of sex, that combined politicizing and depsychologizing of it, may constitute in fact Foucault's chief contribution to gay political theory—as well as the principal reason for his rise to intellectual preeminence as the patron saint of queer activism. Foucault is not only our Marx but also our Freud. At least, *The History of Sexuality, Volume I*, contains the only original account of sexuality that the twentieth century has produced other than Freud's, and it offers the only account of sexuality that can rival Freud's and provide a genuine alternative to the normalizing discourses of conventional psychoanalysis. More specifically, Foucault's antipsychoanalytic approach to sexuality makes it possible, as well as sensible and proper, to treat homophobia as a political, not a psychological, problem: it implies that the causes of homophobia are to be sought not in psychic life, in fantasy, or in the vicissitudes of human development, but rather, as Leo Bersani (rather skeptically) puts it, "[in] a political anxiety about the subversive, revolutionary social rearrangements that gays may be trying out . . . , [an] anxiety about a threat to the way people are expected to relate to one another, which is not too different from saying the way power is positioned and exercised in our society."[231]

Ultimately, the importance of Foucault's work for queer politics does not consist in any improved or more edifying definition of homosexuality but, on the contrary, in the attempt to empty homosexuality of its positive content, of its material and psychic determinations, in order to make it available to us as a site for the continuing construction and renewal of continually changing identities.[232] "Maybe the target nowadays is not to discover what we are," Foucault once wrote, "but to refuse what we are.... We have to promote new forms of subjectivity through the refusal of this kind of individuality.... "[233] Foucault's treatment of homosexuality as strategic position instead of as a psychological essence opens up the possibility of a gay science without objects, of a *queer studies* founded not on the positive fact of homosexuality (and therefore not possessed of a conventional claim to legitimate authority grounded in a privileged access to truth) but on an ongoing process of gay self-knowing and self-formation. Foucault's approach also opens up, correspondingly, the possibility of a *queer politics* defined not by the struggle to liberate a common, repressed, preexisting nature but by an ongoing process of self-constitution and self-transformation—a queer politics anchored in the perilous and shifting sands of non-identity, positionality, discursive reversibility, and collective self-invention. In that sense, perhaps it is not too much to say that Foucault produced the non-theory of which ACT UP is the practice—or, at least, that Foucault's strategic reconceptualization of sex, knowledge, and power has found in certain forms of AIDS activism its most original, intelligent, and creative political embodiment.[234]

By contrast, non-gay-identified critics and philosophers, attached to (because their authority is grounded in) traditional liberal, humanist notions of truth, freedom, and rationality, have found in Foucault's work only counsels of despair on the subject of politics. And they are right to do so, insofar as Foucault's political critique of institutionalized rationality strikes at the root of their epistemological and political privileges. Hence, political resistance to Foucault's interventions has come not from queer activists, not from those who are already in the front lines of the daily battle for survival, but from old-style liberal authorities whose power to define the political *on behalf of everyone* is threatened with delegitimation by Foucault's critique of the various forms of expertise to which they customarily appeal in order to ground their claims to authority. But lesbians and gay men, by contrast—we who, far from having been the beneficiaries of liberal, humanist notions of freedom, truth, and rationality, have tended rather to be the targets of a new kind of terror carried out in their name (a terror all the more terrible in that its nature *as* terror is effectively concealed beneath the disguise of the supposedly nonarbitrary authority of freedom, truth, and rationality)—we who have been denied our *freedom*, our claims to be able to speak the *truth* about our lives, by having been denied a *rational* basis on which to speak at all—we have little cause to bewail the passing of those liberal, humanist notions, to be threatened by their demolition, or to feel deprived of a politics by Foucault's critique of the political economy of discourses. On the contrary, we have tended to find in Foucault's critique of the political economy of discourses a viable basis and inspiration for resistance, just as we have tended to find in *The History of Sexuality, Volume I*, a powerful political charter.

I contend that the nameless activists who fashioned one of the two existing panels for Foucault in the Names Project Quilt, that vast but ever-incomplete memorial to the individuals who have died as a result of AIDS, understood far better than Foucault's liberal critics the political implications of Foucault's notion of power (see Figure 3). The panel consists of a large rectangle with the name MICHEL FOUCAULT written across the

FIGURE 3

top of it in large letters. Underneath, blocked out in smaller lettering, is a long quotation from—what else?—*The History of Sexuality, Volume I* (pages 95–96, to be exact). The text cited on the panel is now famous: "Where there is power, there is resistance . . . a plurality of resistances . . . spread over time and space. . . . And it is doubtless the strategic codification of these points of resistance that makes a revolution possible."

▲   ▲   ▲   ▲   ▲   ▲   ▲   ▲

The Describable Life
of Michel Foucault

> [I]n the order of scientific discourse, the attri-
> bution of a work to an author was, during the
> Middle Ages, indispensable, because such an
> attribution was an index of the work's truth-
> fulness. A proposition was held to derive its
> scientific value from its author. Since the sev-
> enteenth century this function has been stead-
> ily disappearing in scientific discourse; it no
> longer functions except to give a name to a
> theorem, an effect, an example, or a syn-
> drome. In the order of literary discourse, by
> contrast, starting in the same period, the au-
> thor's function has been steadily gaining
> strength. Now, we demand of all those narra-
> tives, poems, dramas, and comedies which cir-
> culated relatively anonymously throughout
> the Middle Ages (and we insist that they tell
> us) where they come from and who wrote
> them. We require the author to answer for the
> unity of the text that we attach to his name;
> we require him to reveal, or at least to display,
> the hidden sense pervading his work; we re-
> quire him to link his writings to his personal
> life and his lived experiences, to the real story
> that witnessed their birth.
>
> —Michel Foucault, *L'Ordre du discours* (1971)

For a long time ordinary individuality—the
everyday individuality of everybody—remained below the threshold of description. To
be looked at, observed, talked about in detail,
followed from day to day by an uninterrupted

126

writing was a privilege. The chronicle of a man, the narrative of his life, a historiography of him composed and revised throughout the course of his existence formed part of the rituals of his power. But disciplinary techniques reverse this relation, lower the threshold of describable individuality, and make of this description a means of control and a method of domination. The description is no longer a monument for future memory, but a document for possible use. And this new describability becomes more marked in proportion as the disciplinary framework becomes more strict: the child, the patient, the madman, the prisoner will become, with increasing ease from the eighteenth century on and according to a rising curve which is that of the mechanisms of discipline, the object of individual descriptions and biographical narratives. This turning of real lives into writing [*cette mise en écriture des existences réelles*] is no longer a procedure of heroization; it functions as a procedure of objectification and subjection/ subjectivation [*assujettissement*]. The carefully assembled life of mental patients or delinquents belongs, like the chronicle of kings or the epic of the great bandits of popular legend, to a specifically political function of writing—but according to an entirely different technique of power.

—Michel Foucault, *Surveiller et punir* (1975)

ALL OF US who write about the life or thought of Michel Foucault are embarrassed—though evidently not sufficiently embarrassed—by the implicit contradiction between Foucault's critical practice and our own. We are embarrassed, in particular, by the contradiction between Foucault's highly skeptical inquiries, instanced by the first passage quoted above, into the discursive function of "the author" and our own rather more pious inquiries into the authorial significance of Foucault's utterances and actions.[1] Foucault's biographers are no exception to the general embarrassment.[2] What is exceptional about them is the cause they have to be embarrassed.

In *L'Ordre du discours*, and in a number of other texts dating from roughly the same period (of which the best known and most important is the 1969 essay "What Is an Author?"), Foucault set out to analyze what he called "the author-function." He subjected the notion of authorship to rigorous and unflinching defamiliarization, treating the author not as a real or natural category of person but as a functional element internal to the operations of discourse—an element, moreover, with a long history and a documented variety of possible uses. Rather than an agent of literary meaning, at once an empirical individual and a regulatory principle of textual signification, "the author" emerges from Foucault's writing as a historically specific and ideologically contingent component of an evolving discursive and institutional technology. "The author," in other words, is ultimately neither a person nor a concept but a practice. And it is a practice that Foucault objected to on a number of grounds, a practice he thought both possible and desirable to do without. He tried, insofar as he could, to resist its effects.[3]

Foucault, to be sure, did not suppose that texts wrote themselves without human agency, or that the people who wrote them did not have lives which might, in some contexts and for some purposes at least, be worth recounting. "Of course, it would be ridiculous to deny the existence of individuals who write," he explained, in response to a hypothetical objection of his own devising; what interested him was "not, of course, the author in the sense of the speaking individual who pronounced or wrote the text in question, but the author as a principle for grouping together discourses, as the unity and origin of their significations, as the focus of their coherence."[4] In the discussion that followed his lecture "What Is an Author?" to the Société Française de Philosophie on February 22, 1969, Foucault made a similar point with reference to his famous remarks, at the conclusion of *The Order of Things* (1966), about the imminent "death of man": "This is a theme that allows me to bring to light the ways in which the concept of man has functioned in knowledge. . . . It is not a matter of asserting that man is dead; it is a matter . . . of seeing in what manner, according to what rules, the concept of man was formed and has functioned. I have done the same thing for the notion of the author." And Foucault concluded, with typical and untranslatable sarcasm, *"Retenons donc nos larmes."*[5]

As with "the death of man," then, so with "the death of the author": the point is not to pronounce "the author" dead, or to prohibit the writing of biographies[6] (although Foucault himself tended to discourage people from studying *him*, urging them to do work of their own instead).[7] The point, rather, is to resist accepting "the author" as a natural or self-evident category—and thus to prevent a naturalized concept of "the author" from blocking further inquiry into the history of "the author" 's formation or the range of its function. Foucault's critique of "the author" is part of a larger political project (which he later thought too narrowly conceived) of identifying "the rules of exclusion" that govern the production of discourse and that thereby limit our freedom to speak and to write.[8]

To compose a *biography* of *Foucault*, then, is to renounce by that very gesture a large part of one's claim to be able to speak with authority about one's ostensible subject; it is to convict oneself, in effect, of having understood nothing about either Foucault's life or his work. And that is not just because biographical criticism reverses the thrust of discursive analysis—treating "the author" as a person rather than as a function, naturalizing and thereby immunizing "the author" against discursive critique—but, more importantly, because the practice of biography, like the practice of case history, as Foucault argues in the passage from *Discipline and Punish* quoted in the second epigraph to this essay, typically operates as a means of normalization[9] and thus as an instrument of disciplinary control. It was precisely in order to expose the strategic conjunction of expert knowledge and institutional power in such socially authorized practices as the narrativizing of individuality, and in order to frustrate (insofar as he could) the complex political technology to which such practices materially contribute, that Foucault pioneered a critique of the political economy of discourses.

▼ ▼ ▼ ▼ ▼ ▼ ▼ ▼

FOUCAULT himself had led an eminently describable life. He could be described, more particularly, and as different occasions might require, as a madman (he had flirted with suicide in his youth), as a left-wing political extremist (he was a member of the Communist party in the 1950s and a Maoist in the late sixties and early seventies), or as a sexual pervert (he was a gay man and a sadomasochist). Foucault, in other words, had good reason to wish to identify, to isolate, and to analyze the "rules of exclusion" that govern "the order of discourse," to uncover the logic behind their operation, and to elucidate the specific strategies that work to deauthorize and to silence social deviants, licensing instead the usual authorities to specify the "truth" of our existence in "objective" (i.e., objectifying and pathologizing) terms. And he had good reason to resist the disciplinary "procedures of objectification and subjection" whereby socially accredited experts "turn real lives into writing." There is nothing remotely so innocuous as to deserve the title of "ironic" or "coincidental," then—rather, there is what could only have been expected—in the fact of Foucault's becoming, especially since his death in 1984, "the object of individual descriptions and biographical narratives." The recent publication of three major biographies of Foucault affords an all-too-apt opportunity both to elaborate Foucault's thesis about the politics of biographical description and to extend Foucault's own explorations of the power-effects produced by truth, and of the discourses of truth produced by power,[10] to the posthumous *mise en écriture* of Foucault himself.

Even before the publication in 1993 of James Miller's *Passion of Michel Foucault* and David Macey's *Lives of Michel Foucault*, even before Didier Eribon's earlier biography *Michel Foucault* appeared in French in 1989 and was translated into English in 1991, sufficient quantities of biographical information were already in sufficiently wide circulation to yield abundant and telling indications of the kind of use to which, in time, the future biographies of Foucault would largely be put. In 1984, for example, in the course of an otherwise very fine appreciation of Foucault's work, Edward Said thought it necessary to emphasize, before he went on to discuss *The History of Sexuality, Volume I*, that the book's "basis in the vicissitudes of Foucault's own sexual identity is notable."[11] (He did not elaborate on what, in particular, was so notable about it.) Said also spoke of the later Foucault's "overdetermined shift from the political to the personal," thereby gesturing toward an implied distinction between Foucault's unfortunate scholarly deviation and the deliberate, principled, *self-determined* shifts that typify the work of normal people—such as the shift in Said's later work from literary studies to orientalism, no doubt—changes of direction that apparently do *not* suffer, in other words, from "overdetermination" (which is to say, "pathological compulsion").[12] Said's darkly unspecific but nonetheless very pointed remarks presumed not only that his readership already knew *exactly* what "sexual identity" of Foucault's (attended by what myriad of "vicissitudes") he was referring to but also that it shared Said's extreme reluctance to see that identity specified; he could there-fore afford to spare himself the indignity of *noticing* the partic-ular sexual identity that he effectively *imputed* to Foucault—treating it, rather, as a matter so strictly personal and private, and at the same time so much in the domain of public knowl-edge, as to be no less indelicate than superfluous to *mention* by name. It is through that effortless demonstration of world-liness, of easy familiarity with and unruffled, if unimpressed, knowingness about the supposed fact of Foucault's homosex-uality, that Said manages to accrue "a surplus value of cultural authority"[13] against which he can then go on to trade, and to trade so unobtrusively—which is to say, so competently (it would have been much more contestable, and therefore much less effective, to come right out and accuse Foucault's work of bearing the disfiguring traces of its author's sexual pathology)—as to insure the political effects of his writing against the risks of political challenge and critique.[14]

Said was writing Foucault's obituary. More recent and more hostile critics of Foucault, especially those who could claim not to suffer from the personal and political disqualifications that now seemed to mark their dead adversary, have shown consid-erably less compunction about invoking the supposedly scan-dalous facts of his life in order to diminish the appeal or to demean the significance of his thought. A typical and instructive example of that common tactic happened to be provided, con-veniently enough for my purposes, by an issue of the *Times Literary Supplement* that appeared just as I was composing the first draft of this paper and that advertised on its cover, under the title "Althusser the Murderous Child," a review by one Mark Lilla of the recently published memoirs and biogra-phies of Foucault's mentor, longtime friend, and intellectual ally.[15] One of Lilla's devices in this essay is to link Althusser with Foucault in ways calculated to denigrate the life and thought of each man by guilty association with the other. Lilla begins, for example, by referring to Althusser's 1980 murder of his wife and subsequent psychiatric confinement "as another morbid episode in the dénouement of *la pensée 68*," in which category he also includes "Michel Foucault's death from AIDS." Later, speaking of Althusser's first bouts of depression which occurred shortly after he had begun teaching at the École Normale Supérieure, Lilla notes, "To their credit, the school authorities reacted quickly and placed him in a separate room in the infirmary, a room where he (like Michel Foucault after him) would frequently seek psychological refuge." Having diagnosed Althusser's work as "one extended effort to make us share his [abnormal, pathological] condition," Lilla concludes, in a tone of undisguised satisfaction, "Biography now permits us [normal, healthy folk] to see what a profoundly intimate meaning the philosophical flight from subjectivity and the attack on humanism had for Althusser, as it did for Foucault." What biography enables Lilla to discover, of course, is not a truth about either Foucault or Althusser so much as an effective strategy of delegitimation and trivialization that avails him in his effort to police the socially established boundaries between the normal and the pathological.

▼   ▼   ▼   ▼   ▼   ▼   ▼   ▼

As THE SUPREMELY confident undemonstrativeness of these innuendos indicates,[16] it does not require any very strenuous effort to discredit the views of an ideological adversary when that adversary has already been branded, in the eyes of some portion of one's readership at any rate, as a madman or a pervert. How seriously, after all, can anyone take the views of someone whose stigmatized personal practices and identity confer upon everyone else a power of irrefutable judgment over him? No wonder, then, that the vulgarity that normally attaches to ad hominem attacks (not to say bashings), at least in intellectual circles, and that normally constitutes a disincentive to engage in them, seems almost magically to dissipate—for reasons that Foucault himself explored throughout his writings in the 1970s—in the vicinity of an insufficiently normalized subject.[17] (Only those tainted by accusations of complicity with Nazism—more tainted by such accusations, I mean, than gay men already are in the straight-liberal imagination—are easier to deprive of their claims to a serious hearing.) Hence the inescapably vexed, treacherous, and volatile politics of any attempt, including my own, to write about the meaning of a socially deviant life.

Take the case of Jean Genet. Much of Genet's prestige both as a literary figure and as a social rebel derived, initially at least, from an extraordinary and extended, if impossibly tedious, homage by Sartre entitled *Saint Genet: Comédien et martyr*. As Earl Jackson observes,

> Jean-Paul Sartre is rightly credited with saving Jean Genet from life imprisonment and with establishing, almost singlehandedly, a place for Genet in the literary canon. Sartre's activity on Genet's behalf is now inextricably linked with his 1952 monograph *Saint Genet*, a work also generally regarded as an act of intellectual courage and as the definitive exposition of Genet's significance—in terms of both his work and his personal life.

Jackson goes on to remark, however, on the curious fact that "it occurred to no one to ask Genet what *he* had thought of the book until 1963" and that "even then Genet's answer was so little noted and so completely forgotten."[18] The exchange Jackson is referring to took place in the course of an inadvertently hilarious *Playboy* interview with Genet, published in April 1964, which does little more than rehearse, at some length, the interlocutors' mutual bafflement and incredulity. *Playboy* is interested in what it is like to be rich and famous, to have Off-Broadway hits, to be a literary star. Genet turns out to be anything but enlightening on those topics; he wants to talk—just as gushingly, perhaps—about poetry and art. But the interviewer, ever hopeful and uncomprehending, persists: "Were you pleased with [Sartre's] unique literary psychoanalysis of you?" Genet replies,

> It filled me with a kind of disgust, because I saw myself stripped naked—by someone other than myself. I strip myself in all my books, but at the same time I disguise myself with words, with attitudes, with certain choices, by means of a certain magic. *I manage not to get too damaged.* But I was stripped by Sartre unceremoniously. My first impulse was to burn the book. . . . It took me some time to get over my reading of his book. I was almost unable to continue writing. . . . Sartre's book created a void which made for a kind of psychological deterioration. . . . I remained in that awful state for six years. . . . [19]

Genet's reaction could hardly have come as much of a surprise to Sartre, since the opening pages of *Saint Genet* document in detail Genet's confessed fears of exposure to the objectifying gaze of the world.[20] It is revealing that anyone who understood Genet as Sartre did should nonetheless have gone on to write and to publish such a book about him.

All biography, to be sure, pits the biographer against the biographical subject in a contest for interpretative sovereignty over the subject's life.[21] Who has the greater authority to discover and to specify the meaning of that life, the person who lived it or the person who is writing it? And almost all biography elects to enter that contest on terms inherently favorable to the biographer, if only insofar as biography is conventionally predicated on the death of its subject (but not, obviously enough, on that of the biographer): the inaugural gesture of most biography is the one so unabashedly performed by Mallarmé in the opening line of his eulogy for Poe. "Tel qu'en Lui-même enfin l'éternité le change": the authentic meaning of the life, its essential truth, appears—once and for all—when it is over. By its very nature, then, biography constitutes an offense to the subject's autonomy, a violation of whatever illusions of hermeneutic control over the meaning of her or his existence a subject may have happened to cherish, and to protest against it is doubtless as misguided, and as futile, as to object to the offense that the critic constitutes to the autonomy of the author, or that literary criticism constitutes to the autonomy of a literary text.[22]

But to pose the problem in such general terms—which is to say, inter alia, in such non-gay-specific terms—is to lose sight of its multiple and particular political dimensions, to miss the special threat that biographical description may represent to those relatively disempowered individuals who are already subject to the process of normalization-by-description, such as "the child, the patient, the madman, the prisoner," and—Foucault might well have added but, for reasons hardly unrelated to the very disciplinary procedures under discussion in this passage, he didn't—the homosexual. It may be that writing still functions as a procedure of heroization in the case of some lives, or at least that some public straight men still live and die, like Homeric heroes, in the fond expectation of having their life's work completed by the narrative that will come after them. But such is not the usual effect of writing on the lives of gay men—as anyone who has ever been publicly identified as gay in a newspaper article will readily testify. On the contrary, the perennial threat of discreditation through biographical description becomes painfully acute, and the need to resist it becomes pressingly urgent, when the biographical subject is gay. The struggle for interpretative authority and for control of representation, intrinsic as it may be to the biographical situation in general, acquires an absolutely irreducible political specificity when it is waged over a gay life.

Now I am not about to formulate either a philosophy or a politics of biography. I do not wish to enter contemporary disputes over the ethics of biographical practice.[23] I am not interested either in policing biographical discourse or in contributing to the production of kinder, gentler biographies of famous perverts. I leave such matters to professional biographers. What I am interested in is the politics of writing a gay life, and the reason I am interested in it is that the issues raised by it directly implicate my own credibility and authority as the writer of this essay and, more generally, as an openly gay intellectual who has, on occasion, attempted consciously to combine credible scholarship with sexual politics in his own practice. If, in other words, the posthumous describing of Foucault's life illustrates and corroborates, as I have argued, Foucault's own thesis about the politics of describability, a similar relation of reflexivity obtains between Foucault's position as an academic with a stigmatized and therefore discreditable identity and my own position as someone whose authority to pronounce on the politics of Foucault's describability is irretrievably compromised by his public embrace of an equally discreditable, and describable, life.

Unfortunately for me, and for Foucault, the mere demystification of the procedures of objectification and subjection does nothing to impede their operation. To anticipate and expose the strategic use of biographical description as "a means of control and a method of domination" is neither to preempt its deployment against oneself nor to disarm its effects (as Foucault's own case amply demonstrates), for the very reason that anyone against whom biographical description can be so deployed in the first place already lacks the requisite cultural authority to frustrate its deployment—which is why the process of being described so often registers on its subjects as violent and can even be experienced as a kind of terrorism. For how can those authorized to describe us be shamed by the prospect of appearing to fit the odious and predictable roles into which we have threatened to cast them, when we aren't sufficiently empowered to be able to do so much as to challenge their very descriptions of us and when they, in any case, can afford not to care whether or not we have anticipated and exposed their strategies, since even so their dismissals of our claims to a serious hearing will pack the same wallop, do the same work, and produce in their audiences the same conviction that everything we may have to say on our own behalf is nothing but special pleading?

If the tone of certain passages in what follows should strike some readers as impassioned (and it seems to me that I have used more italics in this essay than in all the rest of my writings combined), that is in part because of my sense of both the necessity and the futility of what I am about to do. I consider the kind of critique I am undertaking here to be *necessary* if lesbians and gay men are ever to be able to recognize, to expose, and to discredit the rhetorical and discursive tricks that are routinely used to fashion our public representation, but I also acknowledge it to be *futile* as a political intervention, because those dirty tricksters whose habitual practices I would most like to alter are also the ones whose social privileges most insulate them from feeling the force of my objections. And if to speak as a gay man about a topic that directly implicates one's own interests is already to surrender a sizable share of one's claims to be heard, listened to, and taken seriously, then to speak not as the designated representative of a subcultural minority but as a dedicated critic of heterosexual presumption is surely to put the remaining share of one's credibility at risk. One of the difficult things about writing this essay has been the weight of the conflicting imperatives that seemed to bear down on me at every moment of its composition. On the one hand, I didn't want to be dismissed as a mere partisan, as a professional gay polemicist mindlessly and predictably defending his faction against a perceived threat to the party line, and seeming to demonstrate that the only test I could apply to any biographical representation of a gay subject was whether or not it happened to serve the good of my cause. On the other hand, I also didn't want to be lured by the illusory promise of readerly respect and consideration into conforming to some conventionally agreed-upon standard of good behavior, only to find myself dismissed every bit as imperiously and definitively as I would have been if I hadn't restrained myself in the first place. In the end, I have tried to put my case in the most publicly demonstrable terms, according to traditional canons of argument, so as to appear credible, and so as to appeal for the broadest possible consensus on behalf of the social values I wish to champion. At the same time, I have had to reckon with the inescapable limits which my explicit assumption of a politicized gay male speaking-position places on my own credibility, and I have accordingly schooled myself not to moderate my passions in deference to the feelings of the unconverted.

▼   ▼   ▼   ▼   ▼   ▼   ▼   ▼

AMONG FOUCAULT'S biographers, the most recent is also the least ashamed. David Macey introduces *The Lives of Michel Foucault* by invoking Michael Holroyd's claim that "biographies of writers are written in collaboration with the posthumous subject of the biography."[24] He then proceeds, imperturbably, to describe in detail Foucault's own posthumous refusal to collaborate. "Alive, he would have rejected the advances of any biographer," Macey observes, unmoved; "in death, he still struggles to escape them" (xi). Macey does not shrink from struggling with the dead, if still recalcitrant, Foucault. Far from looking to Foucault for authorization, he presumes that the biographical enterprise justifies itself; biography is a well-established literary practice and, as such, it apparently does not require legitimation. Macey practices it in a conventional, as well as in a conventionally responsible, fashion. His comprehensive, well-documented, impassively sober and balanced (though generally sympathetic) account is articulate, detailed, and admirably exact in its formulations; otherwise, it is without special qualities as an intellectual, philosophical, psychological, or institutional biography, and it owes perhaps too much to the questionable influence of Daniel Defert (Foucault's lover of some twenty years), who seems to have authorized the North American edition at least.[25] Nonetheless, Macey's book can reasonably claim to be the single best source to date of complete and accurate information about Foucault's life. Perhaps, as Macey conjectures (480), Foucault himself would have preferred Hervé Guibert's fictional portraits of him—lurid as they are in places—to any biographical representation,[26] but Macey is not disposed to apologize for setting aside Foucault's preferences in favor of his own.

Macey devotes particular attention to matters of bibliographical detail and displays a considerable interest in source criticism (though it should be acknowledged that most of the basic research in these areas had already been carried out by Foucault's French biographer, Didier Eribon, and by those responsible for assembling the library of the Centre Michel Foucault at the Bibliothèque du Saulchoir in Paris). His survey of Foucault's discursive activity takes in not only the major academic books and articles but also Foucault's journalism, literary criticism, radio and television appearances, book and exhibition reviews, political pamphlets and manifestos (both signed and unsigned), interviews and essays in the gay and left-wing press, lectures, course outlines, private letters, and even movie credits, all of which find their proper place in the four-hundred-item, chronologically ordered bibliography at the back of the volume. Macey is also adept at describing the textual sources of Foucault's better-known pronouncements. He notes, for example, that the celebrated passage near the end of *The Order of Things* in which Foucault heralds the "death of man" echoes, first of all, Foucault's unpublished introduction to his translation of Kant's *Anthropologie in pragmatischer Hinsicht*, which Foucault submitted to the Sorbonne in 1961 as his required *thèse complémentaire* (in addition, that is, to *Madness and Civilization*) for the degree of *doctorat d'état*; that passage resembles another in an unpublished manuscript drafted by Louis Althusser in December 1946, which in turn quotes a speech delivered by André Malraux to the inaugural meeting of UNESCO on November 4, 1946; Malraux, moreover, was merely recapitulating a theme he had sounded in an early novel, *La Tentation de l'Occident*, composed in 1921–25; and, in any case, Althusser and Foucault may have found, independently of one another, a common source of inspiration in Alexandre Kojève's commentaries on Hegel. Macey's little rehearsal of what he calls the "history or pre-history" of the "death of man" trope is not the result, to be sure, of any original discovery of own—already in 1989 Eribon had made the connection between *The Order of Things* and Foucault's thesis on Kant, while in 1992 Althusser's biographer, Yann Moulier Boutang, had uncovered and published (as Macey acknowledges) the text in which Althusser quotes from Malraux—but in collecting all this scattered information into one place Macey performs a valuable service, one which he further improves on by quoting liberally from his sources and by specifying the very different meanings attached to the "death of man" in each of the texts and contexts in which it appears (89–90).

That combination of precision and cautiousness turns out to be characteristic of Macey's style as a biographer. He is unwilling to accept hearsay, even when it derives from authoritative sources, in the absence of corroborating evidence, and so he persistently treats as speculation what other biographers present as fact. Rather than attempting to resolve conflicts between competing accounts of even minor details in Foucault's life or work, Macey prefers to lay out the different versions before the reader, sometimes indicating which one he considers to be the most plausible but at other times refusing to adjudicate among them. The mere existence of a variant story or explanation is usually sufficient warrant for Macey to cast doubt on the factual status of the received tradition. The most scandalous items in Foucault's dossier elicit the greatest skepticism, which is perhaps what one might expect from an "official" biographer: Foucault's youthful suicide attempt of 1948, for example, remains in Macey's opinion nothing more than an unconfirmed, if persistent, rumor (28). (Didier Eribon, who presents the suicide attempt as a fact, based his account on the personal testimony of the physician who treated Foucault at the time.)[27] By contrast, Foucault's attitude toward homosexuality—both his own and other people's—receives more detailed and less sensationalistic treatment from Macey than from any other biographer. Macey's evidence indicates that at least from his midtwenties Foucault was out to his brother, probably to his mother as well, and to his friends both gay and straight (28, 81). Far from being tormented by sexual self-loathing, as his other biographers imply, Macey's Foucault seems to have adjusted to being gay at an early age and to have been quite unabashed about his sexual tastes—no mean feat for someone coming out in France in the late 1940s and early 1950s—though he was not so precocious as the younger Defert, who Macey tells us "had been cheerfully and openly . . . gay since his teens" (92). Eribon has recently cast doubt on the veracity of this revisionist interpretation of Foucault's sexual adjustment;[28] the two accounts, however, need not be read as incompatible.

Macey's documentary zeal, his matter-of-fact posture, his skeptical disengagement, and his interpretative restraint offer scant material for commentary, and I shall have comparatively little to say about Macey's Foucault in what follows. For although Macey exercises all the skill necessary to construct a coherent and readable biographical narrative, he does not seem to have a particular story to tell either about Foucault's life or by means of it. He provides a concise and, on the whole, lucid exposition of Foucault's ideas—which is a considerable achievement in itself—but he never indicates what in particular it is about Foucault's life that makes it interesting or worthy of special notice. And it is precisely this failure, or perhaps this deliberate curtailing, of the biographical imagination that ultimately accounts for Macey's success as a biographer of Foucault: Macey manages to reconstruct the *facts* of Foucault's life without attempting to specify its *truth*.[29]

▼ ▼ ▼ ▼ ▼ ▼ ▼ ▼

W**ITH JAMES MILLER** and his extraordinary book *The Passion of Michel Foucault*, what we encounter is exactly the reverse. Not that Miller is either ignorant of or indifferent to the facts of Foucault's life. Though less bibliographically comprehensive than Macey's, Miller's research has been exhaustive in its own way: Miller has read every scrap of Foucault that he could get his hands on; he has talked to everyone who could possibly shed light on any aspect of the story of Foucault's life that he wanted to tell; he has turned up previously unpublished archival material, including a detailed memoir of Foucault's 1975 LSD trip in Death Valley (written shortly afterward by a fellow tripper); and he has made himself an authority on virtually every topic that Foucault took a serious interest in, from the Iranian revolution to fist-fucking. Miller can gloss the meaning of enigmatic words and phrases in Foucault's texts (though he commits occasional errors of translation);[30] he can bring out themes implicit in Foucault's imagery; he can detect the many verbal echoes of modern writers and philosophers in Foucault's prose. Unlike Macey, however, Miller engages only those facts about Foucault that yield him clues to the deeper meaning of Foucault's life, to "the whole truth" *about* Foucault (8), which he then presents to us as the whole truth *of* Foucault. He describes his book not as a conventional biography but as "a narrative account of one man's lifelong struggle to honor Nietzsche's gnomic injunction [in the subtitle of *Ecce Homo*], to become what one is' " (5). Miller seems to understand Nietzsche's phrase in a deterministic sense, as if it posited an individual human essence ("what one is") in advance of all becoming, a truth about the self that constitutes a proper object of historical inquiry. Foucault, by contrast, did not regard *becoming* as a kind of fatality. After all, "one writes," he said (and Miller quotes him [33]), "in order to become other than what one is."[31]

Now it would be neither accurate nor fair to imply that Miller's attempt to put his readers in possession of the truth of Foucault's life shows he hasn't understood Foucault—although, as we shall see, he does systematically scant the political dimension of Foucault's thought, and when he has to account for Foucault's own active participation in various political movements, he does so in highly personalized terms: for example, he attributes Foucault's political reawakening in the late sixties, and his sudden metamorphosis into a street-fighting man, to Foucault's discovery "that politics, like art and eroticism, could occasion a kind of 'limit-experience' " (171). If, then, in his biographical practice, Miller seems intent on presiding over the rebirth of "the author," if he persists in subjecting Foucault to all the traditional demands of authorship—requiring him "to answer for the unity of the text that we attach to his name," "to reveal, or at least to display, the hidden sense pervading his work," and "to link his writings to his personal life and his lived experiences, to the real story that witnessed their birth"—that is not because he has failed to grasp the basic features of Foucault's thought. Miller is a passionate reader of Foucault. His engagement with his subject presents a total contrast to Macey's cool detachment. He takes Foucault's texts and the ideas contained in them with devout seriousness, and he interprets Foucault's life and thought as complementary parts of a single daring existential/intellectual experiment. The resulting novelization of Foucault is unquestionably an original and, for better or for worse, a brilliant achievement. My quarrel with Miller, then, is not that he is uncomprehending of Foucault's project. It is that he is politically opposed to it. He does not say he is. He may not think he is. But he is. The way he goes about describing Foucault's life admits no doubt of it.[32] His account of Foucault's personal and intellectual evolution is not just un-Foucauldian. It is anti-Foucauldian. It purports to "explain" Foucault's thought by tracing its origin to the "truth" of his psychosexual being, thereby combining authoritative historical/biographical knowledge with the power of normalizing judgment in a single gesture whose effect is to strengthen the very disciplinary controls that Foucault's whole life was dedicated to resisting.[33] Far from attempting, as Foucault did, to divert our attention from those spectacles of transgression which the agencies of normalization routinely stage—spectacles whose intended effect is in part to render *un*spectacular if not invisible, by contrast, the agencies responsible for staging them—and, instead, to dramatize, as Foucault did, the conventionally more discreet operations of the disciplinary mechanisms themselves, Miller does exactly the opposite: he consistently produces Foucault as a fascinating and cautionary spectacle of transgression in his own right.[34] *The Passion of Michel Foucault* reads like *Discipline and Punish* in reverse.

The point I am making here is a political one, and it may bear some emphasis, since it is liable to be misunderstood. I am not arguing that the only legitimate way to write the story of Foucault's life is to do so either in a Foucauldian manner or in a Foucauldian idiom—if, indeed, such a thing were even possible. I do not accept the general principle, which might be imputed to me on the basis of these criticisms of Miller, that in order to produce an acceptable biography of a philosopher it is necessary to adopt and to reproduce that philosopher's own doctrines. It is of course abundantly obvious that one's assessment of the significance of a philosopher's life will depend in part on one's estimate of the value of that philosopher's work: an account of Plato's life will be written differently by a realist and a nominalist, because a biographer who believes in the reality and separation of the Forms will feel less need to explain the motivation behind Plato's metaphysics than will one who finds the whole notion counterintuitive and outlandish. That is all as it should be. Miller is under no obligation as Foucault's biographer to agree with anything Foucault said or wrote, nor is he required to ape Foucault's literary or intellectual style. But those of us whose lives may depend on our abilities to resist the power of normalization in its various social and institutional manifestations, whose conception of the political has been crucially shaped by our reading of Foucault's texts, and whose own political and discursive practices have been inspired, however feebly, by Foucault's personal example may perhaps be excused (but, then again, perhaps not) if we protest against an account of Foucault's life and work that in effect reverses his entire political program.

Such a reversal, to be sure, is far from the stated intention of Miller's biography. But the book's reception is, on this point, a more reliable index of its politics than its author's asseverations.[35] A mere glance at the sensational titles of Miller's reviews is sufficient to indicate the disciplinary uses to which his book has so obviously lent itself: "A Taste for Pain" (Mark Lilla [who else?] in the *TLS*); "Subject and Abject" (Alexander Nehamas in *The New Republic*); "The Lure of Death" (Richard Wolin in *Dissent*); "A Philosopher's Death Wish" (Kenneth Woodward in *Newsweek*); "Fatal Attraction" (Jay Tolson in *The National Review*); "Take It to the Limit" (Frank Browning in *Tikkun*); "Philosopher's Groan" (Gary Kamiya in *Artforum*); "The Perversions of M. Foucault" (Roger Kimball in *The New Criterion*); "Paroxysms and Politics" (Richard Rorty in *Salmagundi*).[36] An ominous hint of things to come could already be glimpsed in a prepublication response to Miller's book by Richard Mohr, as quoted by a reporter for the *Chronicle of Higher Education* in a story with the telling headline, NEW FOUCAULT BIOGRAPHY CREATES SCHOLARLY STIR: SOME SAY PERSONAL REVELATIONS IN AS-YET-UNPUBLISHED BOOK COULD OVERSHADOW FRENCH PHILOSOPHER'S CONTRIBUTIONS.[37] Hailing the sort of revisionist thinking about Foucault (whom "people have been viewing," allegedly, "as a saint rather than a thinker") that Miller's book would, he presumed, inspire, Mohr gleefully observed that "it will make the de Man affair look like a picnic." That Richard Mohr, a prominent, original, and courageous gay philosopher and political commentator, could take such obvious pleasure in the anticipated spectacle of a gay-baiting, that he could bring himself to imply that the revelation of Foucault's interest in consensual sadomasochism would prove to be far more scandalous than the disclosure of a prominent critic's wartime literary collaboration with Nazism (which continues to function in Mohr's quip as a figure for sadomasochism),[38] is a shameful indicator of the inexhaustible strength of the cultural imperative—to which even politically active gay men must occasionally submit—to maintain public respectability by pandering to popular prejudices and upholding normalizing standards in matters of sex.

No wonder, then, if those who make it their customary business to defend "traditional values" have seized the opportunity that Miller's book, inadvertently or not, has offered them. "The problem with Foucault, simply put," writes Jay Tolson in *The National Review*, in reference to Miller's biography, "was his profound perversity, a quality that characterized both his life and his work. In fact, it would be all too easy to explain away Foucault's work as the predictable consequence of a tortured psychological make-up: in this case, homosexuality and sadomasochism with a strong suicidal component." Having congratulated Miller for electing not to follow that easy path, Tolson elects to follow it himself, putting "the problem with Foucault," even more simply, in the opening sentence of his review, as follows. "Gore Vidal might have said it best: the French do seem to have both feet firmly planted in the air."[39] While critics working for ostensibly more left-wing publications than *The National Review* seem no less eager to cash in politically on the irresistible spectacle of a radical gay philosopher with his legs in the air, the decorum of straight-liberal commentary evidently requires them to make greater efforts to cover their political tracks (in this they differ, interestingly enough, from Foucault's gay detractors, who, having no public authority to lose, can afford to be just as crude as any professional, right-wing homophobe: Bruce Bawer, for example, is not ashamed to write, "The greatest single influence on Gay Studies today is the late French theorist Michel Foucault, an enthusiast of sadomasochism who analyzed sexual relations almost entirely in terms of power"[40] [not a bad place to begin such an analysis, now that you mention it]). Miller's biography, whose strategy consists in luridly rehearsing Foucault's supposed practices of transgression while elaborately refusing either to endorse or to denounce them explicitly, provides straight liberals with the perfect cover they need from which to conduct *characteristically discreet* forays against the influence of cultural radicals. Thus, "Foucault's politics, whether in theory or in practice, seem no more plausible than before," remarks a suave commentator on the biography in *The New York Review of Books*, "but Miller's account of Foucault's bouts of near-insanity, his flirtations with suicide, with the politics of the 'Maoist' left in 1970s France, and the drug culture of California, gives one a good sense of the kind of [abnormal, pathological] personality that would find modern liberal societies peculiarly oppressive."[41] (You would have to be crazy, after all, wouldn't you, not to just *love* living here? And, indeed, what could be better—for those who want to lay claim to the mantle of "liberal," at least—than a society where the discreditation of "radicals" can proceed without having to resort to the uncivilized expedient of voicing its key disqualifying terms ["abnormal," "pathological"], where the distribution of stigma operates securely because wordlessly, not by means of name-calling but by polite innuendo, and where the demonization of marginalized persons becomes all the more immune to challenge or refutation, and all the more definitive, for never having to make its devaluation of them fully explicit?) In short, the lesson of all this critical commentary on Miller's biography seems to be that when it comes to Foucault, and perhaps to gay issues more generally, the difference between liberals and reactionaries—between *The New York Review of Books* and *The National Review*—is not a difference of politics so much as it is one of strategy.

Miller himself was aware of the risks he was running, but he remained undeterred by them. "No profession of good faith can defuse what is volatile and perhaps tragic in the life that follows," he concedes at the outset of his biography, in a formulation that neatly divides the blame for any unfortunate residual "volatility" between the biographer and his subject—with the latter obligingly assuming the greater share (it is after all "the life," not Miller's own description of it, that is said to contain regrettably "volatile" elements). "Yet despite the many dangers, of scandal and reductionism, of unconscious stereotyping and prurient sensationalism—and last but not least, of offering fresh ammunition to critics hostile to everything Foucault fought for—I have gone ahead, and tried to tell the whole truth, as best I could" (8). What is it about this disarmingly apologetic profession of good faith that nonetheless fails entirely to reassure? Is it that the "many dangers" are brushed aside a bit too quickly, not to say airily, without sufficient indication that the writer grasps the full extent of the peril they may represent to those of us who share Foucault's vulnerability to, say, "stereotyping"? Or is it that Miller too confidently expects his readers to find acceptable whatever risks may be necessitated by a project that describes itself, with obvious sincerity, as a form of truth telling? In any case, Miller's professions cannot wholly dissipate the awareness (which his critics and commentators never cease to heighten) that what our culture typically produces, or recognizes, as "the truth" about gay men and gay sex is not a disengaged, serene, or politically innocuous "knowledge" but an array of contradictory and, it would now seem, murderous knowledge-effects: an illusory *knowingness*, that is, which is not only distinct from "knowledge" but is actually opposed to it, is actually *a form of ignorance*, insofar as it serves to conceal from the supposedly knowledgeable the nature of their own personal and political investments in the systematic misrecognition and abjection of homosexuality.[42]

A good example of that ignorant knowingness at its most politically efficacious can be found in the deceptively bland accusation—surely the most commonly heard criticism of Foucault's work nowadays—that Foucault himself was "unduly preoccupied" or "obsessed" (for which read *abnormally, pathologically, perversely turned on*) by power,[43] an accusation the very making of which expresses nothing if not an unconfessed, though hardly unrelished, *pleasure in power* on the part of Foucault's accusers: a pleasure, specifically, in the power to aggrandize and authorize themselves at the expense of those who all too obviously lack the sexual credentials that immediately accrue to anyone who is willing to make such an accusation in the first place and that underwrite the various social and discursive privileges which Foucault's accusers are typically as adept at exercising as they are careful not to acknowledge.[44] It is precisely this knowingness about Foucault's homosexuality that licenses his detractors to cultivate a corresponding ignorance about the considerable power they both wield and enjoy

in the very act of pathologizing Foucault as someone exces-
sively "interested" in such an allegedly trivial matter as power.
Or, as Foucault himself might have put it, "In our era, the experience of homosexuality remains silent in the composure of
a knowledge which, knowing too much about homosexuality,
forgets it."[45]

That "knowing too much about homosexuality" is not only
not incompatible with knowing too little about it but may actually constitute one of the most powerful and effective vehicles
of such an ignorant knowingness is a possibility that Miller does
not seriously entertain. But he is willing to confront, if only in
passing, the political ramifications of his own detective work,
of his single-minded determination to discover "the truth" about
Foucault's psychosexual life and to refashion that truth into a
key that will unlock the meaning of Foucault's writings by bringing out in them the contours of the writer's personal obsessions.
He quotes, with evident sympathy and respect, D. A. Miller's
cautionary remarks in *Bringing Out Roland Barthes* about the
political dangers of "outing" as a literary-critical practice—of
identifying, that is, or "bringing out" the putatively gay content
in the text of a gay writer (whether closeted or not), and insisting on its gay specificity: "In a culture that without ever ceasing
to proliferate homosexual meaning knows how to confine it to
a kind of false unconscious, as well in collectivities as in individuals, there is hardly a procedure for bringing out this meaning that doesn't itself look or feel like just more police
entrapment" (8).[46] Anyone at all familiar with the English translations of Foucault's writings will have heard in D. A. Miller's
formulation an echo of the famous passage (which James Miller
himself quotes elsewhere [123]) that concludes the introduction
to *The Archaeology of Knowledge* (1969): " 'Do not ask me who
I am and do not tell me to remain the same,' " Foucault, or one
of his personae, declares; " 'leave it to our bureaucrats and our
police to see that our papers are in order. At least spare us their

morality when we write.' "[47] James Miller, however, remains studiously deaf to that plea.

▼   ▼   ▼   ▼   ▼   ▼   ▼   ▼

Not so FOUCAULT'S first biographer, Didier Eribon. That is why he confined himself largely to the outlines of Foucault's career: he recounted in some detail the story of Foucault's academic intrigues, of his political involvements, and of his relations with his mentors, students, publishers, friends, and fans. He touched briefly on Foucault's erotic attachments and he mentioned Foucault's joyous forays, late in life, into the gay "bars and nightclubs" (he doesn't mention the bathhouses) of New York and San Francisco, chiefly because California, Eribon casually implied, was where Foucault contracted AIDS—as if what Eribon elliptically calls "the new plague" (French law made it risky to be explicit about Foucault's cause of death) could not possibly have originated in a civilized place like Paris or been transmitted to Foucault there (315–16). Eribon's refusal to inquire into "the secret territory" of Foucault's life can be attributed partly to native *pudeur* but also, and more importantly I think, to Eribon's own sense that Foucault's "entire oevure can be read as a revolt against the powers of 'normalization' " (x). It was this determination on Eribon's part not to require Foucault to answer for his life before the tribunal of bourgeois morality that led him to treat his protagonist almost as more of an intellectual celebrity than a historical subject; it is also what accounts for the great weakness of Eribon's book as a biography: Eribon's reticence—forced upon him partly by law, partly by "good taste," and partly by political principle— prevents him from demonstrating the extent to which resistance to "normalization" informed and organized the complex interplay among Foucault's personal, professional, sexual, social, academic, and political practices.[48]

If Eribon's mistake is to reduce Foucault's personal life to the merely *private*, neglecting the connections between Foucault's thought and his experiences of sexual, social, and political subjection, Miller's mistake is exactly symmetrical and opposite: it is to seek in the details of Foucault's childhood experiences, fantasy life, sexual preoccupations, and artistic tastes the key to understanding his books, which Miller treats as a series of encrypted autobiographies. What both approaches miss is the specifically *political* character of Foucault's evolving practices of personal life, of his ongoing struggle against the modern "technologies of the subject" whose origins he traced and whose operations he described in book after book. What a different biographer might have enabled us to hear, in the calculated disturbances within the order of the self created by Foucault's supposedly excessive *pratiques de soi* (drugs, sex, philosophy), as "the distant roar of battle"[49] is thus stifled, on the one hand, in the silence of needless discretion and drowned out, on the other, in the chatter of overparticularistic psychologizing.

▼   ▼   ▼   ▼   ▼   ▼   ▼   ▼

DIDIER ERIBON'S biography is certainly entertainment of a very high-class kind. To be sure, it will disappoint those who want to find out the really important facts about Foucault's life, such as when he started to shave his head, and why: Eribon displays an oddly pre-Foucauldian indifference to Foucault's own technologies of the self.[50] But it does contain quantities of reliable information, and anyone intrigued by Foucault will find it both absorbing and instructive.

Here, for example, are some things I learned from it about the publishing history of *The Order of Things*. Foucault preferred the English title to the French, having originally intended to call his book *La Prose du monde*, then (when a posthumous text by Merleau-Ponty turned up with that title) *L'Ordre des choses; Les Mots et les choses* was a backup title which Foucault's editor Pierre Nora ultimately prevailed on him to adopt.[51] The chapter on *Las Meniñas* was added to the book at the last moment, with some hesitation (Foucault thought it "too literary"), having been published earlier as an independent essay in *Le Mercure de France.* Although Foucault's old pal Althusser, as well as Pierre Daix, embraced the book, it was routinely regarded as a right-wing polemic, because its joint critique of phenomenology and Marxism was understood, correctly, as an attack on the tradition of French leftism represented by such figures as Merleau-Ponty and, above all, Sartre (in fact, the proofs contained numerous attacks on Sartre, but Foucault removed them before publication). The book went through six printings in its first year, a total of 21,500 copies. Godard satirized its vogue in *La Chinoise* (1967) and said in an interview that it was against people like "the Reverend Father Foucault" that he wanted to make films so that future Foucaults would be prevented from presuming to say, with reference to the present era, "At such and such a period they thought . . ." "Marxism is the [book's] target," Sartre remarked. "[I]t is a matter of establishing a new ideology, the final dam that the bourgeoisie can erect against Marx." "Poor old bourgeoisie," Foucault commented ten years later, "with only my book for its ramparts!" In the context of this political feud, "structuralism" functioned as a code word for anti-Marxism, and that is one of the reasons Foucault—though an enthusiastic and, at first, admitted practitioner of it—came to repudiate the label, especially once he had belatedly thrown in his lot with the Maoists; he wrote *L'Archéologie du savoir* partly to dissociate himself from the structuralist reading of *The Order of Things.* And at one point he became so dissatisfied with the earlier book that he even asked Nora to stop printing it (155–86).

All that is indisputably fascinating. Eribon has worked hard, read widely, and turned up a vast amount of material, some of it quite obscure: his book is a triumph of historical contextualization. Subsequent biographers of Foucault are in his debt; both Miller and Macey freely acknowledge their dependence on him, although the latter often conceals its precise extent.[52] Eribon knew Foucault and collaborated with him; he even published, under his own initials (at Foucault's urging), a little essay by Foucault on the dismantling of the French homophile organization, Arcadie.[53] Eribon is in a better position than any other biographer to describe the personal, intellectual, and institutional context of Foucault's activities, and he has interviewed all the major and minor players in the French academic and political scene who could illuminate it. The book that results from this method is not a full biography in the conventional sense, as is Macey's, but a kind of "inside story" designed to serve as background to the public life of the man who was for a time France's leading intellectual. It reads in places like an academic version of a Hollywood gossip column (most of the information in the preceding paragraph derives not from archival sources—Eribon has not seen the proofs of *Les Mots et les choses*, for example—but from what various people recounted to Eribon years after the actual events). The name-dropping alone is breathtaking: everybody who was anybody in French social and cultural life turns up in these pages, from Simone Signoret to the Ayatollah Khomeini (although it is left to Macey to conjure up the incongruous image of Foucault cooking vegetarian meals for Julie Christie [239]). What interests Eribon, however, and what he does a superb job of reconstructing, is the shifting network of Foucault's personal, academic, intellectual, and political allegiances over more than three decades. He tells us when Foucault started and stopped being friends with dozens of important people; who wrote letters of recommendation for him, voted to hire or not to hire him, gave his books good or bad reviews; how Foucault positioned himself with respect to numerous intellectual movements and trends; when he joined the Communist party (1950), when he quit the party (1953), when he became a Maoist (1969), and when he exclaimed to a young militant, who had unwisely accosted him in the heat of a demonstration in order to invite him to speak about Marx to a study group, "Don't talk to me about Marx anymore! . . . Ask someone whose job it is. Someone paid to do it. Ask the Marxist functionaries. Me, I've had enough of Marx" (1975). It would be tempting to retitle this book *Michel Foucault: The Career*, to think of it as a highly personalized, behind-the-scenes account of the making of an academic reputation, but that would be to mistake Eribon's principled determination (loosely inspired by Pierre Bourdieu) to foreground the institutional conditions of intellectual work in France: after all, in a country with one (state-run) university system based in the capital, and one centralized intellectual life, philosophical and political fashions cannot meaningfully be disentangled from—just as they cannot simply be reduced to—matters of personal loyalty and professional patronage.

Here, for example, is Eribon's description of Foucault at work on *L'Archéologie du savoir*:

> He wrote furiously and struggled violently with notions of enunciation, discursive formation, regularity, and strategy. . . . Foucault knew that the stakes were considerable. He had been introduced as Sartre's successor, and the challenged master had launched a harsh counterattack. The fight was on, and if he wanted to make off with the winnings, Foucault must not disappoint the expectations of an eager crowd awaiting the next heated exchange. (191)

That Eribon obviously intends this passage to be read not as satire but as high drama conveys more powerfully than anything he could say the agonistic and public character of French intellectual life; it also conveys, more significantly, the disciplinary requirement imposed on Foucault by his public role as a professional "man of knowledge" (and felt occasionally even by those of us lesser folk who work at some remove from the *sixième arrondissement*)—the requirement to play what Foucault himself would later call, in another context, "games of truth."[54]

It was precisely in order to define, expose, and resist the disciplinary regimes that regulated his own discursive practice—whether by compelling him to speak the truth as a state-supported intellectual or by denying him the authority to speak the truth as a madman, left-wing extremist, or homosexual—that Foucault undertook his political critiques of institutionalized rationality. The story of his life makes it possible to interpret his work, as both a thinker and an activist, as a series of evolving responses and resistances to the "conditions of possibility" that governed his own *énoncés*. It is this determination to understand the relations of power immanent in his own intellectual, institutional, and erotic practices, to oppose or renegotiate those relations of power from a position already structured by them, and to discover strategies that might frustrate the technologies of a socially empowered rationality which scrupulously isolates, deauthorizes, and silences the mad, the sick, the delinquent, and the perverse—it is this essentially *political* struggle that represents, for me, the real drama of Foucault's life.

The outlines of that drama, though visible in Eribon's narrative, almost entirely escape its author. This is nowhere more striking than in the pages that document Foucault's virtually simultaneous early experiences as both a patient and a practitioner of psychiatry. While studying for his *license* and *agrégation* in philosophy at the Ecole Normale Supérieure (which he entered in 1946, shortly before his twentieth birthday), Foucault came under the tutelage of instructors who were interested in psychology, who organized classes in psychopathology and even took their students to see patients at the Hôpital

Sainte-Anne and elsewhere. Meanwhile, Foucault was himself experiencing severe psychological difficulties in adjusting to communal life at the ENS: Eribon cites reports of self-mutilation and of a suicide attempt in 1948 (followed by several others, real or staged, during the next years). Foucault's parents sent him to consult a psychiatric expert at—where else?—the Hôpital Sainte-Anne. At the same time Foucault, having obtained his *license* in philosophy at the Sorbonne in 1948, went on to get another one in psychology in 1949, as well as two *diplômes* from the Institut de Psychologie de Paris in 1949 and 1952, where (while working for the second one—in pathological psychology, no less!) he studied with the very specialist whom he had consulted as a patient in 1948. Part of Foucault's training at this stage involved treating patients himself; at the same time, from at least 1950, he had been diagnosing and experimenting on human subjects while working as a technical assistant in electroencephalographic laboratories that a friend had set up in the Hôpital Sainte-Anne as well as at the main hospital of the French prison system. Foucault became fascinated with Rorschach tests in the late 1940s, performing them on as many fellow students at the ENS as he could ensnare, and he retained that fascination for a good twenty years, teaching rigorous classes on Rorschach theory at least as late as 1967. Psychology originally presented itself to Foucault, then, in three guises at once: as a normalizing imposition, as a therapeutic opportunity, and as a self-authorizing practice.

The perennial, inane question as to whether Foucault was a philosopher or a historian could not, in fact, have arisen for the greater part of his career, for the simple reason that he was regarded as neither: "[S]hould his classification be psychology? or history of science?" asked an academic memo in 1960; two years later a dean's recommendation for tenure noted that "his specialty is psychopathology." If Foucault's formal appointments in the 1960s were in philosophy departments, that is partly because psychology, like sociology, had not yet achieved the status of an independent academic discipline in France and was routinely housed within philosophy programs.

How the unhappy youth of 1948 evolved into the suave cultural emissary of 1955–60 (during which time he held quasi-diplomatic appointments at French cultural centers in Sweden, Poland, and West Germany), then into a government apparatchik in the mid-1960s, and ultimately into a consummate academic politician who in 1981 apparently declined Mitterand's offer of the post of cultural attaché in New York in the hope of being named, if not ambassador to the United States, then at least director of the Bibliothèque Nationale—that is one of the many mysteries in Foucault's life which Eribon does not attempt to penetrate and which he barely pauses to notice. In fact, Eribon tries to avoid dealing with messy personal matters: Foucault's serious depression in 1977, for example, whose causes and consequences James Miller probes at length (287–88ff.), elicits from Eribon only perfunctory speculation as to whether "some people close to him . . . had reservations" about the first volume of his *History of Sexuality* (275). While not squeamish about Foucault's gayness, Eribon isn't much interested in it either: he seems to consider it his duty to give us the basic facts; he records various of Foucault's dicta on the subject (over dinner chez Lacan in 1963: "There will be no civilization as long as marriage between men is not accepted" [154]); and he mentions one instance in which Foucault's career suffered from antigay discrimination (Foucault was denied a post as assistant director of higher education in the Ministry of Education in the mid-1960s [133]). Otherwise, homosexuality occupies pretty much the same place in Eribon's account as polio does in the standard progress-narratives of the life of FDR: it is an accidental, and morally neutral, handicap which our hero, in his quest for greatness, managed to overcome (until the end, that is, when it brought him into final, unmerited collision with HIV-disease).[55] Eribon records a sum total of two affairs, with the composer Jean Barraqué in the mid-1950s and later with the philosopher Daniel Defert; the latter crops up, typically enough, at the point in Eribon's narrative when Foucault procured Defert an assistantship in his department at the University of Clermont-Ferrand, thereby incurring the widespread disapproval of his colleagues. In all fairness to Eribon, it should be noted that French law prevented him from providing further details about Foucault's personal life, to say nothing of Foucault's sexual practices, since it would have required him to obtain permission for such disclosures from Foucault's heirs—namely, his mother and, now, his sister—who have never so much as countenanced a public acknowledgment that Foucault's death was caused by AIDS. Still, an inattentive reader might be pardoned for concluding from Eribon's necessarily discreet exposition that after Foucault and Defert became lovers in late 1960 Foucault never had sex with anyone else ever again (an omission more than made up for by Miller and Macey). And yet much of the impetus for Foucault's late work on *pratiques de soi* came from insights into the transformative potential of sex which he gained from his experiences in the bathhouses and S/M clubs of New York and San Francisco, as both Miller and Macey make clear.

Despite these lacunae, Eribon's biography can be combined with Macey's to give us more than enough ammunition to explode the hostile caricatures of Foucault that have been put into circulation recently by assorted theory-bashers. For example, far from being an ivory-tower critic of Marxism who dismissed the realities of oppression and whose notion of power is so totalizing as to exclude the possibility of political resistance, the fifty-year-old Foucault did not shrink from doing physical battle with the police, at considerable personal risk (and, sometimes, cost). Despite his failure to inquire very deeply into female sexual subjectivation in his *History of Sexuality*, despite occasional misogynist remarks to his male friends (all duly recorded by Macey), and despite a recently publicized incident in which he reportedly expressed dismay—and who can blame him?—at the prospect of having to spend an entire evening in the company of Susan Sontag,[56] Foucault was not the antifeminist monster that his gay-baiting detractors often claim him to have been; on the contrary, he worked enthusiastically with female colleagues, was consistent in supporting the establishment of political organizations by marginal groups, including women, and intended *Libération* to give voice to the various emerging tendencies within the women's movement (Eribon, 252). Foucault also took a minor part in the struggle for abortion rights in France (Macey, 321–22). (Paul Rabinow has noted that *Le Désordre des familles* [1982], the one book that Foucault actually coauthored with a woman, the historian Arlette Farge, has yet to be translated into English.)[57] Despite his critique of truth as a regulatory concept in the human sciences, Foucault did not feel at all inhibited about appealing to truth when attempting to expose the realities of torture, police brutality, and governmental injustice. And despite the frequently heard complaint that Foucault's critique of the ideology of authorship harmonized all too cozily in his case with consistent self-promotion as an author, Eribon and Macey both show that Foucault was in fact willing to play fast and loose with the author-function, penning innumerable unsigned tracts, essays, and manifestos, composing a falsely attributed article about himself for a philosophical dictionary, and even writing, in the style of a quasi-Platonic dialogue, the colorful memoirs of a young gay hitchhiker he'd picked up and publishing them under the hitchhiker's own name.[58]

The discontinuities in Foucault's thought, his constant shifts of position, the essentially improvisatory character of much of his work—all of which are well documented by Eribon as well as by Macey—serve as a salutary reminder not only, as Foucault himself often insisted, that he was not a systematic thinker but also that it is both hazardous and superfluous to treat Foucault's oeuvre as a single body of thought, the unitary "work" of a unitary "author." If we learn anything from Foucault, it is not to canonize him as the exponent of some authoritative doctrine but rather to see in him an instructive example of someone whose acute and constantly revised understanding of his own social location enabled him to devise some effective but unsystematic modes of resistance to the shifting discursive and political conditions which circumscribed his own practice. That ability to reflect critically on and to respond politically to the circumstances that both enabled and constrained his own activity may account for why Foucault's life, as much as or perhaps even more than his work, continues to serve as a compelling model for an entire generation of scholars, critics, and activists.

▼   ▼   ▼   ▼   ▼   ▼   ▼   ▼

IF WHAT WAS missing in Eribon and Macey was a willingness to interpret systematically the meaning of Foucault's life, with James Miller we have the return of interpretation with a vengeance. Miller announces his interpretative approach to Foucault's life in the preface to his book: "[T]he crux of what is original and challenging about Foucault's way of thinking, as I see it, is his unrelenting, deeply ambiguous and profoundly problematic preoccupation with death, which he explored not only in the exoteric form of his writing, but also, and I believe critically, in the esoteric form of sado-masochistic eroticism" (7). Whatever one may think of the connection that Miller so casually and alarmingly draws, if only in Foucault's case, between sadomasochism and a preoccupation with death—and whatever one may think of the "critical" importance that Miller assigns to it—one must concede that his approach does at least have the merit, which Eribon's biography signally lacked, of appearing to find genuine philosophical, if not political, interest in Foucault's sexual life and practices. So much for the good news. The bad news is summed up in Miller's postscript: "Unfortunately, Foucault's lifework, as I have come to understand it, is far more unconventional—and far more discomfiting—than some of his 'progressive' admirers seem ready to admit" (384). Foucault, in short, was a weirdo. And—unlike his " 'progressive' admirers," blinded by denial or self-deception—he knew it. All his life he remained a conflicted, anguished, tormented soul, mesmerized by death, by fantasies of suicide, torture, and cruelty; his deepest and most abiding drive was, as he put it in the second volume of his unfinished *History of Sexuality*, to get free of himself (34),[59] which he tried to do by means of a number of "potentially transformative 'limit-experiences' " (30) of mind and body.

This nasty freak, it turns out, was "for better or worse . . . one of the representative men—and outstanding thinkers—of the twentieth century," according to Miller (8), and so it is worth asking, "What value, then, does his work really have? What can it mean for us [normal, healthy folk]? How should it be used?" (19). The ultimate question that Foucault's life poses to Miller is whether various forms of radical politics, radical sex, and other kinds of supposed "limit-experience" actually offer the modern subject a real means of self-transcendence, of escaping domination by an intolerable culture as well as by that culture's outpost in the subject, namely the self (construed as a unique personal essence or identity). Miller's answer to that question—a question of supreme urgency for many cultural activists today—is curiously noncommittal, even dismissive; what draws him to it, evidently, is not the prospect of answering it but the opportunity it provides him for placing Foucault's life and writings under intensified surveillance.

Now if a self-styled "progressive" and confessed admirer of

Foucault like myself is not indeed "ready" to accept Miller's portrait, despite its cumulative rhetorical power, the motive behind my unreadiness does not have to do, as Miller unflatteringly anticipates, with my being "discomfited" by Foucault's apparent weirdness or by his "brave and basic challenge to nearly everything that passes for 'right' . . . among a great many of America's left-wing academics" (384), among whom I am proud to number myself. I do not consider either Foucault's practices of sadomasochism, or the more widely disseminated knowledge of them that Miller's book has facilitated, to be *bad* for Foucault's reputation or for the state of gay politics and cultural theory—although at this point there can be no denying (neither ought there to be any real regretting) the inevitable political damage that such knowledge has done or the many hateful ways in which it has been exploited. Nor would I wish to conceal "the truth" about Foucault's personal life, though I might wish to intervene, to the extent that I can, in the process by which that "truth" is produced and distributed as well as in the institutional practices through which it is made to signify. Rather, my resistance to Miller's portrait of Foucault proceeds from other sources: mistrust of Miller's readerly knowingness, of his ruthless assurance of being able to detect in Foucault's discussion of almost any topic symptomatic expressions of an underlying psychopathology that will unfailingly confirm his diagnosis; reluctance to follow Miller in his tendency to treat Foucault's various practices of nonconformity as idiosyncratic, exceptional, and therefore apolitical; and opposition to Miller's normalizing strategy of reconstituting Foucault's career as a narrative of transgression—and, thus, as an irresistibly, indeed sensationally, describable life.

▼　▼　▼　▼　▼　▼　▼　▼

LET'S BEGIN by looking, very simply, at how Miller's method works at the level of his text. Here, for example, is a typical passage in which Miller poses the sort of unresolvable dilemma that serves chiefly to heighten the suspense and to raise the ostensible philosophical stakes of his own exposition: "Sometimes [Foucault] seems to have considered himself an exemplary seeker of 'clandestine knowledge.' . . . But perhaps, as Foucault himself at other times implies, he was simply a figure of quixotic folly . . . 'something like a nature gone awry' " (30-31). The question, in short, is whether Foucault considered himself a sage or a pervert. Now what is the evidentiary basis for attributing either of those assessments of Foucault (each of which is punitive in its own way) to Foucault himself? In the first case, Miller quotes, as if it were a self-characterization, a sarcastic phrase ("clandestine knowledge") that Foucault actually uses in *The Birth of the Clinic* to caricature the aggrandizing way that nineteenth-century medical scientists represented the work of the pathological anatomists, whom they considered to be their precursors. In the second case, Miller treats as self-referential an evocative formulation ("something like a nature gone awry") from *The History of Sexuality, Volume I*, that Foucault similarly uses in order to convey the rhetorical flavor of nineteenth-century psychiatric accounts of libertinage, which recast the Don Juan of legend in the role of a sexual pervert ("we shall leave it to psychoanalysts to speculate whether he was homosexual, narcissistic, or impotent," Foucault drily comments). In neither passage is Foucault speaking in an authorial persona, let alone in reference to himself. It is Miller's privileged access to the "truth" of Foucault's alleged psychopathology that authorizes him to discover, in each of Foucault's texts, what he elsewhere calls "figment[s] of autobiographical allegory" (112).[61]

That method of reading Foucault produces some astonishing results. Here, for instance, is a sentence from the final chapter of *Madness and Civilization*: "Everything that morality, everything that a botched society, has stifled in man, revives in the castle of murders."[62] And here is Miller's commentary: "An amazing claim—so strange that few readers of *Madness and Civilization* have lingered over it, trying to fathom its implications. Perhaps it is fortunate that the hermetic style leaves shrouded in mystery just what Foucault has in mind" (112). But, fortunately or not, it does not remain shrouded in mystery for long: "To escape from the Castle of Conscience," Miller explains, speaking for Foucault, "we must first enter into a Castle of Murders: against the alleged virtues inculcated by the psychiatrists, transgression will unleash vice; against philanthropic kindness, vengeful cruelty; against a docile animality, a seething lust for corporeal sensation, no matter how painful or self-destructive." And Miller concludes, in a tone of reproof to Foucault's progressive admirers, "This descent into the Inferno is obviously no upbeat 'liberation' " (115–16). Quite so. But does it in fact represent Foucault's personal ethic or political platform? The failure of Foucault's readers to linger over the claim articulated in the text quoted here turns out to be less amazing than Miller supposes when one realizes, upon closer examination of that text, that Foucault does not purport to be speaking in it in his own voice but to be summarizing instead the arguments of the Marquis de Sade. To be sure, the very fervid quality of Foucault's prose might seem to suggest that the Divine Marquis, whose views are so powerfully evoked in it, is in fact speaking for Foucault himself, but more is required to establish such a reading than mere acts of biographical ventriloquism.[63]

Miller has a relatively easy time sustaining his thesis when he can deal with a book like *Madness and Civilization*, which is, after all, about madness. He goes on to claim, however, that "*all* of Foucault's writings [in the 1960s], from the most literary of the essays to the most recondite of his histories, sounded certain themes with revealing frequency. Intimations of evil, madness, and death appear on page after page, a mute echo of the kind of 'limit-experience' apotheosized in *Madness and Civilization*—and a reminder of the personal stakes in Foucault's own 'great Nietzchean quest' " (125; Miller's emphasis). Now this is first of all a strategic error of exposition whose effect is ultimately to make Foucault's books sound as if they're all really about the same thing and thereby to render tediously monotonous a biographical narrative that ought at least, by virtue of its scandalous content, to have been uniformly gripping. Furthermore, since there are, *pace* Miller, long passages in Foucault's books from this period in which such "intimations" do not occur, as well as a number of his shorter works from which they are wholly absent, Miller is obliged to perform some extraordinary critical acrobatics in order to support his generalization and to discover evil and darkness in Foucault's texts wherever he looks. One of his methods is to assert that conventional, or insufficiently lurid, passages in Foucault simply serve to camouflage the author's real intent. "It is precisely in order to disarm" the reaction of "some readers" of *Madness and Civilization*, whom Foucault's "paean to the profane rapture of dying" is likely to strike "as crazy" (112), that Foucault "cunningly disguised" his meaning beneath a vast accumulation of conventional erudition (96), Miller insists. Similarly, *The Order of Things*, despite its lack of comparable flamboyance, "has never ceased to puzzle and provoke"; criticism has raised "the suspicion that this book, like its predecessor, is not what it seems" (151); "the book sooner or later leaves a reader feeling baffled. . . . The longer one ponders the book's argument, the stranger it seems" (153). Here, in other words, is a situation that calls for desperate interpretative measures.

When Miller comes to *The Order of Discourse*, that cool political critique of conventional scholarly and critical language games, he has to claim that it is actually "a high-wire act . . . perhaps [Foucault's] most artfully veiled piece of writing" (183), cleverly concealing as it does Foucault's obsession with evil and violence, with the powers and dangers of discourse—so cleverly, indeed, that no one has ever before read it in such a demonic way. Stepping behind the veil, Miller triumphantly detects one reference to death (though not specifically to Foucault's own, as he claims), plus an ominous characterization of discourse as " 'a violence that we do to things,' a 'practice we impose on them.' " Foucault "also implied that he, for one," had resurrected "a long-forgotten kind of 'true' discourse, one filled with untamed power," capable of provoking ' "respect and terror' " (183–84).[64] This last phrase—the only phrase of Foucault's that Miller quotes in support of his contention that Foucault thought he had resurrected a "true" discourse—does not in fact refer to Foucault's own discourse directly but to the ritualized poetic language of the Greek poets in the seventh and sixth centuries B.C. Miller's attempt to ascribe to Foucault what Foucault himself says about the Greeks is both highly implausible and highly inferential—a far better instance of discursive "violence" than anything in Foucault's own suave performance. Miller, to be sure, isn't pretending to offer full readings of Foucault's texts, but his cavalier and tendentious appropriation of them does not inspire confidence in the thesis that he enlists them to support.

Miller's use of Foucault's texts becomes most "volatile" when he decides to construct a narrative that will dramatize the claim made to him by Daniel Defert (whom Miller is in the odious habit of referring to as Foucault's "longtime companion") that when Foucault "went to San Francisco for the last time [in the fall of 1983], he took it as a *limit-experience*" (29; Miller's emphasis). In Miller's hands, that statement about Foucault's attitude to sex and death in the face of AIDS ultimately turns into the insinuation that Foucault discovered in the AIDS epidemic an opportunity to achieve "his own deliberately chosen apotheosis, his own singular experience of 'The Passion' " (29). Leaving aside the wider social resonances of those phrases—with their suggestion that some gay men knowingly brought AIDS on themselves, that gay male sexuality is masochistic to the point of suicide—which demonstrate just how far Miller is willing to risk, on behalf of gay men and people with AIDS, "the many dangers, of scandal and reductionism, of unconscious stereotyping and prurient sensationalism," let us simply read three consecutive paragraphs of the narrative, in which Miller purports "to tell the whole truth" about Foucault, in order to assess the kind of textual support he chooses to marshal for his interpretation.

> The conditions were chilling. Still, in some bathhouses in San Francisco in the fall of 1983, in the eyes of someone disposed [as Foucault was] to see matters in this light, the scene on some nights may have strangely recalled that conjured up by Foucault ten years before, in his account of plagues and the macabre carnivals of death that medieval writers imagined to accompany them: "Laws suspended, prohibitions lifted, the frenzy of time that is passing away, bodies mingling together without respect, individuals unmasked, abandoning their statutory identity and the figure under which they were recognized, allowing an entirely different truth to appear."
>
> As the lyrical intensity of this passage suggests, the possibility of what Foucault elsewhere called a "suicide-orgy" exerted an unusual fascination over him. Given the anxiety that AIDS continues to provoke, the singularity of Foucault's preoccupations must be stressed: most members of the gay and S/M communities would *never* have seen the situation in such terms. Foucault, by contrast, had long placed death—and the preparation for suicide—at the heart of his concerns: summoning what he once called

"that courage of clandestine knowledge that endures mal-
ediction," he was evidently serious about his implicit lifelong conviction that "to comprehend life is given only to
a cruel, reductive and already infernal knowledge that only
wishes it dead."

That fall, he later told friends, he returned to the bathhouses of San Francisco. Accepting the new level of risk,
he joined again in the orgies of torture, trembling with "the
most exquisite agonies," voluntarily effacing himself, ex-
ploding the limits of consciousness, letting real, corporeal
pain insensibly melt into pleasure through the alchemy of
eroticism. (28)

It is highly doubtful that Miller has ever seen the inside of a gay
bathhouse in San Francisco, or elsewhere, let alone in the fall
of 1983. Nor does he know what Foucault did when he went
there, or how Foucault was affected by what he saw. All that,
it turns out, has to be inferred—not to say fabricated—from
Foucault's texts.

Each of the three overheated, intensely *knowing* paragraphs
in the foregoing passage bolsters its claim on the reader's cre-
dulity by citing the words of Foucault. In the first and last paragraphs, Miller interpolates passages from *Discipline and
Punish*, while in the middle paragraph he quotes again, with
utter solemnity, the bit of sarcasm about "clandestine knowledge" from *The Birth of the Clinic* already discussed, along with
another passage from the same work describing the preoccupation of some nineteenth-century artists with death: in its original context, then, the quoted sentence does *not* convey, except
to Miller, a "conviction" of Foucault's own, as he makes out.[65]
The passage quoted in the first paragraph does indeed evoke,
in the context of *Discipline and Punish*, the carnival of death,
but it does so only to dismiss it as a misleading literary fiction
exactly opposed in all its details to the political fantasies of
disciplinary control, regulation, hierarchy, analysis, division,
and social hygiene that, according to Foucault, also sprang up

around outbreaks of the plague.[66] In the last paragraph, the phrase "the most exquisite agonies" not only does not originate with Foucault, it does not even originate in France: Foucault quotes it from an essay on deterring crime published in 1731 by an English jurist.[67] To find that phrase revived and refashioned into an authentic representation of the physical sensations actually experienced by Foucault (and "later told [to his] friends") in the course of his imagined sexual adventures in 1983 is, to say the least, breathtaking. Finally, "suicide-orgy," the single most offensive term in the entire catalog, comes from a highly facetious little essay on homosexuality and suicide that Foucault published in 1979 in the first issue of *Gai pied* and that, Miller concedes elsewhere, "it is tempting to say, is just a joke" (though Miller himself goes on to imply the contrary [55]); even so, Foucault's only mention of suicide-orgies in that text—"suicide festivals or orgies are just two of the possible methods. There are others more intricate and learned"[68]—hardly bears out Miller's assertion that suicide-orgies "exerted an unusual fascination over" Foucault.[69] Fascination, to be sure, is in plentiful evidence here, but it appears to belong more to the biographer than to his subject.

The enormous persuasive power of Miller's account derives, in any case, not from its factual or textual basis (insofar as it has one) but from the elaborate sexual demonology which it both condenses and disavows. Delusional though Miller's description of Foucault's suicidal orgies in San Francisco's bathhouses may be, it evidently did not fail to strike a responsive chord in the hearts and minds of his straight readers—who somehow seem to have *known*, all along, that *this* was *exactly* what gay men had secretly been up to during the early years of the AIDS epidemic. Miller's genius lies precisely in his unerring ability to perform for such readers the ingratiating service of confirming them in their long-held but hitherto unverified suspicions about the sexual exploits of gay men and sadomasochists, while at the same time providing them with "deniability" should they ever be accused of succumbing to such suspicions merely on the basis of social prejudices. Hence the outpouring of gratitude, praise, and congratulations that greeted Miller's description of the baths; hence, too, the universal impulse to defend that description and to deny or repress any awareness of even its most obvious deficiencies. "There is nothing lurid or voyeuristic about Miller's presentation," stoutly affirms Richard Wolin, in unblinking and almost comic defiance of the evidence directly before his eyes:

> On the contrary, one can *only* admire [well, so much for fussy queens like myself] his unflinching, *nonjudgmental*, and, in many instances, outright sympathetic treatment of the *potentially* sensational aspects of Foucault's personal life. . . . In his vivid descriptions of Bay Area bathhouse life before the "plague," Miller proves a compassionate commentator. . . . Even the most puritanical and closed-minded of readers may find themselves persuaded by Miller's sympathetic, tactful account.[70]

Indeed they may. One might even say that the more puritanical Miller's readers are, the more disposed they may find themselves to be persuaded and the more likely they may be to admire his "bathhouse scene" as a *tour de force*. Wolin's personal conception of what qualifies as sobriety, tact, sympathy, and compassion in Miller emerges with particular clarity from his own attempt to emulate those qualities: his review is entitled, unflinchingly and nonjudgmentally, "The Lure of Death."

▼　　▼　　▼　　▼　　▼　　▼　　▼　　▼

It WOULD BE tedious to multiply examples of Miller's textual abuses beyond what is necessary to justify warning the reader of the need to check Miller's quotations of Foucault against their original contexts before accepting either their documentary value or the various constructions that Miller places on them.[71] For the rest, it will be sufficient to emphasize the strict relationship between reductionism and sensationalism in Miller's portrayal of Foucault: Miller's method is to reduce Foucault's thought to an "autobiographical allegory," then to cluck over its alleged kinkiness. Take, for example, Miller's account of the famous debate between Foucault and Pierre Victor over the question of popular justice.[72] Miller focuses on Foucault's opposition to Victor's proposal for a revolutionary people's tribunal and on his stated preference for spontaneous acts of mass reprisal. Miller plays up Foucault's "astonishing" advocacy of popular massacres, noting that even Foucault's "bloody minded" interlocutor "was obviously taken aback by the implications" of his thinking (204–5). There is, however, another dimension to Foucault's position: Foucault was resisting, from within the ultra-Left idiom that he was compelled to speak in order to take a leading role in French political counterculture at the time,[73] the tendency of certain activists to redeploy (if only in their imaginations) Enlightenment-style norms of rational authority and bureaucratic legitimacy within a supposedly revolutionary framework, to rehabilitate the old political technology of the liberal state under the guise of creating something new and different. Miller understands Foucault's position perfectly well, even if he implicitly reduces it to an expression of self-interest. In a subsequent chapter he notes that, for Foucault,

> to change the world required changing our selves, our bodies, our souls, and all our old ways of "knowing," in addition to changing the economy and society. To "seize" and exercise a dictatorial kind of power might thus simply reproduce the old patterns of subjectification under a new name—as had obviously happened in actually existing

socialist societies, where homosexuals and drug addicts [like Foucault], for example, were often as harshly treated as ever. (234)

It is significant, then, that in his main discussion of the popular justice controversy, Miller ignores the larger political consequences of Foucault's arguments and chooses instead to register shock at Foucault's apparently blithe acceptance of terrorism.

That almost deliberate misconstrual of Foucault's principled resistance to the mechanisms of disciplinary power (whether in their revolutionary or in their bourgeois form), which goes hand in hand with the attempt to repackage such resistance as an expression of Foucault's *personal* attraction to cruelty, torture, bloodshed, and death, is merely one instance of a more general tendency that constitutes the most serious flaw in Miller's account of Foucault: by so thoroughly personalizing Foucault's thought, Miller in effect depoliticizes it.[74] He interprets as idiosyncratic, and therefore as psychologically revealing, what from a different political perspective might well have seemed *exemplary* about Foucault's personal and political attitude—namely, Foucault's consistent and thoroughgoing revolt against normalization—and he presents as peculiar to Foucault the very element in Foucault's political thinking that, far from being an artifact of unique psychological processes, acutely reflects and responds to some of the most common, and most widely shared, experiences of social abjection: namely, Foucault's critique of the procedure by which knowledge and power combine to produce effects of social domination and his opposition to techniques of social authorization, ethical justification, and institutional legitimation that work by constructing, distributing, and enforcing generalizable norms of individual conduct. In fact, Foucault's almost instinctual recoil from any attempt to formulate and to apply universalizing principles of social or ethical value, and from any corollary efforts to impose obligatory standards of social or ethical conformity,[75] is hardly peculiar to anything except the most astute strategies of radical resistance to the normalizing technologies of modern liberal government.

Miller's personalizing treatment of Foucault is all the more remarkable in this context because Miller himself is alive to the absolutely crucial implications of Foucault's politicization of subjectivity for the work of cultural politics, including feminist politics and gay politics. Indeed, what the feminist and gay movements share with other antiauthoritarian political struggles of the 1960s and 1970s, such as the antipsychiatry movement or the children's rights movement, is precisely, according to Foucault, their common resistance to "the government of individualization," their refusal of "abstractions . . . which ignore who we are individually, and also a refusal of a scientific or administrative inquisition which determines who one is." And Foucault concludes,

> To sum up, the main objective of these struggles is to attack not so much "such or such" an institution of power, or group, or elite, or class, but rather a technique, a form of power.
>
> This form of power applies itself to immediate everyday life which categorizes the individual, marks him by his own individuality, attaches him to his own identity, imposes a law of truth on him which he must recognize and which others have to recognize in him. It is a form of power which makes individuals subjects.[76]

By treating modern subjectivity as an effect of power, Foucault brings matters of personal identity into the arena of politics. As Miller himself has observed, Foucault makes political what would otherwise have been considered merely private or psychological: his characteristic approach to the politics of the subject enables what liberal political theorists might dismiss as minor psychological quirks to qualify as rallying points for communal identity and collective struggle.[77] "The politics of the self thus becomes central to Foucault's project," Ed Cohen explains, "precisely because it offers a multiplicity of points of entry into 'the political' and thereby opens up a plurality of spaces for radical creativity."[78] Nothing, then, dramatizes better than Miller's reductively personal account of Foucault's politics the urgency of asserting, against Miller, what may be the cardinal principle of all oppositional cultural politics: namely, the principle that there is nothing personal—at least, that there is nothing *exclusively* personal—about subjectivity.

When Miller chooses to stage his own sense of shock at Foucault's willingness to tolerate political terrorism, moreover, he forfeits the opportunity to convey the horror of a different kind of terrorism, to communicate what Foucault, and many other gay men (together with any number of stigmatized, marginalized, or subaltern people), have experienced as the terror of reason, whose most fearful weapon—as Genet's earlier testimony eloquently implied—is perhaps none other than *the apparatus of unchallengeable description.* To be, and to find oneself being, known and described—rationally (or so it can be made to seem) and therefore definitively, more objectively (or so one is told) than one is capable of describing oneself and therefore irrefutably, resistlessly, with an instantaneous finality that preempts and defeats any attempt on one's own part to intervene in the process by which one becomes an object of knowledge, and that renders one helpless to stave off the effects of a knowledge one has had no share in creating[79]—that is an experience whose peculiar terror is hard to convey to those who have never suffered from the social liabilities that cause the rest of us to be continually and endlessly prey to it. Instead of attempting to make the terror of reason comprehensible as a motive for Foucault's own political resistance, Miller prefers to stage Foucault's weird indifference to the canons of civilized morality as just another item in the dossier of Foucault's "case." As one of Miller's most astute critics remarks,

It was precisely Foucault's appreciation of the way in which normalizing discourses police and subjugate which led him to a profound critique of *identity*, of naming oneself *as* one's sexuality, a critique which Miller eschews as he uses this very modality of domination to cast Foucault's research interests, philosophy, and political investments as unified by and in the character of his "shocking" impulses and obsessions. In this, Miller taps the deepest terror of every socially marked human being—colored, female, queer: that no matter what we write, think about or say, no matter how we fashion ourselves and our work, we will be incessantly returned and reduced to this single marking, that it will be produced again and again as "the truth" of our being, our thinking, our worldly endeavors, as Miller's self-described life with his "wife and three sons in West Roxbury" simply never will.[80]

It is abundantly evident, in short, that the constraints of normalization do not weigh very heavily on James Miller.

▼   ▼   ▼   ▼   ▼   ▼   ▼   ▼

So LET ME try to increase the pressure. Not because I want to normalize Miller—on the contrary, what I like about his book is its passion for Michel Foucault, its crazed intensity and single-mindedness, its visionary excess—nor because I am interested in promoting conventional standards of decency, wholesomeness, and good taste, but because I want to make clearer the political urgency of Foucault's project. How would Miller like it, in other words, if someone did this to him? (Not that any admirer of Foucault, least of all myself, has the credentials to do so—which is what will make my own effort appear to be so *unfair*, so *tasteless*, or at the very least so *unsporting*.) Let me try to subject Miller, then, in the way of an ironic experiment, to the kind of accusatory scrutiny he lavishes on Foucault ("I sometimes had to wonder, while I was writing my book," he admits, "whether I was behaving like some not-so-Grand Inquisitor" [7–8]); my method will be to reverse the panoptic procedure whereby the biographer's authority increases proportionately with both his own invisibility and the describability of his subject, and to treat *The Passion of Michel Foucault*, in its turn, as an autobiographical allegory. What kind of man, I shall ask, emerges from the pages of this bizarre and baffling book? How, in other words, can we (ordinary—if not, by definition, normal and healthy—gay folk) explain this instance of heterosexual pathology, The Passion of James Miller?[81]

The place to embark on such a description is clearly the postscript, in which Miller at least appears to surrender his panoptic privileges and to confess the truth about the source of his monomaniacal fascination with Foucault. He acknowledges that what rekindled his interest in the thinker was "a shocking piece of gossip" (which he now believes to be "essentially false") to the effect that Foucault, when he realized he was dying of AIDS, "had gone to gay bathhouses in America, and deliberately tried to infect other people with the disease" (375). Miller found he could not get this story, along with the dark vistas of secret lust and criminality that it disclosed to him, out of his mind. "What if the story were true?" (376). (Well, what if it were? Miller never follows up that initial question; he prefers to dwell within the field of its shock effect.) Before Miller could even identify the source of this strangely mesmeric rumor, "the idea of writing something" had already crossed his mind (376). He then tried to see if anything in Foucault's major works could be connected with the morbid story he had heard.

Returning to Foucault's books already obsessed by visions of depravity, and applying to them this insane hermeneutic, Miller discovered that "much of Foucault's prose now seemed to me suffused with a strange kind of aura, both morbid and vaguely mystical." Miller responded to this self-induced stimulus exactly as the insightful reader will already have predicted: he became almost instantly "hooked on Foucault. Seduced. . . . " He found himself contemplating "topics that, until then, I had always [*always?*] shied away from. . . . the meaning of death and the human capacity for cruelty . . . the tractable character of pain . . . an ethos of deliberate *ir*responsibility" (376–77). Miller, in short, became intoxicated with fantasies of transgression. And he *still* "didn't yet know whether the initial rumor" about Foucault's antics in the bathhouses was true (377), although when Defert incautiously remarked to him that Foucault took his last trip to San Francisco as a "limit-experience," Miller admits he was "stunned" (380).

The prospect of further research offered to reveal to Miller's fascinated gaze the lineaments of an exotic and forbidden underground world, to make him—like T. S. Eliot's Webster— "expert beyond experience." He started out, he confesses, knowing "virtually nothing about America's gay community— and even less about its sado-masochistic subculture" (377). The first thing to notice about this denial is that it is suspiciously overstated. *Less than virtually nothing?* Does not Miller's wife, as he tells us in his acknowledgments, work in the fields of psychiatry and clinical psychology (466)? And besides, has not American culture been producing images of gay leathermen for some time now? Miller's exaggerated disavowal confesses more eloquently than any mere acknowledgment could do to his own guilty consciousness of the mingled dread, curiosity, and desire produced in him by the imagined spectacle of gay sadomasochism.[82] Consider, moreover, the following statement: "The world of consensual S/M . . . tested my powers of sympathetic imagination. At first, I was shocked: I could not fathom how people could take pleasure in pain, particularly in suffering pain—I'm the kind of person who gets squeamish over having a tooth filled" (377). Is this piece of deliberate banality even remotely credible? The decisive indication against it is provided by the final, stunning irrelevancy: unless Miller's entire picture of S/M was exhausted by *The Little Shop of Horrors*, it hard to see how he could have been so stupid as to confuse an erotic scene with an ordinary dental procedure, simply because both might involve a degree of physical pain. What passes for a personal revelation, then, seems cunningly intended to produce an effect of naïveté, and so to deflect the reader's attention from any potentially discreditable connection between Miller's research project and his psychosexual life.

It is this evident determination to *appear* ingenuous that compromises Miller's attitude of candor and suggests that the purpose behind his abandonment of authorial invisibility in the postscript is not in fact to disclose "the truth" about his obsession with Foucault so much as to construct a cover for the motives that actuated the writing of his biography—and thereby to safeguard the invisibility and objectivity of his authorial persona. Miller's confession of the secret of his interest in the details of Foucault's sexual practices, far from clarifying the nature of his personal and political investments in the project of describing them, seems carefully staged so as to betray signs of what can finally be interpreted only as his own cluelessness. In short, Miller's autobiographical postscript must be read as a genuine instance of that rare and paradoxical literary phenomenon, the straight coming-out narrative. At least it presents us with a characteristic display of heterosexual theatrics. Like the married couple who flirt shamelessly with each other at a dinner party, Miller engages in a highly deliberate performance of ostensibly involuntary self-disclosure which ultimately confesses to nothing but its own innocence and incurs for its performer no graver risk than that of standing accused, by the laughable Oscar Wildes of this world, of washing one's clean linen in public. Miller's gesture of coming out (or should it be called "coming in"?) is just an exercise in coming clean: the self-description by which he exposes himself actually functions to shield him from the dangers of describability.

Despite Miller's professed recoil from the very idea of S/M, there can be no doubt that his powers of sympathetic imagination proved more than equal to the task of entering into it and of graphically representing it. Who could mistake the gusto in the writing of such passages as the following?

> Your hands will be strapped to the ceiling. Bands will be wrapped around each of your arms and tightened. A man with a lancet will approach you, and pierce a vein in each arm. Helplessly you will watch the blood begin to drain from your body.
>
> The ordeal is structured like the "crisis" in medieval medicine. It is a "game," a carefully regulated ritual, a spectacle of "immobile contemplation, of death mimed." Its aim: to *express* passionately and actively an agonizing lust for blood and for death; to turn this lust outward "in a continuous irony"—and so, through a kind of "perverse mysticism," to purge it, to drain it, to "disarm it in advance."
>
> Surrendering to a kind of hallucinatory fever, as the spectacle of your own blood plunges you into delirium, you are going to face your "moment of truth."
>
> You are going to experience directly, in a way that scientific inquiry has never been able to illuminate, "the silent world of the entrails, the whole dark underside of the body lined with endless unseeing dreams."
>
> And through this experience—which will safely whisk you to the threshold of your own imagined death—you are going to feel the pathological process, through its own force, snap the soul's shackles. (279–80)

Despite the frenetic orgy of citations—from de Sade, Deleuze, Foucault, and others—designed to absolve Miller of responsibility for the vividness of the images he conjures up, the nature of his own desire, of his own drive to representation, is all too obvious: he do the perverts in different voices. And what dopey perverts at that; after all, was there ever such a session at any S/M club in the world? Not very likely—and for good reason: however much of a philosophical turn-on the foregoing description may be to Miller, it is perhaps the most singularly *unsexy* dungeon scene ever written.

▼　▼　▼　▼　▼　▼　▼　▼

IT MAY BE instructive in this context to compare Miller's book to a slimmer volume, written at about the same time by a homonymous author, that also deals with the problem of specifying the gay identity of a dead French theorist: namely, D. A. Miller's *Bringing Out Roland Barthes*. Not only is the latter explicitly concerned, as its title indicates, with the project of "gaying" its subject, "bringing out" a writer who did not himself "come out" in his own work; it also acknowledges, as James Miller nowhere does, that in this encounter (as in most erotic ones) the writer's relation to his subject will not "at any moment [be] exempt from the usual vicissitudes of adulation, aggression, ambivalence."[83] D.A. Miller's response to this difficulty is not to attempt to conceal it but rather to stage it, to bring constantly before the reader the nature of the author's own complex investment in the newly insisted-upon fact and significance of Barthes's homosexuality.

In a manner that might be described as "novelesque"—to apply the term that D. A. Miller uses to characterize one of Barthes's queerest literary methods: "an incident dislodged from the teleology of plot; a gesture excised from the consistency of character; a turn of phrase set to drift far beyond the practical exigencies of information or function"[84]—the author here dots his text with a series of austerely impersonal anecdotes from what is presented as his own life, dramatizing precisely his own lack of exemption from the kind of scrutiny that he is fastening upon his subject. "At Gold's, as soon as my set is over, I pass on the dumbbells (with great solicitousness—'Sure you got 'em, now?') to my boyfriend, who will in a moment return the favor; the acceptability, even the necessity, of the gesture to good gym form camouflages the most precious reason for performing it: that our fingers might briefly touch."[85] While scandalizing the cultural imperative that conjoins critical authority with objectivity, objectivity with invisibility, and invisibility with at least presumptive heterosexuality, this deployment of "the novelesque" also neatly evades, by perfunctorily caving into it, some of the disciplinary pressure on the gay subject to "confess": although the anecdote might well be true (though how can the reader tell? and what difference would it make?), it distances itself from the empirical, autobiographical reality of the author by disappearing into the detachment of its own exemplarity.

Now I would hardly want to require everyone who writes about a gay subject to do so in the same way, to stage his or her own subjectivity, to employ D. A. Miller's method, or to imitate the convolutions of his sinuous, self-reflexive prose, which is designed to illustrate and to exemplify the self-discrediting stylistic "hysteria" that Miller ascribes to Barthes: "[W]ho could recognize theory once it enjoined the necessity of looking at its ass in the mirror?"[86] But I do think it is no accident that James Miller, in the interests of preserving his own panoptic privileges, suppressed and evaded the personal and political significance that Foucault's homosexuality and sado-masochism obviously held for him. His self-effacing style powerfully confirms the Foucauldian axiom that the methods of disciplinary power, in order to operate successfully, require (and therefore impose) discretion; they cannot survive their own theatricalization.[87] Perhaps, as D. A. Miller has written elsewhere, "only an ostentation of style and argument can provide the 'flash' of increased visibility needed to render modern discipline a problem in its own right far more fundamental than any it invents to attach its subjects."[88]

▼ ▼ ▼ ▼ ▼ ▼ ▼ ▼

IN ANY EVENT, James Miller's book spares its readers the necessity that Barthesian theory supposedly enjoins: both the author's ass and ours remain firmly, safely, out of sight. We can consume Miller's tale in the complete security of unshaken prior attitudes about sexual politics. Miller advertises his book to us as a mind-altering voyage into uncharted and forbidden territory: he is going to recount Foucault's life, he tells us, "in *all* of its philosophical dimensions, however shocking some of these may seem"; his aim is to "put us in touch with what is most singular—and perhaps most disquieting—about [Foucault's] work" (8–9; Miller's emphasis). That perilous adventure ultimately turns out, however, to be tourism of a tamer sort, rather as if it were a daytime, air-conditioned bus tour of the Castro:[89] it titillates us with imagined spectacles of the illicit while confirming us in the comfort of traditional pieties.

The final point of interest in this ethnographic excursion is its powerful dramatization of what can be made to count as the "truth" about a gay subject, and in whose eyes. Miller's philosophical biography represents a textbook example of what Foucault objected to about "the politics of truth."[90] As Foucault once put it, "True discourse, which the necessity of its form raises above desire and liberates from power, cannot recognize the will to truth that pervades it; and the will to truth, having imposed itself upon us for so long, is such that the truth it wills cannot fail to mask it."[91] "Truth," then, is not the opposite of error; like "the author," or "man," "truth" is a discursive strategy that (among other things) blocks inquiry into the conditions—dynamic and erotic—of its own production; it enables both the exercise of power and the play of desire in discourse to disappear from view. It thereby forecloses what, for many subaltern peoples, are the most pressing political questions to ask of any discourse about us that presents itself as true: Who desires this truth, and why? Who gets to tell it? To whom? For what purpose? With what power-effects? In ways that implicate what other practices or fields of activity? The reason such questions are pressing is that "truth" confers power on those who can claim access to it: it licenses "experts" to describe and objectify people's lives, especially the lives of those who, for whatever reason, happen to find themselves most fully exposed to the operations of disciplinary power. And it licenses such experts to write without ever having to answer *to* the subjects of their descriptions *for* the consequences of those descriptions, because their privileged access to truth enables their power to manifest itself entirely in the guise of a legitimate authority that has no need of further justification. The example of James Miller's book demonstrates with particular vividness, then, why it is that whenever those of us who feel ourselves to be in Foucault's embattled position, or who share his political vision, hear those who aren't, or who don't, invoke the notion of "truth," we reach for our revolvers.

▲ ▲ ▲ ▲ ▲ ▲ ▲ ▲

Notes

Saint Foucault

1. Richard D. Mohr, *Gay Ideas: Outing and Other Controversies* (Boston: Beacon Press, 1992), 221–22.

2. Mohr, *Gay Ideas*, 287 n. 2. Mohr's characterization of my book was inspired—as his quotations from it in that note indicate—by a remark I made in the introduction while reviewing the existing scholarly literature on the subject of sex in ancient Greece. Foucault, I said, took up the theoretical dimension of the history of sexuality as it pertained to ancient Greece "with characteristic brilliance and matchless penetration" (*One Hundred Years of Homosexuality and Other Essays on Greek Love* [New York: Routledge, 1990], 5–6). Not only do I stand by that remark, I consider the judgment contained in it to be both an obvious one and no very great compliment to Foucault: anyone who surveys the pre-1988 classical scholarship on sex from a theoretical perspective will, I believe, all too readily assent to it. Mohr goes on to criticize in some detail a number of the views advanced in my book, but his criticisms lie outside the scope of the present discussion. I hope to address them in a future essay on the reception of my book.

For another example of an attempt to forge a mutually incriminating linkage among Foucault's work, my book, social construction theory, and the current practice of lesbian and gay studies, see Bruce Bawer, *A Place at the Table: The Gay Individual in American Society* (New York: Poseidon Press, 1993), 211–12.

3. In addition to the three points discussed below, let me mention two other respects in which Mohr's characterization of social construction is mistaken. First, the social construction of sexuality applies to heterosexuality every bit as much as it applies to homosexuality; social constructionists do not presume that only homosexuality is constituted culturally or that heterosexuality, by contrast, is constituted naturally. To insinuate that social construction naturalizes heterosexuality but reduces lesbian and gay existence to an accident or artifact of culture is therefore to misrepresent social construction. Second, social construction is not, *pace* Mohr, merely a "variant of cultural determinism." To say that sexuality is constructed is not to say that it is fully determined but only that it is subject to certain constraints. Social constructions are not sufficient to determine personal behavior in any given context; rather, they permit a considerable degree of individual improvisation. To conflate construction with determinism is to make a basic conceptual error. On this point see Judith Butler, *Gender Trouble: Feminism and the Subversion of Identity* (New York: Routledge, 1990), esp. 8–9, 147. (To be fair, I should acknowledge that the distinction I am making here had entirely escaped me when I wrote *One Hundred Years of Homosexuality* [see esp. 40]: I confused construction with determinism exactly as Mohr does. At that time I did not have the advantage, which Mohr has had, of being acquainted with Butler's work.)

4. See, for example, Michel Foucault, "Des caresses d'hommes considérées comme un art," *Libération*, June 1, 1982, 27:

> Bien sûr, on trouvera encore des esprits aimables pour penser qu'en somme l'homosexualité a toujours existé. . . . A de tels naïfs, Dover donne une bonne leçon de nominalisme historique. Le rapport entre deux individus du même sexe est une chose. Mais aimer le même sexe que soi, prendre avec lui un plaisir, c'est autre chose, c'est toute une expérience, avec ses objets et leurs valeurs, avec la manière d'être du sujet et la conscience qu'il a de lui-même. Cette expérience est complexe, elle est diverse, elle change de formes. (Of course, there will still be some folks disposed to think that, in the final analysis, homosexuality has always existed. . . . To such naive souls [K. J.] Dover [in his book *Greek Homosexuality* (1978)] gives a good lesson in historical nominalism. [Sexual] relations between two persons of the same sex is one thing. But to love the same sex as oneself, to take one's pleasure in that sex, is quite another thing, it's a whole experience, with its own objects and their meanings, with a specific way of life and a consciousness on the lover's part. That experience is complex, it is diverse, it takes different forms.)

5. Michel Foucault, *The History of Sexuality. Volume I: An Introduction*, trans. Robert Hurley (New York: Pantheon, 1978), 69.

6. To be sure, a frequently quoted passage from the first volume of Foucault's *History of Sexuality* produces a misleading impression in this respect: "Sexuality," it reads, ". . . is the name that can be given to a historical construct." (Foucault, *The History of Sexuality, Volume I*, 105; see Michel Foucault, *La Volonté de savoir*, Histoire de la sexualité, 1 [Paris: Gallimard, 1976], 139). In fact, the constructionist idiom employed here originates not with Foucault but with his English translator, Robert Hurley; Foucault's own term of choice is *dispositif*, which means something very different from "construct" and which Hurley confusingly translates elsewhere in the same volume as "deployment" (the most apt English equivalent is, in my view, "apparatus"; another possibility is "device"). For more on Foucault's term, see Gilles Deleuze, "What Is a *Dispositif?*" in *Michel Foucault: Philosopher*, ed. and trans. Timothy J. Armstrong (New York: Routledge, 1992), 159–68; see also David Macey, *The Lives of Michel Foucault* (London: Hutchinson, 1993), 355, who summarizes Foucault's own explication of the meaning of *dispositif* as follows: "The term refers to a heterogeneous body of discourses, propositions (philosophical, moral, philanthropic and so on), institutions, laws and scientific statements; the *dispositif* itself is the network that binds them together, that governs the play between the heterogeneous strands. *It is a formation which, at a given historical moment, corresponds to a dominant strategic function.* . . . " (my emphasis; Macey bases this definition on Foucault's statements in an interview entitled "Le Jeu de Michel Foucault," *Ornicar?* 10 [July 1977], 62–93, esp. 63, 65).

7. See "Sexual Choice, Sexual Act: An Interview with Michel Foucault," in *Politics, Philosophy, Culture: Interviews and Other Writings, 1977–1984*, ed. Lawrence D. Kritzman (New York: Routledge, 1988), 286–303 (quotation on p. 288). This interview originally appeared in *Homosexuality: Sacrilege, Vision, Politics*, ed. Robert Boyers and George Steiner, *Salmagundi* [special issue] 58–59 (1982–83), 10–24, and was reprinted in *Foucault Live (Interviews, 1966–84)*, ed. Sylvère Lotringer (New York: Semiotext(e), 1989), 211–32.

8. See my review "Sexual Ethics and Technologies of the Self in Classical Greece," *American Journal of Philology* 107 (1986), 274–86 (quotation on p. 277); *One Hundred Years of Homosexuality*, 64. The sentence is quoted approvingly by James Grantham Turner, ed., *Sexuality and Gender in Early Modern Europe: Institutions, Texts, Images* (Cambridge: Cambridge University Press, 1993), xvi; the terms of his approval, however, indicate something of my reasons for wishing to retract the statement.

9. See, for example, Camille Paglia, "Junk Bonds and Corporate

Raiders: Academe in the Hour of the Wolf," *Arion*, 3rd ser. 1.2 (Spring 1991), 139–212; reprinted in Paglia, *Sex, Art, and American Culture* (New York: Vintage, 1992), 170–248; Mohr, "The Thing of It Is: Some Problems with Models for the Social Construction of Homosexuality," in *Gay Ideas*, 221–42, 285–97; Bawer, *A Place at the Table*, 211; see also Bruce Thornton, "Constructionism and Ancient Greek Sex," *Helios* 18.2 (Autumn 1991), 181–93; Thornton, "Idolon Theatri: Foucault and the Classicists," *Classical and Modern Literature* 12.1 (Fall 1991), 81–100; Micaela Janan, review of *One Hundred Years of Homosexuality* in *Women's Classical Caucus Newsletter* 17 (1991), 40–43; Amy Richlin, review of *One Hundred Years of Homosexuality* in *Bryn Mawr Classical Review* 2.1 (1991), 17–18; Richlin, "Zeus and Metis: Foucault, Feminism, Classics," *Helios* 18.2 (Autumn 1991), 160–80; Richlin, "Not Before Homosexuality: The Materiality of the *Cinaedus* and the Roman Law Against Love Between Men," *Journal of the History of Sexuality* 3.4 (April 1993), 523–73; Judith P. Hallett, "Ancient Greek and Roman Constructions of Sexuality: The State of the Debate," lecture delivered at "Sexualities, Dissidence, and Cultural Change: A Symposium," University of Maryland at College Park, April 10, 1992.

For an excellent general overview and political analysis of recent phobic constructions of Foucault in the United States, see Roddey Reid, "Foucault en Amérique: Biographème et Kulturkampf," *Futur antérieur* 23–24 (1994), 133–65.

10. I adopt Eve Kosofsky Sedgwick's formulation in *Epistemology of the Closet* (Berkeley: University of California Press, 1990), 232.

11. The only other time I had the same experience, it proved to be transformative for my understanding of the topic; see my essay "Why Is Diotima a Woman?" in *One Hundred Years of Homosexuality*, 113–51, 190–211.

12. *Cynthia Griffin Wolff, Plaintiff* v. *Massachusetts Institute of Technology, Defendant*, Commonwealth of Massachusetts Superior Court, Department of the Trial Court, Civil Action No. 92-2430 (April 7, 1992), 1, 7, 13–14 (emphasis not in original, needless to say).

13. Fox Butterfield, "Suit Depicts Fight on M.I.T. Faculty: Literature Professor Asserts Promotions Were Tied to Sexual Preferences," *New York Times*, May 5, 1992, A19.

14. Avik S. Roy and Max Morris, "Behind Closed Doors," *Counterpoint* 2.3 (June 1992), 8–11, 23 (quotation on p. 10).

15. Martha Nussbaum, "The Softness of Reason," *The New Repub-*

lic 207.3–4, July 13 and 20, 1992, 26–27, 30, 32, 34–35; for further details see "Character Studies" (Correspondence), *The New Republic* 207.11–12, September 7 and 14, 1992, 4.

16. Such a complaint, based on a reading of the manuscript of this book, has in fact already been made by Didier Eribon, *Michel Foucault et ses contemporains* (Paris: Fayard, 1994), 11, 51–57. For a more wide-ranging exploration of some of the issues pursued here, see Geoffrey Galt Harpham, " Saint Foucault," *The Ascetic Imperative in Culture and Criticism* (Chicago: University of Chicago Press, 1987), 220–35, 292–95.

The Queer Politics of Michel Foucault

For valuable advice, criticism, and discussion, I am indebted to Douglas Crimp, Arnold Davidson, Lee Edelman, Didier Eribon, Jody Greene, Morris Kaplan, James Miller, Paul Morrison, and Jana Sawicki.

1. "Le pouvoir est partout." Michel Foucault, *La Volonté de savoir*, Histoire de la sexualité, 1 (Paris: Gallimard, 1976), 122; Michel Foucault, *The History of Sexuality, Volume I: An Introduction*, trans. Robert Hurley (New York: Pantheon, 1978), 93, and see, generally, 92–96 (as a general principle, my quotations of Foucault follow the published translations as closely as possible, but I depart from them where necessary). Foucault hastens to explain, in the same passage, that "power is everywhere, not because it surrounds and engulfs everything but because it comes from everywhere," and in a late interview he added, "[I]f there are relations of power throughout every social field it is because there is freedom everywhere. . . . One cannot impute to me the idea that power is a system of domination which controls everything and which leaves no room for freedom." Raul Fornet-Betancourt et al., "The Ethic of Care for the Self as a Practice of Freedom: An Interview with Michel Foucault on January 20, 1984," trans. J. D. Gauthier, *Philosophy and Social Criticism* 12.2–3 (Summer 1987), 112–31 (quotation on pp. 123–24). For my account of Foucault's reception, especially by literary critics and theorists, I am deeply indebted to Mark Maslan, "Foucault and Pragmatism," *Raritan* 7.3 (Winter 1988), 94–114, and to subsequent discussions with the author.

2. Michel Foucault, *Surveiller et punir: Naissance de la prison* (Paris: Gallimard, 1975), 31–32 (*Discipline and Punish: The Birth of* *the Prison,* trans. Alan Sheridan [New York: Pantheon, 1978], 26–27); *La Volonté de savoir,* 121–28 (*The History of Sexuality, Volume I,* 92–97); Jacques Rancière, "Pouvoirs et stratégies: Entretien avec Michel Foucault," *Révoltes logiques* 4 (Winter 1977), 89–97 (Foucault, "Powers and Strategies," in *Power/Knowledge: Selected Interviews and Other Writings, 1972–1977,* ed. Colin Gordon [New York: Pantheon, 1980], 134–45, esp. 140); Fornet-Betancourt et al., "The Ethic of Care for the Self as a Practice of Freedom," 122–24.

3. Foucault, *La Volonté de savoir,* 121–24, esp. 124: "Le pouvoir vient d'en bas" (*The History of Sexuality, Volume I,* 92–94, esp. 94). See, generally, Foucault, *The History of Sexuality, Volume I,* 10–12, 27; Foucault, "Powers and Strategies," 139–42; Fornet-Betancourt et al., "The Ethic of Care for the Self as a Practice of Freedom," 114–15, 122–24.

4. Foucault, *Surveiller et punir,* 196, 218–19 (*Discipline and Punish,* 194, 217); *The History of Sexuality, Volume I,* passim; "Truth and Power," in *Power/Knowledge,* 109–33, esp. 119; "Powers and Strategies," 139–40; "The Subject and Power," in Hubert L. Dreyfus and Paul Rabinow, *Michel Foucault: Beyond Structuralism and Hermeneutics,* 2nd ed. (Chicago: University of Chicago Press, 1983), 208–26, esp. 221–22. As Ed Cohen puts it ("Foucauldian Necrologies: 'Gay' 'Politics'? Politically Gay?" *Textual Practice* 2.1 [Spring 1988], 87–101), "[Foucault] offers a more continuous notion of change which never escapes the fields of power, never longs for the freedom promised by rupture, but rather seeks spaces of creative possibility within the present"(93).

5. Bob Gallagher and Alexander Wilson, "Michel Foucault. An Interview: Sex, Power and the Politics of Identity," *The Advocate* 400, August 7, 1984, 26–30, 58 (quotation on p. 29; see, generally, 28–29); Bernard-Henri Lévy, "Foucault: Non au sexe roi," *Le Nouvel Observateur,* March 12, 1977, 92–93, 95, 98, 100, 105, 113, 124, 130, esp. 124; Fornet-Betancourt et al., "The Ethic of Care for the Self as a Practice of Freedom," 123–24; Rancière, "Pouvoirs et stratégies":

> [Je suggererais] qu'il n'y a pas de relations de pouvoir sans résistances: que celles-ci sont d'autant plus réelles et plus efficaces qu'elles se forment là où s'exercent les relations de pouvoir; la résistance au pouvoir n'a pas à venir d'ailleurs pour être réelle, mais elle n'est pas piégée parce qu'elle est la compatriote du pouvoir. Elle existe d'autant plus qu'elle est là où est le pouvoir; elle est donc comme lui multiple et intégrable à des stratégies glob-

ales. . . . Mais il y a bien toujours quelque chose, dans le corps
social, dans les classes, dans les groupes, dans les individus eux-
mêmes qui échappe d'une certaine façon aux relations de pouvoir. . . . C'est moins l'extérieur par rapport aux relations de
pouvoir que leur limite, leur envers, leur contre-coup. . . . (95, 92;
"Powers and Strategies," 142, 137–38)

See, generally, Foucault, *La Volonté de savoir*, 125–27 (*The History of
Sexuality, Volume I*, 95–96).

6. See Gallagher and Wilson, "Michel Foucault," 29.

7. See especially Michel Foucault, "Politics and Reason" (a version of "*Omnes et Singulatim*: Towards a Criticism of Political Reason," Foucault's Tanner Lectures on Human Values, delivered at
Stanford University in October 1979), in *Politics, Philosophy, Culture:
Interviews and Other Writings, 1977–1984*, ed. Lawrence D. Kritzman
(New York: Routledge, 1988), 57–85, esp. 83–84; Foucault, "The Subject
and Power," 209, 219–24; Fornet-Betancourt et al., "The Ethic of Care
for the Self as a Practice of Freedom," 123–24. The point I am making
here is not an original one; it has been well made, for example, by
Mark Maslan, "Foucault and Pragmatism."

8. Leo Bersani, "The Gay Daddy," *Homos* (Cambridge, Mass.: Harvard University Press, 1995), 77–112 (quotation on p. 81).

9. See Fornet-Betancourt et al., "The Ethic of Care for the Self as
a Practice of Freedom," 113–14, where Foucault explains his objections to sexual liberation as a political strategy in the course of ex-
pounding a larger distinction between "liberation," on the one hand,
and "practices of freedom," on the other.

> I've always been a little distrustful of the general theme of lib-
> eration. . . . I do not mean to say that liberation or such and such
> a form of liberation does not exist. When a colonial people tries
> to free itself of its colonizer, that is truly an act of liberation, in
> the strict sense of the word. But as we also know, . . . this act of
> liberation is not sufficient to establish the practices of liberty that
> later on will be necessary for this people. . . . That is why I insist
> on the practices of freedom rather than on the processes [of lib-
> eration] which indeed have their place, but which by themselves,
> do not seem to me to be able to decide all the practical forms of
> liberty. I encountered that exact same problem in dealing with
> sexuality: does the expression "let us liberate our sexuality" have
> a meaning? Isn't the problem rather to try to decide the practices

of freedom through which we could determine what is sexual pleasure and what are our erotic, loving, passionate relationships with others?

10. Edward W. Said, *The World, the Text, and the Critic* (Cambridge, Mass.: Harvard University Press, 1983), 245–46.

11. Peter Dews, "Power and Subjectivity in Foucault," *New Left Review* 144 (March–April 1984), 72–95 (quotation on pp. 92, 94–95).

12. Charles Taylor, "Foucault on Freedom and Truth," in *Foucault: A Critical Reader*, ed. David Couzens Hoy (Oxford: Basil Blackwell, 1986), 69–102 (quotation on pp. 92, 94; emphasis in original). The article originally appeared in *Political Theory* 12 (May 1984), 152–83.

13. Frank Lentricchia, "Reading Foucault (Punishment, Labor, Resistance)," *Raritan* 1.4 (Spring 1982), 5–32, and 2.1 (Summer 1982), 41–70 (quotation on pp. 51–52).

14. Qtd. in David Macey, *The Lives of Michel Foucault* (London: Hutchinson, 1993), 431, citing Habermas, "Modernity Versus Post-Modernity," *New German Critique* 22 (Winter 1981), 3–14 (quotation on p. 13).

15. Keith Gandal, "Michel Foucault: Intellectual Work and Politics," *Telos* 67 (Spring 1986), 121–34; Maslan, "Foucault and Pragmatism"; Cohen, "Foucauldian Necrologies"; Judith Butler, "Contingent Foundations: Feminism and the Question of 'Postmodernism,'" in *Feminists Theorize the Political*, ed. Judith Butler and Joan W. Scott (New York: Routledge, 1992), 3–21, esp. 12–15; Joseph Rouse, "Power/Knowledge," in *The Cambridge Companion to Foucault*, ed. Gary Gutting (Cambridge: Cambridge University Press, 1994), 92–114.

16. For a brief history of the political activities of ACT UP/New York, see Douglas Crimp, with Adam Rolston, *AIDS DemoGraphics* (Seattle: Bay Press, 1990).

17. Qtd. in Didier Eribon, *Michel Foucault*, trans. Betsy Wing (Cambridge, Mass.: Harvard University Press, 1991), 265.

18. See Macey, *The Lives of Michel Foucault*, 257, 290, 446–48.

19. Richard Rorty, "Foucault and Epistemology," in *Foucault: A Critical Reader*, 41–49 (quotation on p. 47).

20. Macey, *The Lives of Michel Foucault*, 431.

21. Michel Foucault, *Remarks on Marx: Conversations with Duccio Trombadori*, trans. R. James Goldstein and James Cascaito (New York: Semiotext(e), 1991), 37–39.

22. See, for example, Foucault, "The Subject and Power," 211–12; see also Foucault, "What Is Enlightenment?" in *The Foucault Reader,* ed. Paul Rabinow (New York: Pantheon, 1984), 32–50, esp. 46–47; Gallagher and Wilson, "Michel Foucault," 58.

23. I wish to thank Michael Warner for this observation about the mediated character of Foucault's influence on contemporary activists.

24. Perhaps this is the place to say that it is not my aim here to reduce the complexity of Foucault's thought to its utility for gay activists or to uncover the buried gay content in Foucault's texts that supposedly accounts for their distinctive features (cf. Jerrold Seigel, "Avoiding the Subject: A Foucaultian Itinerary," *Journal of the History of Ideas* 51 [April 1990], 273–99). I simply wish to use some aspects of Foucault's reception as a starting point for further inquiry into the political dimensions of his work. I have been much aided in my thinking on this topic by the incisive analyses of Mark Maslan, "Foucault and Pragmatism"; Ed Cohen, "Foucauldian Necrologies"; and Arnold I. Davidson, "Ethics as Ascetics: Foucault, the History of Ethics, and Ancient Thought," in *Foucault and the Writing of History*, ed. Jan Goldstein (Oxford: Basil Blackwell, 1994), 63–80, 266–71. I owe a considerable intellectual debt to all three of these writers, as anyone who consults their texts will immediately see.

25. Foucault, *La Volonté de savoir*, 136. Hurley translates *point de passage*—in what has since become a canonical formulation—as "transfer point" (*The History of Sexuality, Volume I*, 103), but Foucault's image has less to do with switching from one line to another than it does with forced routing through a single point.

26. I certainly don't mean to imply that the politics of gender, race, and class do not also determine in large measure the scope of the AIDS crisis: they all too obviously do. But however complex the politics of AIDS may be, we should not ignore or underrate the element of homophobia that pervades and shapes virtually every dimension of it. On this point see Leo Bersani, "Is the Rectum a Grave?" in *AIDS: Cultural Analysis/Cultural Activism*, ed. Douglas Crimp, *October* [special issue] 43 (Winter 1987), 197–222; Simon Watney, "The Spectacle of AIDS," in *AIDS: Cultural Analysis/Cultural Activism*, 71–86 (reprinted in *The Lesbian and Gay Studies Reader*, ed. Henry Abelove, Michèle Aina Barale, and David M. Halperin [New York: Routledge, 1993], 202–11); and D. A. Miller, "Sontag's Urbanity," *October* 49 (Summer 1989), 91–101 (reprinted in *The Lesbian and Gay Studies Reader*, 212–20).

27. Foucault, *The History of Sexuality, Volume I*, 98.

28. See Thomas Yingling, "AIDS in America: Postmodern Governance, Identity, and Experience," in *Inside/Out: Lesbian Theories, Gay Theories*, ed. Diana Fuss (New York: Routledge, 1991), 291–310, esp. 296.

29. W. H. Auden, "Canzone," lines 1–2, in *Collected Poems*, ed. Edward Mendelson (New York: Random House, 1976), 256–57 (quotation on p. 256).

30. See Esther Newton, *Mother Camp: Female Impersonators in America* (Englewood Cliffs, N.J.: Prentice-Hall, 1972), esp. 104–11; most recently, David Bergman, ed., *Camp Grounds: Style and Homosexuality* (Amherst: University of Massachusetts Press, 1993), and Moe Meyer, ed., *The Politics and Poetics of Camp* (London: Routledge, 1994). For an early understanding of camp as a mode of resistance, see Dennis Altman, *Homosexual: Oppression and Liberation* (1971; reprint, New York: New York University Press, 1993), 150–51, who quotes an article by Mike Silverstein, "God Save the Queen," from *Gay Sunshine* (November 1970), to the effect that "camp is . . . a guerilla attack on the whole system of male-female roles. . . . "

31. I wish to thank Gabriel Gomez for bringing this point to my attention.

32. On this point see D. A. Miller, *The Novel and the Police* (Berkeley: University of California Press, 1988), 206; "Anal *Rope*," *Representations* 32 (Fall 1990), 114–33; reprinted in *Inside/Out*, 118–41, esp. 131–32.

33. See, for example, Ann Pellegrini, "Classics and Closets," *Women's Review of Books* 11.5 (February 1994), 11–12, who describes what it is like for a graduate teaching assistant to come out to a class of undergraduates at Harvard. Compare D. A. Miller, *Bringing Out Roland Barthes* (Berkeley: University of California Press, 1992), 23–24, commenting on a passage by Barthes:

> "To proclaim yourself something is always to speak at the behest of a vengeful Other, to enter into his discourse, to argue with him, to seek from him a scrap of identity. 'You are . . .' 'Yes, I am . . .' Ultimately, the attribute is of no importance; what society will

not tolerate is that I should be . . . *nothing*, or that the something that I am should be openly expressed as provisional, revocable, insignificant, inessential, in a word, irrelevant. Just say, 'I am,' and you will be socially saved." [Thus far Barthes. Miller glosses the text as follows.] The quasi-paranoid mistrust finds its warrant in the undeniable fact that, as a general social designation, the term *gay* serves a mainly administrative function, whether what is being administered is an insurance company, a marketing campaign, a love life, or a well-orchestrated liberal dinner party—as a result of which, even men on whom the overall effect of coming out has been empowering will sometimes also have to submit to being mortified by their membership in a denomination that general social usage treats, as though there were nothing else to say about them, or nothing else to hear them say, with all the finality of a verdict.

34. See Foucault, *The History of Sexuality, Volume I*, 68–69:

The "economy" of discourses—their intrinsic technology, the necessities of their operation, the tactics they employ, the effects of power which underlie them and which they transmit—this, and not a system of representations, is what determines the essential features of what they have to say. The history of sexuality—that is, the history of what functioned in the nineteenth century as a specific domain of truth—must first be written from the viewpoint of a history of discourses.

Cf. also p. 73: "As far as sexuality is concerned, we shall attempt to constitute the 'political economy' of a will to knowledge."

35. See Michel Foucault, *The Birth of the Clinic: An Archaeology of Medical Perception*, trans. A. M. Sheridan Smith (London: Tavistock, 1973), xix: "I should like to make it plain once and for all that this book has not been written in favour of one kind of medicine as against another kind of medicine, or against medicine and in favour of an absence of medicine. It is a structural study that sets out to disentangle the conditions of its history from the density of discourse, as do others of my works."

36. See Foucault, *The History of Sexuality, Volume I*, 98:

One must not suppose that there exists a certain sphere of sexuality that would be the legitimate concern of a free and disinterested scientific inquiry were it not the object of mechanisms of prohibition brought to bear by the economic or ideological requirements of power. If sexuality was constituted as an area of investigation, this was only because relations of power had established it as a possible object; and conversely, if power was able to take it as a target, this was because techniques of knowledge and procedures of discourse were capable of investing it.

37. It has proven profitable for the analysis of other sorts of discourse as well. Let's take the example of abortion discourse. The substantive questions facing polemicists at the moment—whether or not abortion is murder, whether it is right or wrong, when life begins—are not necessarily stupid or irrelevant questions; nor can the answers to them be determined *in principle* by inquiring into the political economy of abortion discourse—by asking, that is, who poses those questions, in what contexts, with what effects, by virtue of what authority, and with what tactical relation to strategic forces manifest in other contested domains of sex, gender, and reproduction. But so long as we continue to be mesmerized by such questions as whether abortion is right or wrong, so long as we continue to accord such questions priority in the debate over legalized abortion, and so long as we continue to assume that the answers to such questions, once we arrive at them, will determine the outcome of that debate (or that one's personal position on legalized abortion ought to be determined by how one has answered those questions in one's mind), we shall be prevented from seeing that what is at stake in this controversy is not only the philosophical question about the rightness or wrongness of abortion but the political question about who controls women's bodies.

To put the matter more forcefully: so long as we insist on obtaining an answer to the most pressing ethical question to do with abortion (whether abortion is murder) *before* we can resolve the policy question about the legalization of abortion, because we believe that only a correct solution to the ethical problem can authorize us to adjudicate correctly the claims of the various "interested" parties to the dispute— so long, in short, as we grant ethics priority over politics—the perhaps equally pressing political question about who controls women's bodies will never be able to get asked. To refuse to allow questions of truth to distract us from questions of politics is not to claim that questions of truth are logically secondary to questions of politics or that they can be settled by political considerations: it is a purely strategic move, a way of shifting the ground of the argument. The point is not that the truth of the matter has or should have no bearing on politics. The point is rather that granting matters of truth precedence over politics is itself a political strategy that may need to be resisted.

Thus, the ethics of abortion can be understood as a philosophical distraction from the political struggle over who gets to make reproductive decisions for women. That is another way of saying that one effect of the strategic decision to shift the ground of argument from matters of truth to matters of power is to settle ethical disagreements pragmatically, not substantively. The question regarding when life begins is not answered in principle by legally permitting abortions to be performed during the first trimester of a pregnancy, for example, but when first-trimester abortions are legalized, the question of when life begins is settled publicly and de facto for all practical purposes. The difficulty of reconciling the views of pro- and antiabortionists may therefore have less to do with substantive disagreements between them than with the way each side deploys its arguments strategically in order to delegitimate (rather than to refute) the claims of the other.

38. Qtd. in James Miller, *The Passion of Michel Foucault* (New York: Simon & Schuster, 1993), 253–54.

39. National Gay and Lesbian Task Force Policy Institute, *Anti-Gay/Lesbian Violence, Victimization & Defamation in 1992* (Washington, D.C.: NGLTF Policy Institute, 1993). The most recent data, for 1993, show a 14 percent decrease in the total number of reported antigay incidents: see National Gay and Lesbian Task Force Policy Institute, *Anti-Gay/Lesbian Violence, Victimization, & Defamation in 1993* (Washington, D.C.: NGLTF Policy Institute, 1994).

40. See Lee Edelman, "Throwing Up/Going Down: *Bushusuru*; or, The Fall of the West," *Homographesis: Essays in Gay Literary and Cultural Theory* (New York: Routledge, 1994), 138–47, esp. 142, emphasizing "the energies of containment [of homosexual meaning] that are central to the dominant representational regime that micromanages perception from moment to moment in everyday life."

41. See Janet E. Halley, "Misreading Sodomy: A Critique of the Classification of 'Homosexuals' in Federal Equal Protection Law," in *Body Guards: The Cultural Politics of Gender Ambiguity*, ed. Julia Epstein and Kristina Straub (New York: Routledge, 1991), 351–77; see also Janet E. Halley, "The Construction of Heterosexuality," in *Fear of* a *Queer Planet: Queer Politics and Social Theory*, ed. Michael Warner (Minneapolis: University of Minnesota Press, 1993), 82–102, esp. 93–94.

42. Eve Kosofsky Sedgwick, *Epistemology of the Closet* (Berkeley: University of California Press, 1990).

43. The characterization of the sexuality of the nineteenth-century homosexual as "a secret that always gave itself away" is, of course, Foucault's: see *The History of Sexuality, Volume I*, 43. For an example of the heterosexist tactic of imposing secrecy on a homosexual's sexuality, all the better to expose it, see George Steiner's comments on Foucault's death in *The New Yorker*, March 17, 1986, 105: "Certain enforced secrecies and evasions veiled his personal existence. This obsessive inquirer into disease and sexuality—into the mind's constructs of Eros and into the effects of such constructs on the body politic and on the individual flesh—was done to death by the most hideous and symbolically charged of current diseases [*sic*]." As Ed Cohen, who quotes this vengeful passage ("Foucauldian Necrologies," 99 n. 12), remarks, Steiner's own veiled allusions to the supposedly well-guarded but transparent secret of Foucault's homosexuality are particularly curious inasmuch as Steiner had published, only four years earlier, in a volume that Steiner himself had coedited, a lengthy interview with Foucault devoted to the topic of homosexuality, a topic which Foucault had addressed from the perspective of an openly gay man: "Sexual Choice, Sexual Act: An Interview with Michel Foucault," in *Homosexuality: Sacrilege, Vision, Politics*, ed. Robert Boyers and George Steiner, *Salmagundi* [special issue] 58–59 (1982–83), 10–24; reprinted in *Foucault Live (Interviews 1966-84)*, ed. Sylvère Lotringer (New York: Semiotext(e), 1989), 211–32, and in *Politics, Philosophy, Culture*, 286–303.

44. On urbanity as a homophobic tactic, see the brilliant analysis by D. A. Miller, "Sontag's Urbanity," *The Lesbian and Gay Studies Reader*, esp. 215.

45. Sedgwick, *Epistemology of the Closet*, 69–70.

46. Foucault, *The History of Sexuality, Volume I*, 27; Sedgwick, *Epistemology of the Closet*, 3.

47. Michel Foucault, *Madness and Civilization: A History of Insanity in the Age of Reason*, trans. Richard Howard (New York: Pantheon, 1965), x–xi (emphasis in original).

48. Qtd. in Macey, *The Lives of Michel Foucault*, 114–15.

49. See Foucault, *Remarks on Marx*, 63–65, esp. 65:

> To the construction of the object madness, there corresponded a rational subject who "knew" about madness and who understood it. In *The History of Madness* I tried to understand this kind of collective, plural experience which was defined between the sixteenth and nineteenth centuries and which was marked by the interaction between the birth of "rational" man who recognizes and "knows" madness, and madness itself as an object susceptible of being understood and determined.

50. Roland Barthes, "Savoir et folie," *Critique*, no. 17 (1961), 915–22; reprinted in Barthes, *Essais critiques* (Paris: Seuil, 1964): qtd. in Eribon, *Michel Foucault*, 117.

51. Michel Serres, "Géométrie de la folie," *Le Mercure de France* (August 1962), 682–96; (September 1962), 62–81: qtd. in Macey, *The Lives of Michel Foucault*, 117.

52. Foucault, *The History of Sexuality, Volume I*, 105.

53. Ibid., 68.

54. See D. A. Miller, "The Late Jane Austen," *Raritan* 10.1 (Summer 1990), 55–79, esp. 57: "All the deployments of the 'bio-power' that characterizes our modernity depend on the supposition that the most effective take on the subject is rooted in its body, insinuated within this body's 'naturally given' imperatives. Metaphorizing the body begins and ends with literalizing the meanings the body is thus made to bear."

55. "comme domaine de vérité spécifique": *La Volonté de savoir*, 92; cf. *The History of Sexuality, Volume I*, 69.

56. Foucault, *The History of Sexuality, Volume I*, 69.

57. For a critical history of sexology as a science, see Janice M. Irvine, *Disorders of Desire: Sex and Gender in Modern American Sexology* (Philadelphia: Temple University Press, 1990).

58. Foucault's emphasis is unfortunately lost on Anglophone readers, because his English translator Robert Hurley renders *dispositif* in the title of Part IV of *The History of Sexuality, Volume I*, as "deployment" but elsewhere (including a much-quoted passage on page 105, quoted later) as "construct." See note 6 to "Saint Foucault."

59. Foucault, *The History of Sexuality, Volume I*, 105–6.

60. Ibid., 139–45.

61. Foucault, *La Volonté de savoir*, 168; cf. *The History of Sexuality, Volume I*, 127.

62. For an early appreciation of the political usefulness of Foucault, see the characteristically prescient remarks by Gayle Rubin, "Thinking Sex: Notes for a Radical Theory of the Politics of Sexuality," in *Pleasure and Danger: Exploring Female Sexuality*, ed. Carole S. Vance (Boston: Routledge and Kegan Paul, 1984), 267–319, esp. 276–78, 284–88; reprinted, with revisions, in *The Lesbian and Gay Studies Reader*, 3–44, esp. 10–11, 16–19.

63. A. M. Krich, ed., *The Homosexuals: As Seen by Themselves and Thirty Authorities* (1954; 6th paperback ed., New York: The Citadel Press, 1968). The book's cover adds the following notation: "A comprehensive, revealing inquiry into the cause and cure of homoerotic manifestations in men and women with *case histories* and *autobiographical accounts*."

64. Ray B. Evans, "Physical and Biochemical Characteristics of Homosexual Men," *Journal of Consulting and Clinical Psychology* 39.1 (1972), 140–47; Muriel Wilson Perkins, "Female Homosexuality and Body Build," *Archives of Sexual Behavior* 10.4 (1981), 337–45 (I quote from the abstracts of the two articles).

65. E.g., Foucault, *Surveiller et punir*, 311 (*Discipline and Punish*, 304): "the chatter of criminology."

66. "Maurice Florence" (*sc.* Michel Foucault and François Ewald), "Foucault," in *Dictionnaire des philosophes*, ed. Denis Huisman (Paris: Presses Universitaires de France, 1984), 1:942–44; trans. Catherine Porter in *The Cambridge Companion to Foucault*, 314–19, esp. 317:

> [T]o refuse the universals of "madness," "delinquency," or "sexuality" does not mean that these notions refer to nothing at all, nor that they are only chimeras invented in the interest of a dubious cause. . . . [Rather, it] entails wondering about the conditions that make it possible, according to the rules of truth-telling, to recognize a subject as mentally ill or to cause subjects to recognize the most essential part of themselves in the modality of their sexual desire.

Cf. Judith Butler, "Critically Queer," *GLQ* 1 (1993/94), 17–32; reprinted in Judith Butler, *Bodies That Matter: On the Discursive Limits of "Sex"* (New York: Routledge, 1993), 223–42: "My understanding of Foucault's notion of genealogy is that it is a specifically philosophical exercise in exposing and tracing the installation and operation of false universals" (p. 282 n. 8).

67. For distinguished recent examples of this synthesis, see Edelman, *Homographesis*, and Butler, *Bodies That Matter.*

68. Harold Beaver, "Homosexual Signs (*In Memory of Roland Barthes*)," *Critical Inquiry* 8 (1981/82), 99–119, esp. 115–16; Sedgwick, *Epistemology of the Closet*, esp. 9–11; Simon Watney, "Troubleshooters," *Artforum* 30.3 (November 1991), 16–18, esp. 17: "Homosexual identity should thus be understood as a *strategic position that privileges heterosexuality*" (emphasis in original); Halley, "The Construction of Heterosexuality."

69. See, for example, Michael Warner, "Homo-Narcissism; or, Heterosexuality," in *Engendering Men: The Question of Male Feminist Criticism*, ed. Joseph A. Boone and Michael Cadden (New York: Routledge, 1990), 190–206, 313–15; D. A. Miller, "Anal *Rope*"; Lee Edelman, "Tearooms and Sympathy, or, The Epistemology of the Water Closet," in *Nationalisms & Sexualities*, ed. Andrew Parker, Mary Russo, Doris Sommer, and Patricia Yeager (New York: Routledge, 1992), 263–84; reprinted, with revisions, in *The Lesbian and Gay Studies Reader*, 553–74, and in Edelman, *Homographesis*, 148–70.

70. Halley, "Misreading Sodomy," 361.

71. Cf. Jacques Derrida, *The Truth in Painting*, trans. Geoff Bennington and Ian McLeod (Chicago: University of Chicago Press, 1987), esp. 332–35, 373–79, on the strange relations or irrelations among and within the terms *two, the pair, parity, the couple, the double, fetishism, homosexuality, heterosexuality*, and *bisexuality.*

72. Halley, "The Construction of Heterosexuality."

73. Paul Morrison, "End Pleasure," *GLQ* 1 (1993/94), 53–78 (quotation on p. 57).

74. Jonathan Katz, *Gay/Lesbian Almanac: A New Documentary* (New York: Harper and Row, 1983), 147–50; David M. Halperin, *One Hundred Years of Homosexuality* (New York: Routledge, 1990), 17, and 158 n. 17.

75. For an elaboration of this point, see Judith Butler, *Gender Trouble: Feminism and the Subversion of Identity* (New York: Routledge, 1990).

76. I owe this formulation to an unpublished paper by Robert A. Padgug.

77. On the practice concealing and exculpating oneself by accusing others, see Eve Kosofsky Sedgwick's remarks on Proust in *Epistemology of the Closet*, 222–30.

78. The notable exceptions include Sigmund Freud, *Three Essays on the Theory of Sexuality*, especially the famous 1915 footnote to the paragraph on "The Sexual Aim of Inverts" in Section 1a of the first essay: "Thus from the point of view of psycho-analysis the exclusive sexual interest felt by men for women is also a problem that needs elucidating and is not a self-evident fact. . . . " See Freud, *Three Essays on the Theory of Sexuality*, trans. and ed. James Strachey, intro. Steven Marcus (New York: Basic Books, 1975), 12. See also Alfred C. Kinsey, Wardell B. Pomeroy, and Clyde E. Martin, *Sexual Behavior in the Human Male* (Philadelphia: W. B. Saunders, 1948); William H. Masters, *Heterosexuality* (New York: HarperCollins, 1994).

79. The history of the concept of sexual perversion abundantly illustrates this point: see Arnold I. Davidson, "Closing Up the Corpses: Diseases of Sexuality and the Emergence of the Psychiatric Style of Reasoning," in *Meaning and Method: Essays in Honor of Hilary Putnam*, ed. George Boolos (Cambridge: Cambridge University Press, 1990), 295–325, esp. 308–9. See also Halley, "The Construction of Heterosexuality."

80. Paul Morrison, *Sexual Subjects* (New York: Oxford University Press, forthcoming).

81. Natalie Angier, "Zone of Brain Linked to Men's Sexual Orientation," *New York Times*, August 30, 1991, A1.

82. See the cover of *Newsweek* for March 12, 1990: THE FUTURE OF GAY AMERICA. MILITANTS VERSUS THE MAINSTREAM. TESTING THE LIMITS OF TOLERANCE.

83. *Bay Times* 14.20, July 1, 1993, 1.

84. For theatricalization as a mode of resistance, see Paul Morrison, "Coffee Table Sex: Robert Mapplethorpe and the Sadomasochism of Everyday Life," *Genders* 11 (Fall 1991), 17–36.

85. Foucault, *The History of Sexuality, Volume I*, 86. Cf. Lévy, "Foucault: Non au sexe roi," 105.

86. Lévy, "Foucault: Non au sexe roi," 93.

87. Qtd. in Eribon, *Michel Foucault*, 237.

88. Macey, *The Lives of Michel Foucault*, 257; see also 269 and, more generally, 255–82. Cf. Foucault, *Remarks on Marx*, 158–60. For the details of Foucault's political activity within the French educational system, see now Didier Eribon, *Michel Foucault et ses contemporains* (Paris: Fayard, 1994), 185–209.

89. Gallagher and Wilson, "Michel Foucault," 58. Cf. Jean Le Bitoux et al., "De l'amitié comme mode de vie: Un Entretien avec un lecteur quinquagénaire," *Le Gai Pied* 25 (April 1981), 38–39, esp. 39 ("Friendship as a Lifestyle: An Interview with Michel Foucault," *Gay Information*, pp. 4–6; "Friendship as a Way of Life," trans. John Johnston, *Foucault Live*, 203–11); Foucault, *Remarks on Marx*, 157: "I absolutely will not play the part of one who prescribes solutions. I hold that the role of the intellectual today is not that of establishing laws or proposing solutions or prophesying, since by doing that one can only contribute to the functioning of a determinate situation of power that to my mind must be criticized."

90. Foucault, *Remarks on Marx*, 174. See, generally, Eribon, *Michel Foucault et ses contemporains*, 289–311, for a lucid account of Foucault's disagreements with Habermas on this point.

91. See "Polemics, Politics, and Problematizations: An Interview with Michel Foucault," in *The Foucault Reader*, 381–90: responding to Richard Rorty's objection that "[Foucault may not be] saying that you and I are as nothing, but [he does] seem to hint that you and I together, as *we*, aren't much—that human solidarity goes when God and his doubles go" (*Consequences of Pragmatism* [Minneapolis: University of Minnesota Press, 1982], 207)—that, as Foucault himself put Rorty's point, he did not locate political projects within the context of a specific community or interest group "whose consensus, whose values, whose traditions constitute the framework for a thought and define the conditions in which it can be validated," Foucault rejoined, "But the problem is, precisely, to decide if it is actually suitable to place oneself within a 'we' in order to assert the principles one recognizes and the values one accepts; or if it is not, rather, necessary to make the future formation of a 'we' possible, by elaborating the question. Because it seems to me that the 'we' must not be previous to the question; it can only be the result—and the necessarily temporary result—of the question as it is posed in the new terms in which one formulates it" (quotation on p. 385). For an extended commentary on this passage, as well as an application of the notions contained in it to the emerging field of lesbian/gay studies, see Ed Cohen, "Who Are 'We'? Gay 'Identity' as Political (E)motion (A Theoretical Rumination)," in *Inside/Out*, 71–92.

92. Gandal, "Michel Foucault: Intellectual Work and Politics," 122–

24, 129. See also the excellent discussion by James W. Bernauer and Michael Mahon, "The Ethics of Michel Foucault," *The Cambridge Companion to Foucault,* 141–58.

93. Qtd. in Eribon, *Michel Foucault,* 227.

94. Qtd. in Macey, *The Lives of Michel Foucault,* 418.

95. Foucault, *Discipline and Punish,* 26, 308; *The History of Sexuality, Volume I,* 93; "Truth and Power," 123.

96. This theme emerges particularly clearly from the history of the struggle for the psychiatric depathologization of homosexuality; see Ronald Bayer, *Homosexuality and American Psychiatry,* 2nd ed. (Princeton, N.J.: Princeton University Press, 1987); see also Martin Duberman, *Cures: A Gay Man's Odyssey* (New York: Dutton, 1991), esp. 204–5, 267–69, and Duberman, *About Time: Exploring the Gay Past,* rev. ed. (New York: Meridian, 1991), 329–41.

97. It is, obviously enough, no easy or safe thing to speak from the position of a homosexual subject—as the case of *Acanfora* (discussed earlier) makes abundantly clear. Nor is every gay speaking always an expression of resistance: as Foucault himself emphasized, it is in part by producing in us the compulsion to speak the truth about ourselves and our sexuality that power has come to invest modern subjects (*The History of Sexuality, Volume I,* 6–12, 18–35). Nonetheless, there is an important distinction to be made, I think, between the kind of speaking that one does to one's psychiatrist or to the members of one's twelve-step group (not to mention one's parole officer) and the kind of speaking that one does in the course of questioning a representative from the Department of Public Health who has been obliged to explain a new standard of confidentiality in HIV-antibody testing to the members of one's local chapter of ACT UP. The kind of gay speaking that, to my mind, would constitute political resistance is not the kind that testifies to the truth of gay being but that contributes to and helps to authorize gay knowledge practices, or that disrupts heterosexist monopolies of heterosexual "free expression."

98. Foucault, *The History of Sexuality, Volume I,* 100–101.

99. Ibid., 101.

100. See Michel Foucault, "Le Gai savoir" (I), *Mec Magazine* 5 (June 1988), 32–36, esp. 32; Gallagher and Wilson, "Michel Foucault," 29.

101. Lévy, "Foucault: Non au sexe roi," 95, 98; my translation is loosely based on that of David J. Parent, "Power and Sex," in Foucault, *Politics, Philosophy, Culture,* 110–24 (quotation on pp. 114–15); this translation originally appeared in *Telos* 32 (1977), 152–61. For other examples of Foucault's reading of the homosexual emancipation movement in these terms, see Gallagher and Wilson, "Michel Foucault," 29; J. P. Joecker, M. Ouerd, and A. Sanzio, "Histoire et homosexualité: Entretien avec M. Foucault," *Masques* 13 (Spring 1982), 14–24, esp. 24.

102. Michel Foucault, "Le Gai savoir" (II), *Mec Magazine* 6–7 (July–August 1988), 30–33 (quotation on p. 31; no English translation). See also Foucault, "Non aux compromis," *Le Gai Pied* 43 (October 1982), 9; Joecker et al., "Histoire et homosexualité," 18, 20; Gilles Barbedette, "The Social Triumph of the Sexual Will: A Conversation with Michel Foucault," *Christopher Street* 6.4 (May 1982), 36–41, esp. 39–40: "Today the important questions are no longer linked to the problem of repression, which doesn't mean that there aren't still many repressed people, and which above all doesn't mean that we should overlook that and not struggle so that people stop being oppressed; of course I don't mean that. But the innovative direction we're moving in is no longer the struggle against repression."

103. Foucault, *The History of Sexuality, Volume I*, 93. See Foucault's more nuanced discussion of the political uses of liberation in Fornet-Betancourt et al., "The Ethic of Care for the Self as a Practice of Freedom."

104. Gallagher and Wilson, "Michel Foucault," 29; in response to this statement Foucault says, "Yes, that is the way I would put it."

105. Hence, for example, the outrage over the recent panel on "AIDS and the Social Imaginary" at the 1992 meeting of the American Anthropology Association in San Francisco, consisting of impeccably credentialed, indisputably left-wing academics (Nancy Scheper-Hughes, Jean Comaroff, Renato Rosaldo, Paul Rabinow, and Michael Taussig; Emily Martin and Arthur Kleinman, scheduled to be on the panel, were absent), none of whom, however, was gay-identified or a person with HIV/AIDS. The panel was thronged by protesters from the Society of Lesbian and Gay Anthropologists, wearing T-shirts that read THESE NATIVES CAN SPEAK FOR THEMSELVES.

106. See Teresa de Lauretis, "Eccentric Subjects: Feminist Theory and Historical Consciousness," *Feminist Studies* 16.1 (Spring 1990), 115–50.

107. On this point see Judith Butler, "Sexual Inversions," in *Discourses of Sexuality: From Aristotle to AIDS*, ed. Domna C. Stanton (Ann Arbor: University of Michigan Press, 1992), 344–61, esp. 354–57.

It is worth emphasizing, however, that the GLF explanation of *why* gay is good resembles very closely the more recent queer-affirmative declarations by Queer Nation: see, for example, Martha Shelley, "Gay Is Good," in *Out of the Closets: Voices of Gay Liberation*, ed. Karla Jay and Allen Young (New York: Douglas/Links, 1972), 31–34.

108. I am drawing here on similar arguments in feminist theory for understanding "woman" not as a nature but as a positionality: see, for example, Linda Alcoff, "Cultural Feminism Versus Post-Structuralism: The Identity Crisis in Feminist Theory," *Signs* 13.3 (Spring 1988), 405–36, esp. 433–35, and the further discussion by Teresa de Lauretis, "The Essence of the Triangle or, Taking the Risk of Essentialism Seriously: Feminist Theory in Italy, the U.S., and Britain," *differences* 1.2 (Summer 1989), 3–37, esp. 11–12; also, de Lauretis, "Eccentric Subjects"; Donna J. Haraway, "A Cyborg Manifesto," in *Simians, Cyborgs, and Women* (New York: Routledge, 1991), 149–81. See, further, Abdul R. JanMohamed and David Lloyd, eds., *The Nature and Context of Minority Discourse* (New York: Oxford University Press, 1990).

109. The distinction between queerness and Queer Nation has been drawn very starkly by Lisa Duggan, "Making It Perfectly Queer," *Socialist Review* 22.1 (January–March 1992), 11–31, esp. 20–21: "Many members of Queer Nation . . . use the term 'queer' only as a synonym for lesbian or gay. Queer Nation, for some, is quite simply a gay nationalist organization." Duggan hastens to point out, however, that attitudes within Queer Nation are more contradictory and complex.

110. A brief summary with documention appears in Arlene Stein, "Sisters and Queers: The Decentering of Lesbian Feminism," *Socialist Review* 22.1 (January–March 1992), 33–55, esp. 50, 55 n. 30.

111. See, for example, the anonymous pamphlet beginning "Queers Read This!" which many take to be the founding document of Queer Nation. I have in mind such passages as the following: "Since time began, the world has been inspired by the work of queer artists. . . . "

112. For further reflections on this topic see Judith Butler, "Critically Queer," and compare her earlier discussion in "Imitation and Gender Insubordination," in *Inside/Out*, 13–31; reprinted in *The Lesbian and Gay Studies Reader*, 307–20.

113. Cover story of *Sister!/My Comrade* (Spring 1990). This was a direct response to a series of articles in the lesbian and gay glossies that had dealt with the fluidity of lesbian identities, most notably a cover story by Jorjet Harper, "Lesbians Who Sleep with Men," *Outweek*

33, February 11, 1990, 46–52. For the reference to *Sister!* I am indebted to Julia Erhart, "The Politics of the Construction of Community: Queerzines," a lecture delivered at "Flaunting It!" (the first annual national graduate student conference in lesbian and gay studies), the University of Wisconsin–Milwaukee, in April 1991.

114. See Michael Warner, "Introduction," in *Fear of a Queer Planet*, vii–xxxi, esp. xxvi–xxvii: "For both academics and activists, 'queer' gets a critical edge by defining itself against the normal rather than the heterosexual. . . . The insistence on 'queer' . . . has the effect of pointing out a wide field of normalization, rather than simple intolerance, as the site of violence. . . . Organizing a movement around queerness also allows it to draw on dissatisfaction with the regime of the normal in general." Similar claims can be made on behalf of the earlier term, "gay"; see Simon Watney, *Policing Desire: Pornography, Aids, and the Media*, 2nd ed. (Minneapolis: University of Minnesota Press, 1989), 18: "Gay culture in the 1970s offered the grounds for the emergence of a social identity defined not by notions of sexual 'essence,' but in oppositional relation to the institutions and discourses of medicine, the law, education, housing and welfare policy, and so on." Dennis Altman (*Homosexual: Oppression and Liberation*, 151) discerned an early example of this oppositional tendency in the Cockettes, a group of gender-fuck performance artists, of whom he wrote, "[T]heir style is an extravagant send-up of all that is normal and respectable. . . . "

For various assessments of "queer" identity as it has evolved, see Teresa de Lauretis, "Queer Theory: Lesbian and Gay Sexualities. An Introduction," *differences* 3.2 (1991), iii–xviii; the sampling of opinion contained in "Birth of a Queer Nation," *Out/Look* 11 (Winter 1991), 14–23; Duggan, "Making It Perfectly Queer," 20–26; Stein, "Sisters and Queers," 50; Lauren Berlant and Elizabeth Freeman, "Queer Nationality," *boundary 2* 19.1 (1992), 149–80 (reprinted in *Fear of a Queer Planet*, 193–229); Henry Abelove, "From Thoreau to Queer Politics," *Yale Journal of Criticism* 6.2 (1993), 17–27; Eve Kosofsky Sedgwick, "Foreword: T Times" and "Queer and Now," in *Tendencies* (Durham, N.C.: Duke University Press, 1993), xi–xvi, 1–20, esp. xi–xiii, 5–9; Jeffrey Escoffier, "Under the Sign of the Queer," *Found Object* 4 (Fall 1994), 133–42, esp. 134–35; Steven W. Anderson, "A Journey into the Queer (and Not so Queer)," unpublished essay.

115. Edelman, *Homographesis*, 114.

116. Gérard Raulet, "Structuralism and Post-Structuralism: An Interview with Michel Foucault," trans. Jeremy Harding, *Telos* 55 (Spring 1983), 195–211 (quotation on p. 207): qtd. in Cohen, "Foucauldian Necrologies," 87. See also Lévy, "Foucault: Non au sexe roi," 130.

117. Bitoux et al., "De l'amitié comme mode de vie," 39 (my emphasis).

118. Macey (*The Lives of Michel Foucault*, 367–78) sums up Foucault's position as follows: "Gays had to do more than assert an identity; they had to create it, and Foucault was wary of any suggestion that its creation was equivalent to the liberation of an essence." See, generally, ibid., 364–70, for an excellent survey of Foucault's writings on gay sex and politics.

119. Michel Foucault, "An Aesthetics of Existence," in *Politics, Philosophy, Culture*, 47–53 (quotation on p. 49). My entire account of the relation between ancient ethics and gay politics in Foucault's thought is deeply indebted to Cohen, "Foucauldian Necrologies," and to Davidson, "Ethics as Ascetics."

120. Michel Foucault, *L'Usage des plaisirs*, Histoire de la sexualité, 2 (Paris: Gallimard, 1984), 16–17; cf. Foucault, *The Use of Pleasure*, The History of Sexuality, Volume Two, trans. Robert Hurley (New York: Random House, 1985), 10–11.

121. Foucault, *L'Usage des plaisirs*, 103 (cf. *The Use of Pleasure*, 89).

122. See, generally, Foucault, *The Use of Pleasure*, 89–98. See also Michel Foucault, "On the Genealogy of Ethics: An Overview of Work in Progress," in *The Foucault Reader*, 340–72, esp. 341 (the interview originally appeared in *Michel Foucault: Beyond Structuralism and Hermeneutics*, 229–52).

123. Michel Foucault, "La Culture de soi," in *Le Souci de soi*, Histoire de la sexualité, 3 (Paris: Gallimard, 1984), 51–85; "The Cultivation of the Self," in *The Care of the Self*, The History of Sexuality, Volume Three, trans. Robert Hurley (New York: Random House, 1986), 39–68. See also Foucault, "L'Écriture de soi," *Le Corps Écrit* 3 (1983), 3–23 (no English translation); Luther H. Martin, Huck Gutman, and Patrick H. Hutton, eds., *Technologies of the Self: A Seminar with Michel Foucault* (Amherst: University of Massachusetts Press, 1988).

124. Foucault, "On the Genealogy of Ethics," 359.

125. Foucault, *The Care of the Self*, 43.

126. Ibid., 50–54. See also Foucault, *L'Usage des plaisirs*, 84–90

(*The Use of Pleasure*, 72–77) for the classical Greek conception of *as-kēsis* as training or exercise.

127. Foucault, *The Care of the Self*, 65–66 (qtd. in Davidson, "Ethics as Ascetics," 68).

128. Ibid., 41 (the passage is quoted by Davidson, "Ethics as Ascetics," 67); see also 67.

129. Paul Veyne, "The Final Foucault and His Ethics," trans. Catherine Porter and Arnold I. Davidson, *Critical Inquiry* 20 (Autumn 1993), 1–9 (quotation on p. 7; my emphasis).

130. Gallagher and Wilson, "Michel Foucault," 27 (my emphasis).

131. Foucault, "What Is Enlightenment?" 39–42 (quotation on p. 41). Cf. Foucault, "On the Genealogy of Ethics," 362: "We have hardly any remnant of the idea in our society, that the principal work of art which one has to take care of, the main area to which one must apply aesthetic values, is oneself, one's life, one's existence. We find this in the Renaissance, but in a slightly academic form, and yet again in nineteenth-century dandyism, but those were only episodes."

132. Hayden White, "Foucault's Discourse: The Historiography of Anti-Humanism," in *The Content of the Form: Narrative Discourse and Historical Representation* (Baltimore: Johns Hopkins University Press, 1987), 104–41, esp. 105–6: "[T]here is no center to Foucault's discourse. It is all surface—and intended to be so. . . . Foucault's discourse is willfully superficial. And this is consistent with the larger purpose of a thinker who wishes to dissolve the distinction between surfaces and depths. . . . Briefly, I argue that the authority of Foucault's discourse derives primarily from its style (rather than from its factual evidence or rigor of argument). . . . "

133. See Cohen, "Foucauldian Necrologies," 92: "While, of course, historically 'style' has been one of the primary ways in which gay men have signified both their existence and their 'difference,' Foucault's suggestion seems to go beyond the formal self-invention which characterizes attitudes such as 'camp' and 'drag' to propose a radical re-imagining which would open up 'new forms of relationships, new forms of love, new forms of creation.' "

134. Foucault, "On the Genealogy of Ethics," 362.

135. Pierre Hadot, *Exercices spirituels et philosophie antique: Deuxième édition revue et augmentée* (Paris: Études Augustiniennes, 1987; 1st ed. 1981); discussion by Arnold I. Davidson, "Spiritual Exercises and Ancient Philosophy: An Introduction to Pierre Hadot," *Crit-*

ical Inquiry 16.3 (Spring 1990), 475–82. In a formal commentary on my paper at the annual meeting of the American Philosophical Association (Pacific Division) in Los Angeles on April 2, 1994, Davidson suggested that my reading of Foucault may be more Hadotian than Foucauldian; I acknowledge that possibility.

136. Pierre Hadot, "La Figure du sage dans l'antiquité gréco-latine," in *Les Sagesses du monde*, ed. Gilbert Gadoffre (Paris: Éditions Universitaires, 1991), 20; qtd. in Davidson ("Ethics as Ascetics," 76), who, however, argues (pp. 68ff.) that Foucault's conception of ascesis is less impersonal and more aesthetic than Hadot's (and, if Hadot is correct, than the ancients'). See also Jean-Pierre Vernant, "One, Two, Three: Eros," in *Before Sexuality: The Construction of Erotic Experience in the Ancient Greek World*, ed. David M. Halperin, John J. Winkler, and Froma I. Zeitlin (Princeton, N.J.: Princeton University Press, 1990), 465–78, esp. 473–77, whose interpretation is influenced by Hadot.

137. See Foucault's remarks in Fornet-Betancourt et al., "The Ethic of Care for the Self as a Practice of Freedom," 121:

> [The subject] is not a substance; it is a form and this form is not above all or always identical to itself. You do not have towards yourself the same kind of relationships when you constitute yourself as a political subject who goes and votes or speaks up at a meeting, and when you try to fulfill your desires in a sexual relationship. There are no doubt some relationships and some interferences between these different kinds of subject but we are not in the presence of the same kind of subject. In each case, we play, we establish with one's self some different form of relationship. And it is precisely the historical constitution of these different forms of subject relating to games of truth that interest me.

For Foucault, then, the "subject" is not an identity or a substance. Moreover, it is always a constructed subject, and the relations of reflexivity that define the subject's "self," its relationship to itself, are constrained by games of truth, practices of power, and historical or social forms. Nonetheless, insofar as the subject is an *ethical* subject, a subject of ethical practices, it is to that extent a free subject, for that is what it means, definitionally, to *be* an ethical subject. Without freedom, ethics is impossible. "Liberty is the ontological condition of ethics," Foucault emphasizes; conversely, "ethics is the deliberate form assumed by liberty" (115). And he adds, in reference to the classical Greeks, "[A] slave has no ethics" (117).

138. "On écrit pour être autre que ce qu'on est": Charles Ruas, "Archéologie d'une passion," *Magazine Littéraire*, no. 221 (July–August 1985), 100–105 (quotation on p. 104); translated as "An Interview with Michel Foucault," in Foucault, *Death and the Labyrinth: The World of Raymond Roussel*, trans. Charles Ruas (London: Athlone Press, 1986), 169–86 (quotation on p. 182). See also Rux Martin, "Truth, Power, Self: An Interview with Michel Foucault (October 25, 1982)," in *Technologies of the Self*, 9–15, esp. 9: "I don't feel that it is necessary to know exactly what I am. The main interest in life and work is to become someone else that you were not in the beginning"; Foucault, *Remarks on Marx*, 25–67, esp. 27: "When I write, I do it above all to change myself and not to think the same thing as before." Foucault's association of death and writing dates back to his literary essays in the early 1960s; that is a theme of the study by James Miller, *The Passion of Michel Foucault*.

139. Fornet-Betancourt et al., "The Ethic of Care for the Self as a Practice of Freedom," 113.

140. Davidson, "Ethics as Ascetics," 70.

141. Foucault, *L'Usage des plaisirs*, 14–15; cf. *The Use of Pleasure*, 8–9.

142. Foucault, *L'Usage des plaisirs*, 15; cf. *The Use of Pleasure*, 9 (qtd. in Davidson, "Ethics as Ascetics," 70).

143. Foucault, *L'Usage des plaisirs*, 14.

144. Joecker et al., "Histoire et homosexualité," 24 (my emphasis).

145. Bitoux et al., "De l'amitié comme mode de vie," 38 (my emphasis); cf. Joecker et al., "Histoire et homosexualité," 24: "I'd say that one should make use of one's sexuality to discover, to create some new relationships."

146. Lévy, "Foucault: Non au sexe roi," 98; "Power and Sex," 116.

147. Bitoux et al., "De l'amitié comme mode de vie," 39 (my emphasis).

148. Ibid.; Foucault, "Non aux compromis," 9.

149. Bitoux et al., "De l'amitié comme mode de vie," 38 (my emphasis); expanded in Joecker et al., "Histoire et homosexualité," 24.

150. Barbedette, "The Social Triumph of the Sexual Will," 36. Cf. Michel Foucault, "Des caresses d'hommes considérées comme un art,"

Libération, June 1, 1982, 27 (the passage is quoted in note 4 of "Saint Foucault").

151. Barbedette, "The Social Triumph of the Sexual Will," 38.

152. Gallagher and Wilson, "Michel Foucault," 27; cf. Foucault, "Le Gai savoir" (I), 32.

153. Bitoux et al., "De l'amitié comme mode de vie," 38.

154. Cf. Warner, "Introduction" to *Fear of a Queer Planet*, xiii, citing Harold Garfinkel, "Passing and the Managed Achievement of Sex Status in an Intersexed Person," *Studies in Ethnomethodology* (Cambridge: Polity Press, 1984), 116–85 (essay first published in 1967): "Queers do a kind of practical social reflection just in finding ways of being queer."

155. Bitoux et al., "De l'amitié comme mode de vie," 39; cf. Lévy, "Foucault: Non au sexe roi," 100.

156. Barbedette, "The Social Triumph of the Sexual Will," 38.

157. Ibid. Macey (*The Lives of Michel Foucault*, 367) reports a story told by Claude Mauriac in his memoirs to the effect that Foucault consulted a lawyer, shortly before his death, in order to inquire about the possibility—evidently abandoned—of adopting his lover of twenty years, Daniel Defert.

158. Qtd. in de Lauretis, "The Essence of the Triangle," 14.

159. Ibid., 14–15.

160. Ibid., 22.

161. Ibid., 18.

162. Fornet-Betancourt et al., "The Ethic of Care for the Self as a Practice of Freedom," 129. I wish to thank Jana Sawicki for calling my attention to this passage. I should emphasize, in this context, that Foucault did not easily or lightly make distinctions between power inequalities and domination; nor did he look on pedagogy as a politically neutral or harmless activity. It was not, for him, so much a matter of conceptually separating supposedly benign exercises of power (such as teaching) from nonconsensual impositions of force (such as imprisoning) as it was a matter of scrutinizing relations of power in order to discern the precise effects (of domination or otherwise) produced by them. For an example of his skepticism about the supposed benignity of certain power asymmetries, see Foucault, "Politics and Ethics: An Interview," in *The Foucault Reader*, 373–80, esp. 378–79.

163. Gallagher and Wilson, "Michel Foucault," 29–30 (emphasis in original).

164. Ibid., 27–28 (emphasis in original).

165. The interview, conducted on July 10, 1978, was published in Dutch as "Vijftien vragen van homosexuele zijde san Michel Foucault," *Interviews met Michel Foucault*, ed. M. Duyves and T. Massen (Utrecht: De Woelrat, 1982), 13–23, and finally printed in two installments under the title "Le Gai savoir" in *Mec Magazine* during the summer of 1988. There is a transcription of the original interview in the Centre Michel Foucault in Paris; the text has unfortunately been omitted—it is one of several important omissions—from the new, four-volume collection of Foucault's papers, *Dits et écrits 1954–1988*, ed. Daniel Defert and François Ewald (Paris: Gallimard, 1994). (I wish to thank Diana Fuss for originally calling to my attention the existence of this interview, and to Michael West for supplying me with a copy of the text and sharing his unpublished translation with me).

166. Foucault, "Le Gai savoir" (I), 34:

Il faut néanmoins y regarder de plus près, pour saisir que toute cette mise en blason de la masculinité ne coïncide aucunement avec une revalorisation du mâle en tant que mâle. Au contraire, dans la vie quotidienne, les rapports entre ces hommes sont empreints de tendresse, avec des pratiques communautaires de vie et de sexualité. Sous les signes et à l'abri de ces blasons masculins, les rapports sexuels qui se déroulent se révèlent être plutôt des valorisations de type masochiste. Les pratiques physiques de type fist-fucking sont des pratiques que l'on peut nommer comme dévirilisées, voire désexuées. Ce sont en fait d'extraordinaires falsifications de plaisir que l'on atteint en s'aidant d'un certain nombre d'instruments, de signes, de symboles ou de drogues telles que le poppers ou le MDA. Si ces signes de masculinité sont là, ce n'est pas pour revenir à quelque chose qui serait de l'ordre d'un phallocratisme, d'un machisme, mais plutôt pour s'inventer, pour faire de son corps un lieu de production de plaisirs extraordinairement polymorphes, et en même temps détachés des valorisations du sexe et particulièrement du sexe mâle. Car il s'agit de se détacher de cette forme virile de plaisir commandé qu'est la jouissance, jouissance prise au sens éjaculatoire, au sens masculin du terme.

167. Richard D. Mohr, *Gay Ideas: Outing and Other Controversies* (Boston: Beacon Press, 1992), 135–203.

168. Gallagher and Wilson, "Michel Foucault," 29.

169. For the sake of clarity I'll quote Gayle Rubin's definition of fist-fucking (which, she notes, "is also known as fisting or handballing"): "It is a sexual technique in which the hand and arm, rather than a penis or dildo, are used to penetrate a bodily orifice. Fisting usually refers to anal penetration, although the terms are also used for the insertion of a hand into a vagina." See Rubin, "The Catacombs: A Temple of the Butthole," in *Leatherfolk: Radical Sex, People, Politics, and Practice,* ed. Mark Thompson (Boston: Alyson, 1991), 119–41 (quotation on p. 121 n). Macey, *The Lives of Michel Foucault,* 370, defines fist-fucking as "the gradual penetration of the rectum by a lubricated *and clenched* fist" (my emphasis); the last detail in this definition is an error (as well as a physical impossibility).

170. See Morrison, "End Pleasure."

171. Rubin, "The Catacombs," 126.

172. Madeleine Chapsal, "Michel Foucault: A bas la dictature du sexe," *L'Express,* January 24, 1977, 56–57: qtd. in Macey, *The Lives of Michel Foucault,* 364.

173. For a powerful challenge to Foucault's description and interpretation of S/M, see Bersani, "The Gay Daddy."

174. Edgar Gregersen, *Sexual Practices: The Story of Human Sexuality* (New York: Franklin Watts, 1983), 56–57. I wish to thank Gayle Rubin for giving me this reference and David Kent for reminding me that twentieth-century sexual inventions did not end with fist-fucking.

175. Macey, *The Lives of Michel Foucault,* 370.

176. See Gayle S. Rubin, "The Valley of the Kings: Leathermen in San Francisco, 1960–1990," Ph.D diss., University of Michigan, 1994.

177. My source for this quip of Foucault's is Arnold Davidson.

178. Gallagher and Wilson, "Michel Foucault," 28.

179. Ibid., 28. Cf. Foucault, "On the Genealogy of Ethics," 347: "If we compare [the Greek ethical experience which implied a very strong connection between pleasure and desire] to our experience now, where everybody—the philosopher or the psychoanalyst—explains that what is important is desire, and pleasure is nothing at all, we can wonder whether this disconnection wasn't a historical event, one which was not at all necessary. . . . "

180. Macey, *The Lives of Michel Foucault,* 365; see Dews, "Power and Subjectivity in Foucault," for an extended comparison of Foucault to Lyotard and Deleuze.

181. Foucault, "Le Gai savoir" (II), 32 (I adapt Macey's translation p. 365] whenever possible):

> J'avance ce terme parce qu'il m'apparaît échapper à ces conno-
> tations médicales et naturalistes que porte en elle cette notion de
> désir. Cette notion a été utilisée comme un outil, une mise en
> intelligibilité, un étalonnage en terme de normalité: "Dis-moi quel
> est ton désir et je te dirai qui tu es, si tu es normal ou pas, donc
> je pourrai qualifier ou disqualifier ton désir." On repère bien cette
> "prise" qui va aller de la notion de concupiscence chrétienne jus-
> qu'à celle freudienne de désir, en passant par la notion d'instinct
> sexuel dans les années 1840. Le désir n'est pas un événement,
> mais une permanence du sujet, sur laquelle se greffe toute cette
> armature psychologico-médicale. Le terme de plaisir de son côté
> est vierge d'utilisation, quasiment vide de sens. Il n'y a pas de
> "pathologie" du plaisir, de plaisir "anormal." C'est un événement
> "hors sujet," ou à la limite du sujet, dans ce quelque chose qui
> n'est ni du corps ni de l'âme, qui n'est ni à l'intérieur, ni à l'ex-
> térieur, bref une notion non assignée et non assignable.

182. Gallagher and Wilson, "Michel Foucault," 28.

183. "Le Gai savoir" (I), 36. My translation follows the corrected French text supplied by Eribon, *Michel Foucault et ses contemporains*, 286, based on the transcript of the interview in the Centre Michel Foucault in Paris. Cf. Gallagher and Wilson, "Michel Foucault," 28:

> [I]f the perennial question [people] ask is "Does this thing con-
> form to my identity?" then, I think, they will turn back to a kind
> of ethics very close to the old heterosexual virility. If we are
> asked to relate to the question of identity, it has to be an identity
> to our unique selves. But the relationships we have to have with
> ourselves are not ones of identity, rather they must be relation-
> ships of differentiation, of creation, of innovation. . . . We must
> not exclude identity if people find their pleasure through this
> identity, but we must not think of this identity as an ethical uni-
> versal rule.

184. See David M. Halperin, "Platonic *Erôs* and What Men Call Love," *Ancient Philosophy* 5 (1985), 161–204.

185. Foucault, *Remarks on Marx*, 49.

186. Qtd. in Macey, *The Lives of Michel Foucault*, 364. See, further, Eribon, *Michel Foucault et ses contemporains*, 265–87.
187. Gallagher and Wilson, "Michel Foucault," 28.
188. Foucault, "Le Gai savoir" (II), 31:

> [C]e n'est pas parce que cette notion de sexualité nous a permis de nous battre qu'elle ne comporte pas pour autant un certain nombre de dangers. Il y a tout un biologisme de la sexualité et par conséquent toute une prise possible par les médecins et par les psychologues, bref par les instances de la normalisation. Nous avons au-dessus de nous des médecins, des pédagogues, des législateurs, des adultes, des parents qui parlent de sexualité!... Il ne suffit pas de libérer la sexualité, il faut aussi... se libérer de la notion même de sexualité.

Cf. the slogan DÉTRUIRE LA SEXUALITÉ ("Destroy Sexuality"), which appears as a section heading on page 97 of the March 1973 special issue of the periodical *Recherches*. The issue, subtitled "Grande Encyclopédie des Homosexualités," seems to have been the work, at least in part, of Félix Guattari, but Foucault (among many others) lent his name to the list of collaborators, in order to offer the periodical some insurance against government suppression. I wish to thank Alain Vizier for bringing this text to my attention.
189. Michel Foucault, "Sade, sergent du sexe," *Cinématographe* 16 (December 1975–January 1976), 3–5: "Il faut inventer avec le corps, avec ses éléments, ses surfaces, ses volumes, ses épaisseurs, un érotisme non disciplinaire: celui du corps à l'état volatile et diffus, avec ses rencontres de hasard et ses plaisirs sans calculs...."
190. Foucault, *La Volonté de savoir*, 207–8 (cf. *The History of Sexuality, Volume I*, 157).
191. Bersani, "The Gay Daddy," 81.
192. Bersani, "Is the Rectum a Grave?" 222; for reasons that escape me, Bersani puts forward this slogan in what he claims to be direct opposition to Foucault's view.
193. Bitoux et al., "De l'amitié comme mode de vie," 38.
194. Ibid. Foucault expands on this theme in Gallagher and Wilson, "Michel Foucault," 30.
195. Bitoux et al., "De l'amitié comme mode de vie," 38.
196. Foucault, "Le Gai savoir" (I), 35.
197. Rubin, "The Valley of the Kings."

198. Foucault, "Le Gai savoir" (I), 36.

199. Barbedette, "The Social Triumph of the Sexual Will," 38–39.

200. Bitoux et al., "De l'amitié comme mode de vie," 39.

201. Cohen, "Foucauldian Necrologies," 91.

202. Davidson, "Ethics as Ascetics," 73.

203. Barbedette, "The Social Triumph of the Sexual Will," 39; cf. Foucault, "Non aux compromis," 9, where Foucault speaks in similar terms about the importance of pleasure as a "site of creation of culture."

204. Foucault, "On the Genealogy of Ethics," 349.

205. Rubin, "The Catacombs," 127–28.

206. Charles Taylor, "Foucault on Freedom and Truth," 98, makes the exactly opposite claim that history is what underwrites and defines our *identity*. One could hardly ask for a better dramatization of the difference in outlook between Foucault and his humanist critics.

207. Edward W. Said, "Michel Foucault, 1927[*sic*]–1984," *Raritan* 4.2 (Autumn 1984), 1–11, esp. 5.

208. Foucault, *Remarks on Marx*, 33–34.

209. Foucault, "What Is Enlightenment?" 46.

210. Foucault, *Remarks on Marx*, 121.

211. A searingly eloquent and powerful argument to this general effect has been made by Bersani in "Is the Rectum a Grave?," but even he concludes by recommending to gay men getting fucked as a means of mortifying "the masculine ideal of proud subjectivity" and advocates practicing "*jouissance* as a mode of ascesis" (222).

212. See D. A. Miller, "Secret Subjects, Open Secrets," in *The Novel and the Police*, 192–220, esp. 219–20.

213. Foucault, "On the Genealogy of Ethics," 351.

214. See Arnold Davidson's forthcoming paper on Foucault's attraction to the "queerness" of the ancient Cynics.

215. Foucault, *The Use of Pleasure*, 23; see also 30–31, 36, 53–54, 62, 77, 89, 92–93, 97, 138–39, 250–53.

216. See, for example, David Cohen and Richard Saller, "Foucault on Sexuality in Greco-Roman Antiquity," in *Foucault and the Writing of History*, 35–59, 262–66.

217. Foucault, *L'Usage des plaisirs*, 111, 275–77 (cf. *The Use of Pleasure*, 97, 250–53).

218. See Lauren Berlant ("' '68: or, The Revolution of Little Queers," forthcoming), who distinguishes between "a version of queerness that is . . . referential . . . and an understanding of queer as a placeholder term, opening a wedge into a history and a world that doesn't exist, one into which we might, at some time, be able to translate ourselves."

219. See de Lauretis, "Queer Theory," esp. iii–xi. For a description of the historical and ideological conditions that once seemed to be particularly auspicious for the emergence of a queer culture, see de Lauretis's economical formulation of "the speculative premise" from which "queer theory," as she originally conceived it, might be expected to take off:

> [H]omosexuality is no longer to be seen simply as marginal with regard to a dominant, stable form of sexuality (heterosexuality) against which it would be defined either by opposition or by homology. In other words, it is no longer to be seen either as merely transgressive or deviant vis-à-vis a proper, natural sexuality (i.e., institutionalized reproductive sexuality), according to the older, pathological model, or as just another, optional "life-style," according to the model of contemporary North American pluralism. Instead, male and female homosexualities—in their current sexual-political articulations of gay and lesbian sexualities, in North America—may be reconceptualized as social and cultural forms in their own right, albeit emergent ones and thus still fuzzily defined, undercoded, or discursively dependent on more established forms. Thus, rather than marking the limits of the social space by designating a place at the edge of culture, gay sexuality in its specific female and male cultural (or subcultural) forms acts as an agency of social process whose mode of functioning is both interactive and yet resistant, both participatory and yet distinct, claiming at once equality and difference, demanding political representation while insisting on its material and historical specificity. (iii)

To the extent that de Lauretis's speculative premise accurately describes a real and ongoing social and discursive state of affairs, both queer culture and queer theory still remain genuine possibilities.

220. Foucault, "Le Gai savoir" (I), 35–36.

221. Michel Foucault, "An Interview with Michel Foucault," *History of the Present* (February 1985), 2 (translated from an article in *Les Nouvelles Littéraires*, March 17, 1975): qtd. in Gandal, "Michel Foucault: Intellectual Work and Politics," 131. When asked how "can we be sure that these new pleasures [that gay culture has invented] won't be exploited in the way advertising uses the stimulation of pleasure as a means of social control?" Foucault replied, "We can never be sure. In fact, we can always be sure *it will happen*, and that everything that has been created or acquired, any ground that has been gained, will, at a certain moment, be used in such a way. That's the way we live, that's the way we struggle, that's the way of human history" (Gallagher and Wilson, "Michel Foucault," 28).

222. Foucault, "On the Genealogy of Ethics," 229–52 (quotation on pp. 231–32). The passage is quoted by Gandal ("Michel Foucault: Intellectual Work and Politics," 129), who cites the following parallel: "As soon as it's a matter . . . of an institution of power, everything is dangerous. Power is neither good nor bad in itself. It's something perilous" ("Interview de Michel Foucault," *Actes* [June 1984], 5).

223. Joecker et al., "Histoire et homosexualité," 24.

224. D. A. Miller, *Bringing Out Roland Barthes*, 31.

225. See, generally, ibid., 28–31, esp. 30:

> In a culture that since the eighteenth century has massively depreciated male embodiment . . . we must register the distinctiveness of those practices of post-Stonewall gay male culture whose explicit aim, uncompromised by vicissitudes of weather or fashion, is to make the male body visible to desire. The men of the Muscle System or the Chelsea Gym, who valuing tone and definition over mass give as much attention to abs and glutes as to pecs and lats; who array their bodies in tanks and polos, purchased when necessary in the boys' department, in Spandex and Speedos, in preshrunk, reshrunk, and, with artisanal care, perhaps even sandpapered 501s—let us hail these men . . . for lending whatever inchoate social energies would resist the boxer shorts ethic the brave assistance of an advance guard that proceeds insensible to the pompous charges of exhibitionism, or hectoring accusations of body terrorism, thrown in the way.

226. Michel Foucault, "Politics and the Study of Discourse," *Ideology and Consciousness* 3 (Spring 1978), 7–26 (quotation on p. 24): qtd. in Gandal, "Michel Foucault: Intellectual Work and Politics," 124 (Foucault, "Réponse à une question," *Esprit* 371 [May 1968], 850–74 [quotation on p. 871]).

227. Cf. Donna J. Haraway, "A Cyborg Manifesto" and "The Biopolitics of Postmodern Bodies: Constitutions of Self in Immune System Discourse," in *Simians, Cyborgs, and Women*, 149–81, 203–30.

228. Foucault, *Power/Knowledge*, 193 (qtd. in Cohen, "Foucauldian Necrologies," 100 n. 24); cf. Foucault, *Remarks on Marx*, 33, 36:

> [I]t is evident that in order to have [a transformative experience] through a book like *The History of Madness*, it is necessary that what it asserts is somehow "true," in terms of historically verifiable truth. But what is essential is not found in a series of historically verifiable proofs; it lies rather in the experience which the book permits us to have. And an experience is neither true nor false: it is always a fiction, something constructed, which exists only after it has been made, not before; it isn't something that is "true," but it has been a reality.

229. Foucault, "Structuralism and Post-Structuralism," 207 (qtd. in Cohen, "Foucauldian Necrologies," 87).

230. Cf. Mark Blasius, "An Ethos of Lesbian and Gay Existence," *Political Theory* 20.4 (November 1992), 642–71; see now Blasius, *Gay and Lesbian Politics: Sexuality and the Emergence of a New Ethic* (Philadelphia: Temple University Press, 1994).

231. Bersani, "The Gay Daddy," 78. Bersani's essay presents a lucid exposition of Foucault's depsychologizing approach to sex and poses the most direct and radical theoretical challenge to it that I know of.

232. Cf. Stuart Hall, "Cultural Identity and Diaspora," in *Identity: Community, Culture, Difference*, ed. Jonathan Rutherford (London: Humanities Press International, 1990), 222–37.

233. Foucault, "The Subject and Power," 216.

234. Cf. James Meyer, "AIDS and Postmodernism," *Arts Magazine* 66.8 (April 1992), 62–68; Douglas Crimp, "Right On, Girlfriend!," in *Fear of a Queer Planet*, 300–320.

The Describable Life of Michel Foucault

Portions of this essay have previously appeared in *Salmagundi* 97 (Winter 1993), 69–93, under the title "Bringing Out Michel Foucault"; in the *Bryn Mawr Classical Review* 3.2 (1992), 104–9; and in the *Lesbian and Gay Studies Newsletter* 19.2 (July 1992), 32–35, under the title "Saint Foucault." I wish to thank D. A. Miller for his comments and encouragement; my thinking and writing here have been inspired—all too obviously, perhaps—by his work. I am particularly grateful to Paul Morrison for his numerous and sympathetic but unsparing readings of this essay, as well as for his extremely useful criticisms and suggestions. I also benefited from helpful discussions with Arnold Davidson, Lee Edelman, Didier Eribon, Gayle Rubin, and my colleagues at the Society for the Humanities at Cornell University in November 1993 (especially Natalie Kampen and Naomi Scheman). And I stole a good line from Jeffrey Carnes.

1. For an exceptionally adroit but otherwise typically shamefaced attempt to escape this contradiction, see Roger Chartier, "The Chimera of the Origin: Archaeology, Cultural History, and the French Revolution," in *Foucault and the Writing of History*, ed. Jan Goldstein (Oxford: Basil Blackwell, 1994), 167–86, 291–94, esp. 167–69.

2. Didier Eribon spends two pages attempting to defuse what he acknowledges to be the "paradoxical" quality of his enterprise: see his *Michel Foucault*, trans. Betsy Wing (Cambridge, Mass.: Harvard University Press, 1991), ix–x. James Miller voices similar misgivings about the project of subjecting Foucault to biographical criticism: see *The Passion of Michel Foucault* (New York: Simon & Schuster, 1993), 6–7. (All further page references to these two books will be included in the text of my essay.)

3. See David Macey, *The Lives of Michel Foucault* (London: Hutchinson, 1993), xi–xxiii, for a partial catalog of Foucault's efforts to resist becoming a subject of biography, much less an "author." (Further references to this work will be included in my text.)

4. Michel Foucault, *L'Ordre du discours. Leçon inaugurale au Collège de France prononcée le 2 décembre 1970* (Paris: Gallimard, 1971), 30, 28; cf. Foucault, "The Discourse on Language," trans. Rupert Swyer and reprinted as an appendix to Michel Foucault, *The Archaeology of Knowledge*, trans. A. M. Sheridan Smith (New York: Pantheon, 1972), 215–37, esp. 222, 221. Swyer's translation generally requires to be emended; in the case of the latter passage quoted, I have substituted the literal translation provided by Macey, *The Lives of Michel Foucault*, 244, for Swyer's version.

5. "So let's not get all broken up over it just yet" is the best I can do to convey the tone of Foucault's remark. The rest of my translation follows, with minor corrections, the version provided in the English-language edition of Eribon, *Michel Foucault*, 210. The transcript of the session is published under the title "Qu'est-ce qu'un auteur?" *Bulletin* *de la Société française de Philosophie* 64 (1969), 73–104 (quotation on p. 101).

6. Cf. Michel Foucault, "Foreword to the English Edition," *The Order of Things: An Archaeology of the Human Sciences* (New York: Pantheon, 1970), xiii: "I do not wish to deny the validity of intellectual biographies [for the history of science]."

7. See, for example, the anecdote told by Jana Sawicki, *Disciplining Foucault: Feminism, Power, and the Body* (New York: Routledge, 1991), 15 (and confirmed in its typicality by François Delaporte in conversation with me): "I told [Foucault] I had just finished writing a dissertation on his critique of humanism. Not surprisingly, he responded with some embarrassment and much seriousness. He suggested that I not spend energy talking about him and, instead, do what he was doing, namely, write genealogies." See also James Miller, *The Passion of Michel Foucault*, 185: "Unlike many other professors [at the Collège de France], Foucault made no effort to establish an independent base in one of Paris's research centers; he continued to evince no interest whatsoever in recruiting disciples," citing Pierre Bourdieu, "Preface to the English Edition," *Homo Academicus*, trans. Peter Collier (Stanford, Calif.: Stanford University Press, 1988), xix, who notes in turn that "until the end of his life, and even when he became professor at the Collège de France [Foucault] remained almost entirely bereft of specifically academic and even scientific [i.e., disciplinary] powers, and therefore of the clientele which these powers afford. . . . "

8. Hence, Foucault continued not just to preach but also to practice (on a scale whose dimensions have only recently begun to emerge) anonymous publication. As he explained to an interviewer two months before he died, "[O]ne would like [one's books] to be read for their own sake" (qtd. in Macey, *The Lives of Michel Foucault*, 426, citing Foucault, "Une esthétique de l'existence," *Le Monde Aujourd'hui*, July 15–16, 1984, xi; English translations of this text by John Johnston and by Alan Sheridan are available, respectively, in Michel Foucault, *Foucault Live (Interviews 1966–84)*, ed. Sylvère Lotringer [New York: Semiotext(e), 1989], 309–16, and in Michel Foucault, *Politics, Philosophy, Culture: Interviews and Other Writings, 1977–1984*, ed. Lawrence D. Kritzman [New York: Routledge, 1988], 47–53).

9. For a working definition of what Foucault understands by "normalization," see Michel Foucault, *Surveiller et punir: Naissance de la*

prison (Paris: Gallimard, 1975), 185–86; *Discipline and Punish: The Birth of the Prison*, trans. Alan Sheridan (New York: Pantheon, 1978), 182–84:

> In short, under a regime of disciplinary power, the art of punishing . . . brings five quite distinct operations into play: it refers individual acts, performances, and conducts to a group ensemble that is at once a field of comparison, a space of differentiation, and a source of the rule to be followed. It differentiates individuals in relation to one another and in terms of that group rule, whether the rule be made to function as a minimal threshold, as an average to be looked to, or as an optimum to be approximated. It measures in quantitative terms and hierarchizes in terms of value the abilities, the level of attainment, and the "nature" of individuals. It imposes, through this "valorizing" measurement, the constraint of a conformity to be achieved. Lastly, it traces the limit that will define difference in relation to all other differences, the external frontier of the abnormal. . . . [To recapitulate, it] compares, differentiates, hierarchizes, homogenizes, excludes. In a word, it *normalizes.* . . . Like surveillance and together with it, normalization becomes one of the great instruments of power at the end of the classical age. The marks that once indicated status, privilege, and group membership come to be replaced, or at least to be supplemented, by a whole range of degrees of normality: these are signs of membership in a homogeneous social body, but they also play a part themselves in classification, in hierarchization, and in the distribution of ranks. In one sense, the power of normalization enforces homogeneity; but it individualizes by making it possible to measure deviations, to set levels, to define specialties, and to render differences useful by calibrating them one to another. The power of the norm functions easily within a system of formal equality, since within a homogeneity that is the rule, the norm introduces, as a useful imperative and as the result of measurement, all the gradations of individual differences [translation extensively modified].

10. See Michel Foucault, "Qu'est-ce que la critique? [Critique et *Aufklärung*] (Séance du 27 mai 1978)," *Bulletin de la Société française de philosophie* 84 (Paris: Armand Colin, 1990), 35–63, esp. 39. No English translation has as yet appeared.

11. Edward W. Said, "Michel Foucault, 1927[*sic*]–1984," *Raritan* 4.2 (Autumn 1984), 1–11 (quotation on p. 5).

12. Ibid., 8. See Ed Cohen, "Foucauldian Necrologies: 'Gay' 'Politics'? Politically Gay?" *Textual Practice* 2.1 (Spring 1988), 87–101, esp. 88, on Said's refusal to take seriously the politicization of subjectivity in what Said terms Foucault's "more private and esoteric" (p. 10) later work.

13. I quote from Lee Edelman's analysis of the insinuating rhetoric at work in a 1963 *Time* magazine article on James Baldwin and the Black civil rights movement in the United States: by "demonstrat[ing] access to the fetishized knowledge the commerce in which defines the worldliness of those 'in the know,' " Edelman writes, the article "takes part in the enforcement of a normalizing sexual taxonomy, generating, for those positioned to exploit it, a surplus value of cultural authority through the policial recognition and identification of the gay man whose sexuality must be represented as legible precisely because it 'threatens' to pass unremarked"; see Lee Edelman, "The Part for the (W)hole: Baldwin, Homophobia, and the Fantasmatics of 'Race,' " in *Homographesis: Essays in Gay Literary and Cultural Theory* (New York: Routledge, 1994), 42–75 (quotation on p. 43).

14. Not all of Said's performances achieve the same high standard of suavity. Elsewhere in the same essay, for example, Said speaks less guardedly about Foucault's final lapses into "the personal": "It was noticeable that he was more committed to exploring, if not indulging, his appetite for travel, for different kinds of pleasure (symbolized by his frequent sojourns in California), for less and less frequent political positions" (9). Quoted and discussed by Cohen, "Foucauldian Necrologies," 88.

15. Mark Lilla, "Marx and Murder," *TLS*, no. 4669, September 25, 1992, 3–4. On Foucault and Althusser, see now Didier Eribon, *Michel Foucault et ses contemporains* (Paris: Fayard, 1994), 313–50.

16. See D. A. Miller, "Sontag's Urbanity," *October* 49 (Summer 1989), 91–101; reprinted in *The Lesbian and Gay Studies Reader*, ed. Henry Abelove, Michèle Aina Barale, and David M. Halperin (Routledge: New York, 1993), 212–20:

> As anyone adept in the *bon usage* of homophobia knows, too much of it is as apt to be thought to betray homosexual desire as too little; becoming a fully entitled man in our society . . . means not just learning homophobia, but also learning to acquire the calculation-become-intuition that would moderate it, or rather silence its expression just short of the point where it might start to show. It is homophobia, not homosexuality, that requires a

closet, whence it characteristically makes its sorties only as a multiply coded allusion, or an unprovable, if not improbable, connotation. Such featherweight pressure, however, is all that is required to activate—via a chain of displacements to rival a Freudian dream—fantasy positions and defenses whose cumulative effect on gay men and on gay desire has been thus almost inarticulably harmful. (215)

17. See, for example, Michel Foucault, "L'Evolution de la notion d'individu dangereux' dans la psychiatrie légale," *Revue Déviance et Société* 5 (1981), 403–22 (English translations: "About the Concept of the 'Dangerous Individual' in Nineteenth-Century Legal Psychiatry," trans. Carol Brown, *International Journal of Law and Psychiatry* 1 [1978], 1–18; "The Dangerous Individual," trans. Alain Baudot and Jane Couchman, in Foucault, *Politics, Philosophy, Culture*, 125–51). See also Michel Foucault, "La Vie des hommes infâmes," *Cahiers du chemin* 29, January 15, 1977, 19–29; translated by Paul Foss and Meaghan Morris as "The Life of Infamous Men," in Michel Foucault, *Power, Truth, Strategy*, ed. Meaghan Morris and Paul Patton (Sydney: Feral Publications, 1979), 76–91.

18. Earl Jackson Jr., *Fantastic Living: The Speculative Autobiographies of Samuel R. Delany* (New York: Oxford University Press, forthcoming).

19. *Playboy* 11.4, April 1964, 45–53 (quotation on pp. 51–52; emphasis added).

20. See Jean-Paul Sartre, *Saint Genet: Actor and Martyr*, trans. Bernard Frechtman (New York: George Braziller, 1963), 3–4, 18ff. Cf. Eribon, *Foucault et ses contemporains*, 24–26.

21. I wish to thank Kevin McLaughlin for formulating the issue in these broader terms and for obliging me to confront it.

22. Cf. Michel Foucault, "Monstrosities in Criticism," trans. Robert J. Matthews, *Diacritics* 1.1 (Fall 1971), 57–60.

23. For a recent survey, see Karen J. Winkler, " 'Seductions of Biography': Scholars Delve into New Questions About Race, Class, and Sexuality," *Chronicle of Higher Education* 40.10, October 27, 1993, A6–7, A14, reporting on a conference at Harvard University on October 15–16, 1993, entitled "Life Likenesses: The Seductions of Biography."

24. Macey cites Holroyd's *Bernard Shaw*. Vol. 1: *1856–1898. The Search for Love* (Harmondsworth, Eng.: Penguin, 1990), 4.

25. The inside flap of the book jacket contains the notation "written with the full cooperation of Daniel Defert, Foucault's former lover. . . . " (The edition I bought in Australia, which I take to be identical with the British edition, and which appeared half a year earlier, boasts only that Macey "has enjoyed the co-operation of many people close to Foucault. . . . ") I am told that Defert did not, in fact, approve the use of his name to market Macey's book.

26. See Hervé Guibert, "Les Secrets d'un homme," in *Mauve le vierge* (Paris: Gallimard, 1988), 103–11; and *A l'ami qui ne m'a pas sauvé la vie* (Paris: Gallimard, 1990). English translations: "A Man's Secrets," trans. Arthur Goldhammer, *Grand Street* 39 (1991), 67–77; *To the Friend Who Did Not Save My Life*, trans. Linda Coverdale (New York: Atheneum, 1991).

27. Eribon defends his version of the events in his recent book *Michel Foucault et ses contemporains*, 55–56.

28. Ibid., 55–56, 116.

29. I borrow this distinction from Richard Meyer, "Robert Mapplethorpe and the Discipline of Photography," in *The Lesbian and Gay Studies Reader*, 360–80, esp. 370, who invokes it in the course of a similar argument about the politics of the production of sexual knowledge: in a series of detailed visual analyses, Meyer convincingly shows that Mapplethorpe's project in his portfolio of S/M photographs is to record the fact of a sadomasochistic subculture but not, quite pointedly, to attempt to render its "truth."

30. See Eribon, *Michel Foucault et ses contemporains*, 26–27n., for examples of particularly tendentious mistranslations by Miller.

31. "On écrit pour être autre que ce qu'on est." Charles Ruas, "Archéologie d'une passion," *Magazine Littéraire*, no. 221 (July–August 1985), 100–105 (quotation on p. 104); translated as "An Interview with Michel Foucault," in Michel Foucault, *Death and the Labyrinth: The World of Raymond Roussel*, trans. Charles Ruas (London: Athlone Press, 1986), 169–86 (quotation on p. 182). Miller gives Foucault's dictum a slightly different spin by translating it as "One writes to become someone other than who one is." For an extended critique of Miller on this point, see Eribon, *Michel Foucault et ses contemporains*, 26–30. John Guillory, "The Americanization of Michel Foucault," *Lesbian and Gay Studies Newsletter* 20.2 (July 1993), 35–37, also protests against the way Miller's narrative strategy "renders the life entirely intelligible by reducing every contingency to a *fatality*" (p. 35).

32. At least *some* of Miller's reviewers were undeceived: see Lisa Duggan, "Biography = Death: Michel Foucault, Passion's Plaything,"

The Village Voice 38.18, May 4, 1993, 90–91; Wendy Brown, "Jim Miller's Passions," *differences* 5.2 (Summer 1993), 140–49. See also Jonathan Dollimore, "Desire in the Face of Death," *The Times Higher Education Supplement*, no. 1077, June 25, 1993, 17; Guillory, "The Americanization of Michel Foucault."

33. Cf. Brown, "Jim Miller's Passions," 147: "Miller's book is a case study in what Foucault identified as the power of discursive normalization."

34. See the press release issued by Miller's publishers, Simon and Schuster, to promote the book:

> For the first time, Miller reveals the full extent of Foucault's involvement in San Francisco's sadomasochistic underground . . . gives a detailed account of Foucault's death from AIDS . . . and examines the rumor that Foucault knowingly attempted to give AIDS to others. . . . Miller also investigates Foucault's growing fascination in the 1970s with drug use and with California's freewheeling gay culture. . . . In frank detail, Miller relates how Foucault sought both to find and to transcend himself through his experiences with sex and drugs. (qtd. in Brown, "Jim Miller's Passions," 140)

35. By far the best account of the political context in which Miller's book was written and received, and of the book's own political effects within the larger framework of recent cultural struggles in the United States, is Roddey Reid, "Foucault en Amérique: Biographème et Kulturkampf," *Futur antérieur* 23–24 (1994), 133–65.

36. Mark Lilla, "A Taste for Pain: Michel Foucault and the Outer Reaches of Human Experience," *TLS*, no 4695, March 26, 1993, 3–4; Alexander Nehamas, "Subject and Abject: The Examined Life of Michel Foucault," *The New Republic*, no. 4074, February 15, 1993, 27–36; Richard Wolin, "The Lure of Death," *Dissent* 171 (Spring 1993), 259–63; Kenneth Woodward, "A Philosopher's Death Wish," *Newsweek* 121.5, February 1, 1993, 63; Jay Tolson, "Fatal Attraction," *The National Review* 45.3, February 15, 1993, 47–48; Frank Browning, "Take It to the Limit," *Tikkun* 8.3 (May/June 1993), 65–67; Gary Kamiya, "Philosopher's Groan," *Artforum* 31.7 (March 1993), 13; Roger Kimball, "The Perversions of M. Foucault," *The New Criterion* 11.7 (March 1993), 10–18; Richard Rorty, "Paroxysms and Politics," *Salmagundi* 97 (Winter 1993), 60–68. I owe a number of these references to Reid, "Foucault en Amérique," who similarly calls attention to the remarkable continuity between the Miller biography's sensationalistic style and the idiom of journalistic and critical reports of it.

37. Scott Heller, "New Foucault Biography Creates Scholarly Stir: Some Say Personal Revelations in As-Yet-Unpublished Book Could Overshadow French Philosopher's Contributions," *Chronicle of Higher Education* 39.6, September 30, 1992, A8, A13–14.

38. Similarly, Tolson, "Fatal Attraction," 48, berates Foucault for his alleged failure to "resist the German virus." Although the phrase alludes, in its context, to "a fatal attraction to German ideas among . . . French intellectuals," it condenses a remarkable number of other sinister associations in just a few words.

39. Ibid., 47.

40. Bruce Bawer, *A Place at the Table: The Gay Individual in American Society* (New York: Poseidon Press, 1993), 211.

41. Alan Ryan, "Foucault's Life and Hard Times," *The New York Review of Books* 40.7, April 8, 1983, 12–17 (quotation on p. 14).

42. See, generally, Eve Kosofsky Sedgwick, *Epistemology of the Closet* (Berkeley: University of California Press, 1990), esp. 4–8, who speaks eloquently in this connection of the "privilege of unknowing."

43. Cf. Miller, *The Passion of Michel Foucault*, 15: "Though Foucault first explicitly addressed the issue of power in [*Discipline and Punish*], it had always been one of his preoccupations. All of his work, from *Madness and Civilization* on, pivots around asymmetrical relationships in which power is exercised, sometimes thoughtfully, often wantonly. The figures haunting his pages enact an allegory of endless domination, from the hangman torturing the murderer to the doctor locking up the deviant." From here it is a short step to Bruce Bawer's statement, already quoted: "The greatest single influence on Gay Studies today is the late French theorist Michel Foucault, an enthusiast of sadomasochism who analyzed sexual relations almost entirely in terms of power."

44. For a brilliant and sustained analysis of this homophobic strategy, see D. A. Miller, "Sontag's Urbanity."

45. Michel Foucault, *Madness and Civilization: A History of Insanity in the Age of Reason*, trans. Richard Howard (New York: Pantheon, 1965), xii. (I have substituted "homosexuality" for "madness" in Foucault's formulation.)

46. D. A. Miller, *Bringing Out Roland Barthes* (Berkeley: University of California Press, 1992), 18 (James Miller quotes a version slightly different from the published one quoted here). Perhaps even more pertinent in this context is another passage from the same work that the author of *The Passion of Michel Foucault* did not choose to quote: "For in the guarding of that Open Secret which is still the mode of producing, transmitting, and receiving most discourse around homosexuality, the knowledge that plays dumb is exactly what permits the abuses of an ignorance that in fact knows full well what it is doing" (16–17).

47. Michel Foucault, *L'Archéologie du savoir* (Paris: Gallimard, 1969), 28; *The Archaeology of Knowledge*, 17 (with corrections, but retaining the explicit reference to the police, which is not in the original). For an example of biographical criticism that makes use of the "fact" of Foucault's homosexuality to unlock the meaning of his work—an example, that is, of an interpretative approach to Foucault that looks and feels exactly like what D. A. Miller calls "police entrapment"—see Jerrold Seigel, "Avoiding the Subject: A Foucaultian Itinerary," *Journal of the History of Ideas* 51 (1990), 273–99. Quoting the passage from *The Archaeology of Knowledge* just cited, Seigel imperturbably rejoins, "If, ignoring Foucault's injunction, we seek to discover stable features behind his projected facelessness and a definable pattern underneath his labyrinthine movements, we need not accept his claim that we do the work of police and bureaucrats" (274). Since "we" can evidently do whatever "we" fucking please, why (I wonder) do we even trouble to dispute Foucault's claim? Why not admit straight out that we understand our analysis of Foucault to be an extension of the work of the police, a means of enforcing standards of health and social decency? What would we lose by making that admission—the ability to pretend that our undertaking is not irretrievably homophobic? Did we think that we had fooled anyone by such transparent subterfuges? For a similar attempt, albeit undertaken in a different spirit, to read Foucault's *History of Sexuality, Volume I,* as a closet drama, see Eve Kosofsky Sedgwick, "Gender Criticism," in *Redrawing the Boundaries: The Transformation of English and American Literary Studies,* ed. Stephen Greenblatt and Giles Gunn (New York: Modern Language Association of America, 1992), 271–302, esp. 278–85, who argues that "the closet of homosexual-heterosexual definition" is " 'the unconscious' of this text" (284).

48. Eribon has now partly made up for his earlier omissions in a new book, *Michel Foucault et ses contemporains*, esp. 49ff., 265–87, and passim. He has also responded, strenuously but not always comprehendingly, to my criticisms of his biography (51–57).

49. I quote Alan Sheridan's translation of the concluding words of Foucault's *Surveiller et punir* (1975). The phrase also serves as a chapter title in *The Passion of Michel Foucault*, and Miller does, to be sure, treat Foucault's personal life as an arena of (sometimes quite heroic) struggle, the scene of a Nietzschean quest "to become what one is." But Miller does not understand that struggle to be a political one (nor, in fact, did Foucault so understand it until the late 1960s), and in any case Miller's eloquent final assessment of it makes Foucault sound less like Zarathustra than like Dr. Strangelove:

> Foucault struggled bravely: against conventional ways of thinking and behaving; against intolerable forms of social and political power; against intolerable aspects of himself. . . . Harboring his maddest impulses in the books that he wrote, he tried to understand these impulses, simultaneously explaining and expressing them, exorcising his desires while struggling to establish their innocence, in part by methodically documenting the historical origin of the divisions we customarily make between good and evil, true and false, the normal and the pathological. (384)

50. Macey, *The Lives of Michel Foucault*, 209, tells us that Foucault began the practice of shaving his head while he was living in Tunisia (from the autumn of 1966 to the autumn of 1968). He characteristically reports two different explanations that Foucault later offered for it: (1) it stopped him from worrying about losing his hair; (2) it enabled him to reveal his true face.

51. Macey, *The Lives of Michel Foucault*, 160–61, however, provides two other competing accounts of how Foucault ultimately fixed on that title.

52. Compare, for example, the following points in Macey's biography and in Eribon's: Foucault's teaching assignments at Lille; Foucault's report to Raymond Polin that his thesis would be on "the philosophy of psychology"; Foucault's meeting with Maurice Chevalier in Stockholm; the possible origin, in Foucault's 1956 seminar on Racine's *Andromaque* in Uppsala, of his later discussion of Orestes's madness in *Madness and Civilization*; Foucault's request to Stirn Lindroth to be allowed to submit his doctoral thesis to the University of Uppsala;

Dumézil's procurement of an appointment for Foucault in Poland through contact with Philippe Rebeyrol. Macey cites Eribon as the source of the primary documents he reproduces, but he does not credit him (or any source that might have been common to both of them) for the rest of his information.

53. "Le Départ du prophète," *Libération*, July 12, 1982, 14. Eribon reprints this text, and tells the story of how it came to be written and published, in his new book, *Michel Foucault et ses contemporains*, 277–81.

54. Michel Foucault, *L'Usage des plaisirs*, Histoire de la sexualité, 2 (Paris: Gallimard, 1984), 12 (Foucault, *The Use of Pleasure*, The History of Sexuality, Volume Two, trans. Robert Hurley [New York: Random House, 1985], 6–7).

55. To be fair to Eribon (who has come out, discreetly, in *Michel Foucault et ses contemporains*, 52), I should point out that the second, revised French edition of his biography contains a more extended discussion of the significance of Foucault's homosexuality (to which Eribon has also devoted considerable space in his more recent book on Foucault): see Didier Eribon, *Michel Foucault (1926–1984)* (Paris: Flammarion, 1991), 44–47.

56. See Edmund White, "Love Stories" (a review of the works of Hervé Guibert), *London Review of Books* 15.21, November 4, 1993, 3–4, 6, esp. 3.

57. Rabinow made his observation at a public symposium on Foucault and biography at the University of California, Berkeley, on May 14, 1993.

58. "Maurice Florence" (*sc.* Michel Foucault and François Ewald), "Foucault," in *Dictionnaire des philosophes*, ed. Denis Huisman (Paris: Presses Universitaires de France, 1984), 1:942–44; trans. Catherine Porter in *The Cambridge Companion to Foucault*, ed. Gary Gutting (Cambridge: Cambridge University Press, 1994), 314–19; Thierry Voeltzel, *Vingt ans et après* (Paris: Grasset, 1978): described in detail by Macey, *The Lives of Michel Foucault*, 372-73.

59. See Foucault, *L'Usage des plaisirs*, 14: the much-quoted phrase is *se déprendre de soi-même*, literally "to fall out of love with oneself."

60. For the first passage, see Michel Foucault, *Naissance de la clinique* (Paris: Presses Universitaires de France, 1963), 125; *The Birth of the Clinic: An Archaeology of Medical Perception*, trans. A. M. Sheridan Smith (New York: Pantheon, 1973), 124. For the second passage, see Michel Foucault, *La Volonté de savoir*, Histoire de la sexualité, 1 (Paris: Gallimard, 1976), 54–55; *The History of Sexuality, Volume I: An Introduction*, trans. Robert Hurley (New York: Pantheon, 1978), 39.

61. Miller is here echoing Foucault, but the original formulation has a rather different import in context:

> Each time I tried to do a piece of theoretical work, it had as its starting point elements of my own experience and was always in relation to processes that I saw going on around me. It's because I thought I could recognize in the things I saw, in the institutions that I was dealing with, in my relations with others, some cracks, mute tremors, malfunctionings, that I undertook a particular piece of work—some fragments of autobiography [*quelque fragment d'autobiographie*].

I translate from the corrected text (which Miller also quotes [31]) of an interview with Didier Eribon, "Est-il donc important de penser?" *Libération*, May 30/31, 1981. The published English version, which is based on the uncorrected text, is Foucault, "Practicing Criticism," *Politics, Philosophy, Culture*, 152–56 (quotation on p. 156). For a nuanced attempt to distinguish Foucault's meaning from Miller's interpretation of it, see Eribon, *Michel Foucault et ses contemporains*, 59–67; Eribon points out (60n.) that the text originally published in *Libération* erroneously contained the phrase *quelques fragments d'autobiographie*, which gives the misleading impression that Foucault was being much less tentative about the autobiographical dimensions of his theoretical work than, in fact, he was.

62. Michel Foucault, *Histoire de la folie à l'âge classique*, rev. ed. (Paris: Gallimard, 1972), 552; *Madness and Civilization*, 282 (I adopt the translation Miller provides on p. 112).

63. See Eribon, *Michel Foucault et ses contemporains*, 39–42, for a critique of Miller's interpretation of Sade's significance for Foucault.

64. See Foucault, *L'Ordre du discours*, 10, 55, 17; "The Discourse on Language," 216, 229, 218.

65. See Foucault, *Naissance de la clinique*, 175; *The Birth of the Clinic*, 171.

66. See Foucault, *Surveiller et punir*, 199–200; *Discipline and Punish*, 197-98.

67. See Foucault, *Surveiller et punir*, 38; *Discipline and Punish*, 34.

68. See Michel Foucault, "Un plaisir si simple," *Le Gai Pied*, no. 1 (April 1979), 10; I have been working from the English version, "The Simplest of Pleasures," trans. Mike Riegle and Gilles Barbedette, *Fag Rag*, no. 29 (n.d.), 3.

69. Here is what Roger Kimball concludes from Miller's account: "Foucault came to enjoy imagining 'suicide festivals' or 'orgies' in which sex and death would mingle in the ultimate anonymous encounter" ("The Perversions of M. Foucault," 11).

70. Wolin, "The Lure of Death," 260 (emphasis added). Wolin himself, evidently, is more than merely "persuaded": note, for example, the excited tone in which he remarks, "[T]he *riveting* account of [Foucault's "LSD-induced *epiphany* concerning the familial origins of his homosexuality"] is one of *the high points* of Miller's narrative" (260; my emphasis).

71. For a somewhat defensive discussion of another instance of Miller's misreading, see Gary Gutting's introduction ("Foucault: A User's Manual") to his recent *Cambridge Companion to Foucault*, 1–27, esp. 23, 27 n. 35. A detailed and devastating (though not, admittedly, a complete) survey of Miller's misinterpretations can be found in Eribon, *Michel Foucault et ses contemporains*, 27–30, 35–45, 289.

72. Michel Foucault, "On Popular Justice: A Discussion with Maoists," in *Power/Knowledge: Selected Interviews and Other Writings, 1972–1977*, ed. Colin Gordon (New York: Pantheon, 1980), 1–36. For an excellent and illuminating corrective to Miller's reading of this text, see Eribon, *Michel Foucault et ses contemporains*, 43–44.

73. Cf. Macey, *The Lives of Michel Foucault*, 300: "Although no Maoist, [Foucault] did use some Maoist terminology, simply because of the need to engage with the discourse of his interlocutors."

74. And so Mark Lilla, "A Taste for Pain," 3, is able to conclude, incredibly, from Miller's book that "Foucault now appears as an essentially private Nietzschean moralist who begins and ends his career trying to orient himself in relation to society and his own drives. The political Foucault stands out as the exception, the product of an unfortunate historical conjuncture." But Lilla's deduction is tame compared to the bizarre uses to which Frank Browning manages to put Miller's reading of Foucault as an apostle of transgression:

> Though later in his life Foucault would revise his enthusiasm for popular vengeance, he insisted that to be fully human *required* the individual to taste, touch, and feel the inner tissues of cruelty that are released through rebellion and revolution. It was not

enough for him to be a celebrated radical professor. He had to experience the revolt in his body, to feel the adrenaline coursing through his veins as he joined the students atop an occupied classroom building heaving bricks onto the police below. That was the "limit experience" of revolution, of breaking through his role as professor, merging into the unified disorder of common action. It gave him a glimpse of human transcendence.

Alas, the courts of the post-revolution seem to look pretty much like the courts of the *ancien régime*. Political revolt seemed only to replace one power pyramid with another, never to disrupt it for longer than a moment. In the end, as a philosopher driven to the question of what it means to be human, driven to know what it meant for him to be human, he was left with nothing more than the flesh, his flesh. The only way remaining for us (him) to know the living self is through the ruthlessly cruel sacrifice and obliteration of that self. Whence to the chamber of S/M horrors in San Francisco [no address provided]. . . . (Browning, "Take It to the Limit," 66; my emphasis)

75. Macey, *The Lives of Michel Foucault*, 269, commenting on Foucault's political efforts in the early 1970s to facilitate alliances among prisoners, lawyers, bureaucrats, and doctors for the purpose of challenging the administration of the prison system in France, observes that these "new social strata," as Foucault dubbed them, "were not being asked to speak in the name of supposedly universal values such as justice, but from the position within which their own specific practices bring them into conflict with the demands of power." For a lucid exposition of the political principles behind Foucault's resistance to universalizing notions of value and refusal to advocate specific values, see Keith Gandal, "Michel Foucault: Intellectual Work and Politics," *Telos* 67 (Spring 1986), 121–34; compare Eribon's lucid account of the issues at stake in the disagreements between Foucault and Habermas, in *Michel Foucault et ses contemporains*, 289–311.

76. Michel Foucault, "The Subject and Power," in Hubert L. Dreyfus and Paul Rabinow, *Michel Foucault: Beyond Structuralism and Hermeneutics*, 2nd ed., (Chicago: University of Chicago Press, 1983), 208–26 (quotation on p. 212).

77. Miller's remarks were made at a roundtable discussion of "The Life and Politics of Michel Foucault," which he chaired, at the annual meeting of the American Political Science Association on September 5, 1992, in Chicago.

78. Cohen, "Foucauldian Necrologies," 93.

79. For a brilliant exposition of the horrific consequences of gay male describability, see Sedgwick, *Epistemology of the Closet*, 224–30, who expounds on Proust's portrayal of "the invert" as "that person over whom everyone else in the world has, potentially, an absolute epistemological privilege" (232).

80. Brown, "Jim Miller's Passions," 148. It may be worth quoting, yet again, D. A. Miller, *Bringing Out Roland Barthes*, 23–24:

> [A]s a general social designation, the term *gay* serves a mainly administrative function, whether what is being administered is an insurance company, a marketing campaign, a love life, or a well-orchestrated liberal dinner party—as a result of which, even men on whom the overall effect of coming out has been empowering will sometimes also have to submit to being mortified by their membership in a denomination that general social usage treats, as though there were nothing else to say about them, or nothing else to hear them say, with all the finality of a verdict.

81. Duggan ("Biography = Death," 91) remarking on "Miller's own preoccupations and anxieties," suggests in a similar spirit that "perhaps the volume would be more appropriately titled *The Passion of James Miller*." Wendy Brown ("Jim Miller's Passions," 141) goes further and interprets Miller's alleged "linking of poststructuralism with Nazism, philosophical anti-foundationalism with AIDS, gay sadomasochistic sex with love of political cruelty, and the 'death of the subject' with indifference to life" as "the metonymic workings of Miller's psyche"; she also accuses Miller more specifically of resentment, obsession, voyeurism, pornography, passive aggressiveness, vengefulness, and hostility.

82. See D. A. Miller, "Anal *Rope*," *Representations* 32 (Fall 1990), 114–33; reprinted in *Inside/Out: Lesbian Theories, Gay Theories*, ed. Diana Fuss (New York: Routledge, 1991), 118–41. See also Lee Edelman, "Seeing Things: Representation, the Scene of Surveillance, and the Spectacle of Gay Male Sex," in *Inside/Out*, 93–116; reprinted in Edelman, *Homographesis*, 173–91.

83. D. A. Miller, *Bringing Out Roland Barthes*, 7–8.

84. Ibid., 48.

85. Ibid., 14.

86. Ibid., 28.

87. Paul Morrison, "Coffee Table Sex: Robert Mapplethorpe and the Sadomasochism of Everyday Life," *Genders* 11 (Fall 1991), 17–36 (my formulation is a near quotation of Morrison, pp. 17–18).

88. D. A. Miller, *The Novel and the Police* (Berkeley: University of California Press, 1988), ix.

89. I borrow this image from D. A. Miller, *Bringing Out Roland Barthes*, 32.

90. Foucault, "Qu'est-ce que la critique?" 39.

91. Foucault, *L'Ordre du discours*, 19, 22; "The Discourse on Language," 219 (translation revised).

Index

Freedom (*continued*)
practices of, vs. liberation, 30, 56,
68–97, 101–6, 109–12, 193–94n.
See also Liberation; Resistance
French prison system, 24–25, 55–56,
158, 173–76, 236n
Freud, Sigmund, 121, 204n
*Three Essays on the Theory of
Sexuality*, 204n
Friendship
in classical antiquity, 82
sexual pleasure and, 103–4
Fuss, Diana, 215n

Gai pied, first issue of, 171
Gandal, Keith, 22, 53–54, 220n, 221n,
236n
Garfinkel, Harold, 214n
Gay vs. queer, 62–63
Gay activism, 6, 7, 14, 16, 25–33, 56–
67, 107–8, 112–15, 120–25, 162.
See also ACT UP; AIDS activism;
Resistance
Foucault's influence on, 195n
Gay authority, institutional crisis of,
8, 11–14, 130–39, 146–53
Gay culture, 73, 99–101, 210n, 220n
Gay identity
vs. queer identity, 62
as social designation, 197n, 237n
Gay liberation, 31–32, 207–8n
history of, 56–57
political strategy of, 57–62. *See
also* Homosexual emancipation
movement, political strategy of;
Liberation; Sexual liberation
Gay Liberation Front, 61, 207–8n
Gay-bashing, 32, 199n
Genet, Jean, 134–35, 176
Genitals, male
de-eroticization of, 87–91
re-eroticization of, 88–89
German homosexual emancipation
movement. *See* Homosexual
emancipation movement,
political strategy of
German ideas, 230n

Goldstein, Jan, 195n
Greek philosophy, ethical self-
fashioning and, 109–11
Greene, Jody, 191n
Groupe d'Information sur les Prisons
(GIP), 55
Guattari, Félix, 218n
Guibert, Hervé, 78, 140
Guillory, John, 228n
Gutting, Gary, 235n
Gym culture, 115–19

Habermas, Jürgen, 22, 205n, 236n
Hadot, Pierre, 75, 211–12n
Harpham, Geoffrey Galt, 191n
Hermaphrodites, 95
Heterosexual/homosexual binarism,
43–44
Heterosexuality
contradictory notions about, 46–48
as default, 44–45
definition of, 43–44
dependence of, on homosexuality,
44–47
as norm, 46
pathology of, 177–82
History
determination by, 104–5
identity and, 219n
personal in, 106
as spiritual exercise, 104–6, 222n
study of, 105–6
transformative potential of, 104–6,
119–20
HIV-antibody testing, 28, 206n
Holroyd, Michael, 139
Homophobia, discursive analysis of,
30–31, 33–34, 37–38, 42–48, 51–
52, 120–22
Homophobic discourses, 32–37, 42–
52
"the homosexual" defined by, 43–
48, 61
refuting lies of, 37–38
resistance to, 30–33, 48–52, 120
reversal of, 56–62, 66–67
Homosexual ascesis. *See* Ascesis